SLOE GIN
AND
BEESWAX

JANE NEWDICK

SLOE GIN AND BEESWAX

SEASONAL RECIPES & HINTS FROM TRADITIONAL HOUSEHOLD STOREROOMS

PHOTOGRAPHS BY
PIA TRYDE

First published in 1993
by Charles Letts & Co Ltd
Letts of London House
Parkgate Road
London SW11 4NQ

ISBN 1 85238 333 X

A CIP catalogue record for this book is available from
the British Library.

Project editor: Gillian Haslam
Designer: Kit Johnson
Illustrator: Vana Haggerty
Typeset by Dorchester Typesetting Group Ltd
Colour reproduction by Daylight Colour Art Pte Ltd
Printed and bound in Singapore

IMPORTANT: In the recipes use only one set of measurements. The quantities given in metric are not always exact conversions of the imperial measurements.

CONTENTS

INTRODUCTION

grew up in a household where both growing and preserving food was a normal daily activity. I took for granted the fresh eggs, soft fruit and home-made marmalade and, as a child, presumed that everyone lived as we did. This was at a time when freezers were a new and expensive novelty, but the baker and butcher delivered to our door every other day. Our food through the year was very seasonal as most of our vegetables and fruit came from a not very large but well organised garden. My father won prizes at the local produce show and we made use of wild food such as blackberries, just as every person living in the country seemed to. There was still a sense of thrift and a fear of being extravagant after years of wartime food rationing but I remember living extremely well, almost luxuriously.

■ *The soft fruits of summer are short-lived but the pleasure they give can extend throughout the whole year. Take time to preserve a little of the sweet* largesse *while you can (right).*

Since my childhood days I have lived briefly in a city but mostly in the country and I find that old habits die hard. I feel a faint sense of guilt if the season for bitter oranges has passed and no marmalade has been made or the apples lie wasting in the orchard because I am too busy to deal with them. Some days I enjoy the therapy of spending time making something special which can be stored away. Stirring a pan and dreaming a bit or neatly labelling a row of shining jars is both relaxing and useful and that is quite a rare combination these days. The doing and making is every bit as enjoyable as the pride in the finished result and there is a tremendous pleasure in the physical tasks of peeling,

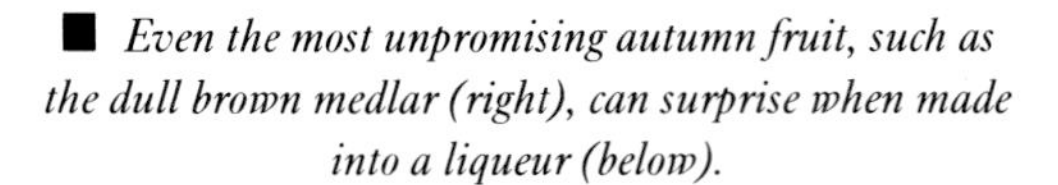

■ *Even the most unpromising autumn fruit, such as the dull brown medlar (right), can surprise when made into a liqueur (below).*

chopping and mixing ingredients which are invariably beautiful, colourful and fresh and which taste and smell delicious. It is a task which appeals to all our senses as well as our hoarding instincts.

I believe that most of us have something of the folk memory in us, of storing up for leaner days and filling storecupboards, though few of us have to out of necessity. We have the greatest choice of foods in our developed countries, almost too much choice, but something which has been made by you with care and pleasure doubly rewards the output of time and energy you spend making it. However good something is that has been bought, we still feel instinctively that home-made is best. There are also some things which simply can't be bought so, if you want to enjoy them, you will just have to make them yourself. Where can you buy praline, for example, or melon pickle? We are rapidly losing our sense of the seasons as more and more of us live in an urban environment but there are still things which can only be done at certain times of the year. This gives us a pattern through the year of jobs to do which I think most people enjoy or even need. While routine is dull, a seasonal task is something to look forward to or regret missing in a real way and gives shape to our hectic, over-busy lives.

THE STILLROOM

It seems that since the earliest times, most settled households contained a room or area in which to do certain important tasks for the house and estate. This was known as the stillroom quite simply because it would have contained a still or distillation device of varying degrees of sophistication for making flower oils and essences.

The name was still in use until quite recently, and even in the 1930s Chatsworth House in Derbyshire had stillroom maids with quite specific jobs to do. By this period their sole function was to prepare special foods for meals such as afternoon tea, so they might make jams and preserves and scones and biscuits to take up to the drawing room where the family gathered together at four o'clock. A stillroom of, say, the sixteenth century had a much more varied purpose, including mixing powerful medicines and cures for illnesses, distilling essential oils and possibly alcohols, preserving and conserving fruits, vegetables and flowers and making polishes, soaps, sweetmeats, dyes, inks, perfumes and lotions. Day-to-day cooking was done in a main kitchen and special jobs such as brewing, laundry, butchery, dairy work and baking all had their own workspace. The stillroom had to be functional but one imagines it was also a pleasant place to be, with thick wooden and slate surfaces, a rush and herb-strewn floor and shelves to store the results of the work carried out there. It might have had only small windows letting in a stream of light but the atmosphere would have been scented with the strange and wonderful smells of musk, orange peel, roses and resin.

This was the place where the woman of the house was all important. While many households were run by male stewards, the stillroom tasks were invariably overseen by the mistress of the house. She alone had the keys to unlock precious cupboards and coffers containing expensive and sometimes rare ingredients and the lovingly compiled recipe books which contained her own very special ways to make things. Recipes were passed down by mother to daughter or through a household so there was a long unbroken link between the generations and the years. Even now we can trace so many stillroom recipes back through the years and see the influence of past generations on one branch of our day-to-day lives.

The woman at this period needed to be a gardener, a herbalist, a cook, a good organiser, a nurse and a perfumer. Certain times of year would have been desperately busy, trying to keep pace preserving the flow of produce reaching the stillroom. In winter months there would have been more time to take stock and make things from the stored ingredients, lining the walls with jars and crocks. Regular checking of items in store would have been necessary in an age before refrigeration or central heating, when damp, insects and vermin were constant problems in the storecupboards. But there would have been rewards too, for example during seasonal feasting such as Christmas when a well stocked stillroom would provide the luxurious and very special foods and drinks which helped to make the festival a lavish occasion during a frugal time of year.

A modern day stillroom can be wherever you choose. An average kitchen would provide all the equipment and space that you are likely to need, though storage for the results of your labours may need some thought. Few new houses are built with any cool larder space, presuming people rely on the fridge and freezer for their food. Ideally a cool, dark space is necessary for keeping jams and marmalades, but you may have to make do with boxes stored under the bed in an unheated spare room or an outside building.

Where once there were just knives and pestles and mortars, we now have food processors, liquidisers and other tools to speed up jobs. Some preparation is infinitely better done with the help of a machine, some is not, but, unless you want to, there is no need to do things the hard way for the sake of authenticity. Some people take pride and pleasure in cutting peel as thin as they can for their own special marmalade, others would be happy to roughly mince it and not bother with niceties. It is up to you how you go about things, but remember that sometimes the pleasure of making something is often bound up with the processes it takes to do it. A quiet, gentle session stoning and skinning a bowlful of peaches is a soothing and pleasing, if somewhat sticky, task. The trick is always to make enough time to do the job uninterrupted and properly.

JARS AND BOTTLES

I have collected and inherited storage and preserving jars over the years. Some are so old fashioned I can no longer get rubber rings and replacement fittings for them, but I can still use the jars with home-made tops. Manufacturers of modern glass preserving jars have an irritating way of changing the design every few years and making your older jars obsolete. Probably the most useful jars to buy are the spring-top French Le Parfait jars which come in a basic shape in a variety of sizes. Their design has hardly changed for years so new rubber rings are easy to get. After opening a sealed jar the rings have stretched and cannot be used again.

You will probably find these jars useful for chutneys, pickles, marmalade and fruit jams made in large quantities and recipes such as vegetables in oil or where you need to sterilize the jar in a water bath. This is the process of bringing the jars up to a certain temperature in a large pan of water either on top of a stove or in an oven. The temperature is held for a particular length of time according to what you are sterilizing and then, when the jars have cooled down, the seal is tested to make sure you have a perfect airtight fit. My

■ *Bottles of liqueurs and country wines collect dust on an attic ledge (right).*

mother bottled fruits in this way before the days of freezing and it is still useful for some preserves, especially fruit syrups, ketchups and essences, such as mushroom essence. As a guide, the filled jars or bottles are stood well apart up to their lids in a deep water bath, standing on a trivet so they do not touch the pan base. Over an hour the water temperature is slowly brought up to 38°C (100°F) and then on to 74°C (165°F) and maintained for 10 to 15 minutes. Remove jars after this and leave them to cool, then check that the seal is firm. If all this sounds far too complicated, then the good news is that we hardly need to bother with this practice these days. We can combine the best of the old and new ways of doing things and simply keep anything in the fridge which is doubtful stored at room temperature.

Collect small, shaped glass jars and bottles for storing lotions, polishes, and other things. These days it sometimes means that you have to eat your way through rather a lot of

■ *In an efficient stillroom, notes and recipes are collected through the years (above).*

■ *Old-fashioned green glass jars shine from their recent wash and scrub before being filled with good things (above).*

special yoghurt or something similar to acquire a reasonable amount of small glass jars. I buy old fashioned jam jars without screw thread tops and old 2 lb jars whenever I see them. They are getting scarce now but sometimes one is lucky. The old thick glass jars are uneven and charming. Obviously dating from a time when weights and measures had not been heard of, their shapes and thickness of glass varies. Whatever you put in them, though, looks good. It is not often possible to buy empty plain glass jars for preserves, though there is a good choice of new glass bottles and larger storage jars made from recycled glass. Some of these have cork stoppers or you can buy corks from wine-making shops.

ONLY THE BEST

Old recipes tend to use malt vinegars where needed and large amounts of sugar. Strong vinegars are still vital ingredients in some pickle recipes, but now we usually prefer to use wine and cider vinegars which don't have quite such an acidic kick to them.

The question of sugar is tricky – while of course we should all eat less for our teeth and bodies' sake, there is nothing to replace its preserving qualities which is why it is in jams and preserves to start with. Commercial manufacturers are inventing sugarless spreads and low sugar jams but my view is that I'd rather have the real thing very occasionally than something less good more often. That is not to say that we can't reduce the sugar levels enormously in recipes and produce fresher tasting and more delicious results. Again, by using the fridge to help in their storage, jams can have less sugar in them than the classic 1-to-1 fruit to sugar balance. To keep well and not go mouldy jams and jellies should have 60% sugar content. There is a way to work this out in the finished jam. The weight of sugar put in the jam is multiplied by 100 and divided by the weight of jam made. This should be a minimum of 60% to keep well. Much depends on the raw ingredients and the method that you use. The chances are that you will not be making kilos of preserves to keep for ages so long term storage should not be a problem. Experiment and use less sugar when you can.

The key to good results is good ingredients and in every case the quality of the produce you started out with will show through in the final jar. It goes without saying that fruit and vegetables are needed as fresh as possible and nothing too ripe or past its prime is worth preserving. Generally there are no corners to be cut except, perhaps, when you have to buy alcohol for a fruit liqueur and here at least there is generally no point in buying fine cognac or expensive branded vodka. Proper preserving sugar is costly but does work well, otherwise use cane sugar rather than beet sugar if possible. There is jam-making sugar available containing pectin to help fruits set but generally this isn't necessary except, perhaps, for tricky fruits such as strawberries. I find that lemon juice helps and I never aim for stiff jam but jam with lots of fruit so at least it doesn't run off the bread.

GIFTS AND GREAT OCCASIONS

When storing and preserving foods was a matter of life and death rather than a pleasing thing to do occasionally, the religious festivals and traditional feast days lit up the year's calendar in more ways than one. In the depths of winter came Christmas and Twelfth Night and the celebration of the shortest day having passed gave great optimism. Food was brought out from the storecupboards and special things made during the summer for just such feasting were spread with ceremony upon a groaning table. Particular foods became associated with a time of year, such as mincemeat and almond marzipan and rich enormous puddings made from dried and candied fruits.

We continue to this day to make special occasion foods such as this, so people still make Christmas puddings in November on 'Stir-up Sunday' or thereabouts and densely fruited cakes not just for Christmas but for weddings and christenings, anniversaries and birthdays. Family traditions still continue so in the first spell of warm weather in spring, for example, I make a jug of lemonade to drink in the garden just as my mother did for us every year.

Many of the recipes and ideas for items to make in this book are the kind of things which everyone loves to be given. A home-made present, particularly one of food, has none of the stigma of 'Where did it come from and how much did it cost?' or is it to the recipient's sophisticated taste. None of that matters as it is just a simple friendly expression of time having being spent on someone else's behalf and that is always touching.

If you are clever you can probably make all the gifts you might want to give at Christmas from one session making fruit ratafias or herb jellies. Nearer the time, shorter term things such as home-made olive paste and potted cheeses make excellent presents and are more welcome and unexpected than sweet concoctions.

■ *Fruits, berries and leaves left over from a harvesting need not be wasted (below).*

AUTUMN

Never-ending days of summer give way to a change in the air. The days shorten rapidly, the first frosts appear and there is a sense of urgency to collect and use all the seasonal good things which are still to be found in the garden and hedgerows. Tree fruits of all kinds need to be dealt with and preserved or stored. There are nuts and fungi, too, and any garden root crops must be lifted and protected in order to last until spring.

■ *Autumn means it is time to hoard and store all the produce that will keep. Nuts in their convenient storage shells are definitely worth the space they take up.*

EARLY AUTUMN

'And fruit and leaf are as gold as fire
And the oat is heard above the lyre.'

A. C. SWINBURNE
Atlanta in Calydon

ALTHOUGH MOST of us see plenty of fresh produce throughout the year, this is still the season of abundance and harvest. Gardens, shops and countryside are laden with good things. Some of the richest pickings are free from the hedges and trees and the soft, damp weather brings out clutches of fungi on the forest floor. If the weather has been kind to the trees, and you've stolen a march on the birds and animals, there should be nuts to find amongst the turning leaves. In some years many gardens have one or more trees simply laden with so much fruit that produce cannot even be given away, and for those without time to deal with the baskets of apples or windfallen pears guilt is induced as the harvest lies waiting. But one need not feel bad if every last bit of this bounty isn't stored away. Nothing is wasted by the time birds, insects and mice have eaten their fill. Watching butterflies feed from the sweet syrup of over-ripe plums is as satisfying as having preserved the fruit in jars or made it into chutney. But even one or two pots of home-made jam or chutney induces a glow of satisfaction and thrift so an hour

■ *The fleeting milky bloom on the surface of plum skins is one of the best things about these delicious fruits, whether they come from orchard trees or free from the hedgerows (above).*

or two found to use up and preserve some of the delicious seasonal produce is always worthwhile.

At this time of year the last of the garden plums and damsons are still in season and later wild sloes and bullace are free in the hedges. Related to the damson, wild bullace are like small round gages, green to begin with and ripening to a translucent, freckled apricot colour. Wild fruits have an astringency and strength of flavour which makes them best of all for recipes which require a large quantity of sweetening. While garden varieties of plums are good to eat raw or simply cooked, fruits such as elderberries and sloes are intensely flavoured, making them ideal for jellies and fruit pastes. One exception to this is the humble blackberry or bramble which is sweet and mild in flavour and, though children love the soft purple jelly made from it, the inclusion of plenty of lemon or sour crab apple juice is necessary to spark up the taste.

This time of year finds space for storage at a premium especially if you have garden crops to keep through the winter. By the end of the summer everything from the previous year should have been finished up and shelves free once more, apart from summer preserves. Much of what is made through the autumn will be destined for long term storage and for eating through the whole year, so spend some time organising what goes where. For example, put jars of chutney, which need time to mellow, on the highest shelves or at the back of cupboards.

Garden crops and root vegetables will also need to be harvested and ripened and a suitable place made ready for their storage. In milder climates it is often best to leave crops such as carrots and parsnips in the ground to pick as needed, but onions, potatoes, beetroot and turnips must be kept from frost. Marrows and pumpkins if really sound should keep well in an outhouse or cellar and it is sensible to get as much as possible put away so at least it can be dealt with later through the winter when there is more time to do something with it. For example, beetroot will keep for many weeks so if you want to make pickles or chutneys they can be done when the pressure is off and all perishable produce used up.

Certain things such as mushrooms will need to be dealt with as soon as possible after picking, as will any really ripe fruit or vegetable but other items are more good natured, so there is no rush for example with nuts and solid-hearted red and white cabbage will hang quite safely from strings or in netting for weeks in a cool, dark place.

FRUIT PASTES AND CHEESES

From medieval times to the nineteenth century great importance was placed on the number of preserved fruits a household could produce. Colour was everything, so a simple apple cheese recipe would be adapted to produce shades from the palest green through amber to red. The stiff fruit pastes and cheeses were used to fill elaborate sectioned pastry tarts with patterns as complex as a seventeenth-century parterre or cut into jewel-like decorations. A remnant of this tradition survived until this century in the multicoloured jam tarts often seen at country tea tables.

At this phase of the year time is concentrated on storing and preserving food for the larder with less thought of making lotions and perfumes and other things for the house. The last of the summer roses can still be harvested for their petals as many of the old-fashioned types have a good second blooming now. Late lavender should be plentiful along with many other herbs, though most will have lost their summer freshness and pungency. If you have grown any plants for their seeds then now is the time to pick and dry these. Often the simplest way is to pick the whole seed head and place in a large paper bag, then shake it to extract seeds if they are ripe and ready. Liqueurs, ratafias and all manner of drinks made by steeping ingredients in an alcoholic base can be started now. Many are quick to mature and will be ready to drink by the time winter sets in but some are well worth keeping for twelve months to broach with ceremony a whole year on.

WILD PLUM SWEETMEATS

This is a variation on the ancient recipe for quince paste or membrillo, eaten as a dessert or sweetmeat. Its success depends on using a very sharp, strongly flavoured fruit such as sloe or bullace which holds its own against long cooking and the sweetness of the sugar. There is no need to stone the fruit before cooking.

1.4 kg (3 lb) wild plums or sloes
300 ml (10 fl oz) water
1 kg (1 lb 4 oz) sugar
caster sugar for decorating

Cook the plums with water very gently until completely soft. Push the fruit through a sieve and return to the pan with the sugar. Cook stirring often until it forms a thick purée. Keep simmering and the fruit paste will get thicker and thicker, spitting and bubbling dramatically. When it comes away from the sides of the pan, pour it into a shallow tin to cool and set. Cut into small squares and roll them in sugar. Store in an airtight container until required.

■ *The dense and richly flavoured paste made from wild plums will keep well into the winter and beyond, to eat as a dessert at the end of a meal or with soft fresh cheeses (above).*

ROSE-HIP MARMALADE

This is based on a Danish recipe for a delicious cross between jam and conserve. The result does not set solid but is very full of fruit. In Denmark it is often stored away to be eaten in late winter or early spring when it is as welcome as a tonic. Any large fruited, fleshy rose-hips will do either from the wild, or from bushes such as the Japanese *rugosa* garden roses.

1 kg (2 lb) rose-hip shells, cleaned of all seeds
175 ml (6 fl oz) distilled malt vinegar
275 ml (10 fl oz) water
½ vanilla pod
500 g (1 lb) sugar
Juice of 1–2 lemons

Put rose-hips, vinegar, water and vanilla in a large pan. Simmer gently until almost completely soft. Add the sugar and cook until the hips are really soft and the marmalade thickened a little. Add lemon juice to taste. Remove the vanilla pod and pot into large jars, preferably china, not glass, to stop the preserve losing its colour.

■ *Rose-hips are high in Vitamin C but are often overlooked as fruits to use for preserves (above). They come into their own in a subtle jam made from an old Danish recipe (right).*

HOUSES IN the country lucky enough to have productive fruit trees often have space in outbuildings to store sound surplus fruit, but however well-built for the purpose, it is always difficult to keep mice, rats and insects away from the tempting plunder. At one time large kitchen gardens had special fruit stores, often built in a circular shape with a thatched roof and row upon row of well ventilated shelves. Here all the top fruit such as pears, apples, medlars and quinces, as well as grapes with their stems in special jars full of water, would be stored. Slatted shelves arranged in tiers in a frame are still a good way for smaller households to keep fruit through the winter. These should be put in a cellar,

■ *In the crook of the tall old Sussex tree which produced them, a clutch of red Lady Sudeley apples wait while the rest of the crop are picked (above).*

■ *Perfect Comice pears ready to be stored and ripened slowly. A tiny dab of shiny sealing wax helps to keep each pear fresh (left).*

attic or cool larder and filled with fruit, allowing air to circulate through the racks but never letting the apples or pears touch their neighbours. Conditions during storage should be cool and not too dry otherwise the fruits shrivel and turn leathery or ripen and spoil too fast.

Commercial warehouses are kept refrigerated to hold fruit until wanted for sale and this does little for fruit which is usually picked too early, anyway, for flavour to develop. Pears for example should normally be picked before they are ripe and then ripened slowly in store where they can be regularly checked. Held in cold conditions until required, they are then brought into a warm room to ripen to just the right degree of soft juiciness.

The vast number of old varieties of apples and pears is proof that different types were bred for different purposes with a view to spreading their use from the earliest harvested summer fruits right round to stored fruits kept almost until the next year's new crop. Some types of apple, such as the sweetly named Norfolk biffin, were bred specifically to be dried whole, usually strung on long ropes like a giant necklace. Many of the long forgotten apples were used for cider which was once the everyday drink of rural England and in medieval times apples were used almost exclusively to make verjuice or cider, or the fruit preserved in some way while the fresh fruit was scorned – perhaps those very early varieties were mouth-puckeringly sour. Some varieties of apple keep beautifully off the tree while many of the early types just don't store and need eating as soon as they are picked. Greasy skinned varieties such as Bramley's seedling are definitely happy to be stored and will keep sound for several months especially if each fruit is individually wrapped in a little protective coat of newspaper. A glut of non-keeping apples means a session at the stove making a simple apple sauce or purée to be bottled or frozen, or variations on the chutney theme using apples as a base with other seasonal fruits and vegetables.

SIMPLE APPLE PURÉE

This is endlessly useful in the storecupboard as a basis for puddings, cakes and sauces. A mixture of apples is often good though certain cooking varieties will turn to a perfect fluffy sauce without help. You must decide whether to add sweetening depending on the future use.

Peel and core apples and slice finely into a large heavy pan. Cook over a gentle heat with no extra liquid, watching that it does not catch. Cook until the apple softens or turns fluffy then take off the heat and beat vigorously or liquidise it if you want it completely smooth. This makes a delicious purée full of flavour to which you can add some pure vanilla, a few scrapings of lemon zest, sugar if you like, and a small knob of unsalted butter. You could also spice some batches with cinnamon or ginger. This can be bottled into preserving jars then sealed and sterilised.

Yet another solution to baskets of ripe fruit is to dry the apples in rings. This is only really practical if you have a constant gentle heat source such as a cooking range which is

permanently warm, though small batches can be dried in a very cool oven or airing cupboard. Once dried, the finished slices, which are like curly pieces of soft chamois leather, can be stored in big glass jars or tins in a cool dark cupboard. For culinary use it is best to remove the peel before drying but if you plan to use the rings for more decorative purposes then the red or green skin looks pretty left on the fruit. Dried apple rings can be made into wonderful garlands, ropes and wreaths for decorating the house at Christmas. One of the prettiest ideas is to thread dried apple rings (use either red- or green-skinned fruit) amongst dried eucalyptus leaves to make a subtle garland in shades of deep burgundy or lime mixed with the blue-green foliage of the eucalyptus.

DRIED APPLE RINGS

Use fruit which is unblemished and sound and peel each apple if you wish. Either core the whole apple with an apple corer, or wait until you have sliced each apple into rings and then use a small circular metal cutter to remove a circle of core. Leave the core intact if the rings are for decoration. Cut the rings about 4 mm (1/8 inch) thick or 'as thick as a Victorian wedding ring' which is a charming description but somewhat vague. Put the cut apple rings into a large bowl containing a salt solution of 40 g salt to 3.4 litres water (1½ oz to 6 pints). Steep the rings for about 10 minutes then thread them on bamboo canes and hang above a heat source. They dry quite quickly depending on the warmth, probably two to three days. They remain slightly soft and leathery to the touch.

■ *A simple bamboo cane and a gentle heat source are the only things required to dry metres of red and green apple rings batch by batch throughout the autumn (above and left).*

HOME-GROWN tomatoes often linger on the vine long after the summer has gone if there are no early frosts to spoil the fruit. The tough stringy stems of outdoor grown plants can be pulled, complete with root and plenty of green tomatoes, and hung to continue ripening in a dry place such as a barn or greenhouse. The fruits do not need sun to ripen though the flavour will not be as good as during the hot summer months. These bonus fruits can be used to make chutneys and jams and are one of the great standbys for people with kitchen gardens. French cooks have no qualms when it comes to making jams with wonderful and weird combinations of ingredients. They make a delicious preserve out of green tomatoes, walnuts and lemons which has a subtle and rather sophisticated taste. Use any basic jam recipe with the proportion of about two thinly sliced lemons and 150g (5oz) of chopped walnuts to a kilo (2lb) of tomatoes.

■ *The bright yellow of fresh ingredients transforms to a rich gold once fruits, vegetables and spices have been simmered to make chutney (above and right).*

YELLOW TOMATO AND PEPPER CHUTNEY

Hardened chutney addicts are always looking for a new recipe. Yellow tomatoes form the base of this one with other flavours all taking their cue from the colour yellow. Chutneys give the cook the chance to be truly inventive but judicious tasting is necessary as 'less is more' is often the best approach and restraint gives better results than adding more and more different ingredients. Remember that flavours do change and develop in storage.

2kg (4½lb) yellow tomatoes
450g (1lb) onions
450g (1lb) yellow peppers
salt
700g (1½lb) sugar
900ml (1½pints) white wine or cider vinegar
10g (½oz) whole mustard seed
10g (½oz) ground cayenne
10g (½oz) ground turmeric
10g (½oz) ground cumin
3 cloves garlic, chopped

Peel tomatoes if you have the patience – some people do not mind the bits of skin in the finished chutney. To skin tomatoes drop into boiling water, leave for 4 minutes then plunge into cold water and peel. Slice tomatoes, onions and yellow peppers. Put them into a large shallow dish and sprinkle with salt. Leave overnight then rinse off salt and drain. Put sugar, vinegar and spices into a large pan and stir until sugar is dissolved, then add the drained fruit and vegetables. Simmer gently for about three hours, stirring frequently. The chutney is ready when it has a good jammy texture but you may need to add more vinegar or simmer it a bit longer to reach this stage. Remove from the heat and leave to cool slightly before potting into jars and sealing. Leave to mature for several weeks.

A liking for spiced and pickled foods seems to be a worldwide indulgence and what started as a means to store and preserve foods has developed into a branch of cooking in its own right. Steeping foods in vinegar or verjuice, which was an early version of the preservative, has been practised for centuries. The medieval stillroom produced pickled flowers, including whole rose buds and various stems and roots, to garnish winter salads. In the seventeenth century samphire and broom buds received similar treatment and by the eighteenth century recipes abound for pickled radish, golden pippins, fennel, green walnuts, and for catsup and strong keeping sauces to spice bland foods and plain boiled or roasted meats. By the nineteenth century the Indian colonial influence had added mango chutney to the list as well as more homely things such as pickled cabbage and pickled eggs.

MID-AUTUMN

'I desired to know what Mushrooms they had in the Market. I found but few, at which I was surpris'd, for I have all my Life been very cautious and inquisitive about this kind of Plant, but I was absolutely astonish'd to find, that as for Chamignons, and Moriglio's, they were as great strangers to 'em as if they had been bred in Japan.'

WILLIAM KING
Journey to London 1699

THE SUSPICION of fungi of all sorts is often as common today as it appears to have been in London in the seventeenth century, but we are beginning to take a new approach inspired by the attitude of other countries. An autumn sortie out into the woods and forests in Italy or France, for example, is seen as both a pleasurable and a useful occupation, often producing a basket of fragile delicacies to be made into tempting soups or sauces or dried for winter use.

Of course there are risks in eating unidentified mushrooms but in most cases the best varieties to eat are distinctive and easy to recognise and identify. The best guide to what is safe to eat is always someone who is already knowledgeable but there are dozens of specialist books which give guidance and encouragement.

Certain types of mushroom lend themselves perfectly to drying as a means of storage. The boletus varieties, or ceps as they are often called, are large, meaty mushrooms with a curious spongy flesh rather than the more common delicate gills usually found under the cap. Beech woods are a good hunting ground for *Boletus edulis* in late autumn and their season is quite long. They should be sliced across into thin pieces, discarding the stem if it is very tough. The pieces can be strung onto threads or spread out on a fine mesh or muslin and put in a warm place with plenty of air movement to hasten the drying process. If you do not have a suitable constant gentle heat source, the mushrooms can be dried in an oven at the lowest temperature setting, leaving the door slightly ajar to let the moisture escape. Ordinary field mushrooms or even bought cultivated ones can be preserved in this way and, unless they are enormous, can be dried whole. Once dry they should be stored in a jar and used to add flavour to soups and stews after a soak in water to re-constitute them.

Another delicious variety of wild mushroom which is easy to identify is the girolle or chanterelle (*Cantherellus cibarius*), a pretty apricot-coloured trumpet-shaped fungus usually found in woodland. It has a delicious, subtle earthy flavour, best eaten as a dish alone or with nothing to overshadow its taste. Italian cooks who love and respect all kinds of wild fungi make wonderful marinated and oil-preserved mushroom recipes to eat as hors d'oeuvres while cooks with a passion for sauces and strong condiments follow traditional recipes to make rich mushroom essences or ketchups to add judiciously to soups, stews and gravies.

■ *Any unknown mushrooms must be identified carefully with books and spore prints or by an expert (left above).*

■ *Beautiful mauve-stemmed wood blewits appear in autumn and are easily recognisable. Their name comes from their delicate bluish colouring (left below).*

MUSHROOM ESSENCE

Use large black-gilled field mushrooms. The result is dark and thin, like soy sauce, and beautifully flavoured. The quantities can be varied according to your harvest but base amounts around these proportions.

1.8 kg (4 lb) large black gilled field mushrooms
110 g (4 oz) sea salt
3 cloves garlic
1 litre (1¾ pints) red wine vinegar
½ teaspoon ground ginger
½ teaspoon ground allspice
½ teaspoon ground mace
¼ teaspoon ground black pepper
2 tablespoons port
2 tablespoons brandy, optional

Slice the mushrooms and layer with salt in a large bowl. Leave overnight. Wash off the salt and put the mushrooms into a large saucepan with garlic, vinegar and spices. Simmer very gently for about one hour, stirring occasionally. Strain through muslin and add port and brandy. Pour into small bottles and sterilize for 30 minutes. If to be used immediately, cork it and keep in the fridge.

■ *Use small bottles to store the concentrated essence and, after sterilizing, seal over the cork with sealing wax. Once opened store in a fridge (above).*

The fiery chilli pepper is believed to have been grown as a cultivated crop as early as 7000 BC in the mountains of Mexico but it did not reach the wider world until very much later. Countries such as India, which we imagine have always cooked with the heat of chillies, only acquired the plant as late as the sixteenth century.

The capsicum family of which hot chillies are just one type is vast and probably all types originate from central and South America. In general the mild sweet peppers all belonging to the *Capsicum annuum* genus grow in temperate zones, while the hot varieties from both *Capsicum annuum* and *Capsicum frutescens* come from the tropics. The chilli spread via the Portuguese spice route to the Far East and to Africa and down to the southern part of North America and Brazil through the slave trade.

DRIED HEAT

Chillies are very simple to dry and store. Thread each fruit on to strong thread using a big darning needle. Just remember not to lick the end of the thread to get it through the needle eye half way through the process! Hang the rope of chillies above a warm stove to dry then store in jars until needed. Chillies threaded like this are incredibly colourful and decorative, particularly if the orange and red types are used.

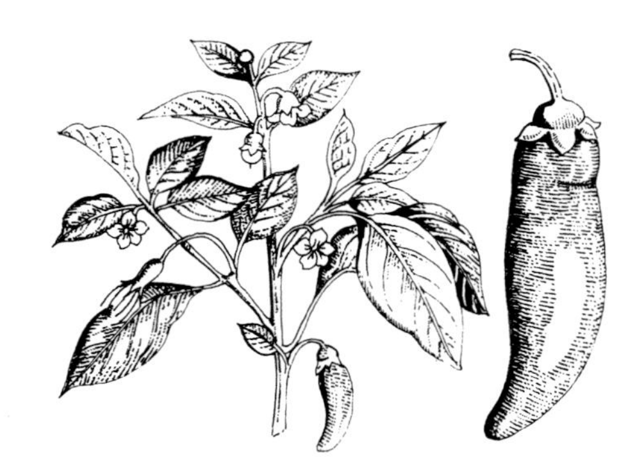

The Spanish brought seeds to Europe as a substitute for Asian pepper (*Piper nigrum*) and different varieties of capsicum immediately became popular, unlike many south American crops such as maize and tomatoes which took far longer to become accepted.

The chilli is now the most widely used spice in the world. Dried chillies and ground chilli powder have found their way into many pickle and chutney recipes over the years but it is only since we have all embraced ethnic foods into our everyday eating that we know what to do when faced with a fresh red or green chilli. There are more than 150 known types of chilli but, depending where you live, you will be lucky to find a choice of more than two or three fresh, though it is possible to buy them dried as well as canned and pickled. The hottest chillies are bird peppers known as *pequin* in Mexico while others such as *poblanos*, another Mexican type, are less fiery and therefore have a more distinctive flavour of their own above the heat. The seeds and tissue inside a chilli contain the alkaloid capsaicin which burns and irritates skin and is extremely painful if it touches the eye. Always take care when preparing chillies as it is so easy to forget and rub your face or eye with a chilli-covered finger. Wear gloves if you can and discard the seeds unless you are a complete masochist. The painkiller effects of capsaicin have been used to relieve aching muscles, asthma and even sore throats but there have been as many unpleasant uses of the stuff through history too. Chilli is supposed to help a hangover, hence the Tabasco in various hair-of-the-dog cures.

Sweet peppers are far more familiar as they are linked in our minds with mediterranean dishes and memories of squeaky fresh piles of peppers glowing in market baskets in France, Spain or Italy. Grown commercially as a year-round crop in an ever increasing rainbow range of colours, they have become an everyday sight to us. The best way to preserve their warm, sweet taste is to remove the skin by grilling them, then store them in olive oil. This method gives them a smoky, melting quality miles away from their over-assertive raw crunch and flavour.

■ *Fiery chillies burn with an intense colour as well as a powerful heat when they are fresh or as here, when dried and strung into long decorative garlands for storing (right).*

RED PEPPERS IN OIL

Jars of red peppers preserved in oil are useful for providing a last minute first course or part of a mixed cold table. The strips of peppers can also be drained well from the oil and added to pasta sauces or other dishes where you need the colour, texture and smokey taste of peppers prepared this way. You could also make this with yellow or orange peppers or a mixture of all three colours. Precise quantities are difficult to give so adapt according to your harvest. Remember that after grilling, the peppers lose a good deal of moisture and reduce in volume. A small preserving jar will hold roughly four fresh peppers.

Ripe red peppers
Olive oil

To remove the pepper skin spear each fruit on to a fork and hold over a naked gas flame or put under a very hot grill, turning regularly until the skin is blistered, charred and black. Put the peppers into a large paper bag and close it, letting the peppers sweat. When they are cold the skin should peel off easily. Cut each pepper into half and remove pith and seeds, then cut flesh into small strips and pat dry. Pack the strips into clean jars and top up with olive oil, being sure to cover the peppers completely. Seal the jars and keep in a cool place. As you eat the peppers, keep the rest submerged beneath the oil.

■ *A selection of red peppers and chillies preserved in oil. Peppercorns can also be added to the oil and the corks can be sealed with sealing wax (overleaf).*

ONE PART of the great autumn harvest which we often overlook these days are seeds and the uses that they can be put to. We are all familiar with the huge variety of fruits, vegetables and nuts available today, but the seeds contained within many fruits are just as edible and delicious and usually packed with minerals, healthy oils and good things which are hard to obtain from other foods. Seeds are little powerhouses of energy waiting to be set in motion as anyone who has sprouted them and watched the fast and astonishing transformation from apparently dead brown husk to fat green shoot will realise.

A few traditional seeds have come back into favour recently so now it is not unusual to find delicious seeded bread containing such things as linseed and sunflower seeds. Flavouring seeds such as caraway and aniseed are also making a welcome come-back into fashion. At one time a seed-cake was food worthy of derision and considered a plain and boring tea-time staple. Now we might think such a cake a true delicacy because of its rarity and it can certainly be quite scrumptious if properly made with butter and good eggs. Large fruits like pumpkins contain huge quantities of seeds which are often wasted when only the rich orange inner flesh is used but they can easily be separated from the stringy inner core and washed clean. Spread them out on a baking sheet and leave to dry in a warm place, then store in jars. You can toast them later in a moderate oven for about 25 minutes after tossing them in a mixture of salt and a little vegetable oil.

A delicious spice mixture which includes pumpkin seeds is easy to make and excellent eaten with baked potatoes, sprinkled on salads or used to dip hard boiled eggs into. Simply dry-fry an equal quantity of hazelnuts, pumpkin seeds, and sesame seeds together and sprinkle in some cumin seeds and coriander seeds. Add a pinch of chilli powder and salt and pepper. Grind this mixture roughly in a coffee grinder or food processor then store in an airtight jar and use as needed. Roasting or dry-frying the seeds releases their aromatic oils, increasing their flavour. However, they must be heated gently.

Sunflower seeds should be husked from their hard outer shell to reveal the sweet and soft inner kernel.They, too, can be toasted for more flavour or spiced up with soy sauce or flavourings such as chilli or cumin. Add sunflower seeds to salads and cereals and wholewheat breads or sprinkle them on thick yoghurt with honey.

SUNFLOWER AND PUMPKIN SEED BREAD

This is good, solid, chewy real bread that is delicious enough to eat without butter. The oats and seeds add a slight sweetness and make the loaf taste particularly good if eaten with slightly salty cheese or spiced foods. To make two large loaves.

FIRST STAGE

1 sachet Fermipan dried yeast, approx 6g (1/4 oz)
350g (12 oz) unbleached strong white flour
350g (12 oz) wholemeal flour
300ml (1/2 pint) warm milk
570ml (1 pint) warm water

SECOND STAGE

1 teaspoon salt
75g (3 oz) melted butter
350g (12 oz) wholemeal flour
450g (1 lb) rolled oats
75g (3 oz) chopped pumpkin seeds
75g (3 oz) chopped sunflower seeds

FIRST STAGE Put the white flour and first quantity of wholemeal flour into a large bowl and mix in the dried yeast. Add the warm milk and water and mix well. Cover with a damp cloth and leave to rise for about an hour in a warm draught-free place.

SECOND STAGE Next add the salt, melted butter, remaining wholemeal flour, oats and seeds and knead until you have a smooth fairly soft dough. Add more liquid if it seems necessary. Leave to rise again, covered with a damp cloth, for about 50 minutes. Knock back the dough once more and leave for a third proving, this time for about 40 minutes. Finally shape into two loaves, either round or oval, and put on to large greased and floured baking sheets. Leave covered in a warm place to prove for about one hour or doubled in size. Bake in a hot oven 220°C (425°F) Gas Mark 7 for about one hour. Cool on a rack.

Another seed now widely used is the poppy seed. The tiny blue-grey seeds are often seen sprinkled on bread but in Eastern European cookery they are used more inventively and in a quantity large enough to taste their unique flavour. Soaked and ground up with honey or other sweeteners, they fill delicious cakes and pastries. They are easy to harvest from their pepper pot seed heads. Be sure to grow the type which has the culinary seed (*Papaver somniferum*).

■ *A solidly satisfying rustic kind of bread which is good enough to eat alone. The pumpkin and sunflower seeds add sweetness and texture (above).*

In the kitchen seeds and nuts seem to be linked together as ingredients but they both have very different qualities which are not really related. Nuts have always been an important food source as in most cases they contain protein, vitamins and minerals and have their own built-in storage in a most convenient form.

Once shelled, nuts quickly turn stale and the fats they contain become rancid so husk them as you want them and use them up quickly. Shelled nuts should be kept in a cool, dry, dark place in an airtight container. In the past various ways have been found to store nuts for as long as possible and while we can now buy many types now more or less all the year round there can still be seasonal gluts.

When walnuts fall ripe from the tree they very often still have some of the fibre from the green fruit around them. This should be scrubbed off and the shell made perfectly clean before storing them. They are of course at their most delicious when perfectly new and fresh and make a meal with bread and butter and salt to dip the milky kernels into. In medieval times nuts were stored in earth or salt to hold in their natural moisture and stop them drying out. Hazelnuts are always smooth and perfect in their shells when ripe and can be simply stored in old fashioned hessian or string bags. All nuts are best kept in a cool, dark and airy place.

■ *Gathering the harvest of nuts (left). Walnuts in their shells can be stored in coarse salt to keep them fresh and sweet (below).*

PRALINE

The true confectioners' and pâtissiers' praline is made from a mixture of hazelnuts and almonds. A perfect way to store both types of nut! The nuts are roasted first then put into the caramelled sugar. From such simple ingredients comes one of the best flavourings for ice-creams, cakes and all kinds of puddings. In a sheet it is a kind of nut brittle. Ground into powder it keeps well in an airtight jar or can be frozen if you prefer. Make as little or as much as you want simply using the same weight of mixed almonds and hazelnuts as sugar.

75g (3oz) whole unblanched almonds
75g (3oz) whole unblanched hazelnuts
175g (6oz) granulated sugar

Put the nuts on separate baking trays and toast in a moderate oven for about 6 minutes, checking them often and shaking the trays to turn the nuts. When they are slightly browned and toasted take them out of the oven and put almonds aside. Shake the hazelnuts in a dry cloth and most of the loose papery skin will come off. In a heavy-based pan slowly melt the sugar over a gentle heat. Stir occasionally until the sugar has completely melted. When every grain has dissolved, let it bubble and boil until it turns to a light golden colour. Toss in the nuts, stand back and let it cook a bit longer until it is a dark golden brown but don't let it scorch. Draw off the heat and pour it quickly into a shallow tin lined with non-stick paper and leave to cool. When cold and set, break it into rough pieces. Either store it like this or grind to a crunchy powder in a liquidizer or with a rolling pin.

■ *Almonds, hazelnuts and walnuts are transformed into the wicked temptations of praline and candied walnuts (above).*

CANDIED WALNUTS

These tempting walnut halves are coated in a candied spiced sugar coating. Packed tightly into pretty paper cones they make an ideal gift.

100g (4oz) walnut halves
225g (8oz) granulated sugar
Juice of one orange, made up to 150ml (5fl oz) with water
Grated rind of one orange
1 teaspoon powdered cinnamon

Pre-heat the oven to 180°C (350°F) Gas Mark 4. Spread walnuts on to a baking sheet and put in the oven for about 15 minutes. Meanwhile, put the sugar into a pan and add the strained orange juice. Dissolve slowly over a low heat, then bring to the boil and cook rapidly, without stirring, until the temperature reaches 116°C (240°F) on a sugar thermometer (soft ball stage). Take the pan off the heat and add the orange rind, cinnamon, and walnuts. Stir until the mixture becomes creamy. Turn out onto a plate and separate the walnuts. Store in an airtight container.

LATE AUTUMN

'Autumn, I love thy parting look to view
In cold November's day, so bleak and bare,
When thy life's dwindled thread worn nearly thro',
With ling'ring, pott'ring pace, and head bleach'd bare . . .'

JOHN CLARE
Written in November

THE PROSAIC cabbage, though a humble thing, is nevertheless a king among vegetables and is still one of the largest and most important crops grown throughout the world. The original varieties came from shore-growing plants of the Brassica family and are leafy, tough and hardy. Coleworts or worts, as early types of cabbage and kale were known, have always been an important part of poor peoples' diet from Roman times onwards and the medieval stew of beans and worts was a daily staple for centuries. Good ways of preserving cabbage are not easy but pickles of both white and red varieties are excellent and the solid white Dutch cabbages store well hanging in a cool, dark storeroom.

■ *Maligned and underated, the cabbage deserves a finer place in our affections (left). Varieties range from dark red to crinkled Savoy to Dutch white (above).*

SAUERKRAUT

Originally a German dish, this is simply fermented white cabbage produced by layering salt with the shredded leaves. Home-made sauerkraut is far tastier than the shop-bought variety and is well worth the time and effort it takes. The juniper berries add extra flavour. It is only worth making in fairly large quantities so you will need equipment to match. A straight-sided, glazed stoneware jar of about 9 litres (2 gallons) capacity is needed and a big mixing bowl for the first stage.

4 large heads of solid white cabbage
150g (5oz) approx sea salt
Caraway seeds
Juniper berries

Scald the jar and line the base with a few whole leaves. Shred the cabbage very finely, removing the tough stem and core. Weigh the cabbage and put in a very large mixing bowl with 50g (2oz) salt for every 2.5kilos (5lb) cabbage. Leave for about 20 minutes then pack layers of cabbage into the jar adding a few juniper berries and caraway seeds as you go. Add any moisture from the bowl. Cover the top of the cabbage with a double thickness of butter muslin and put a plate on top which fits neatly into the neck of the jar. Stand a heavy weight on the plate and leave jar in a warm room [21°C (70°F)] for several days. When froth appears, remove weight and plate and skim it away. Leave for two more days and re-skim, then continue this for a further two weeks. It is now ready to eat. Either keep it in the fridge, freeze it or store by heating sauerkraut to just below boiling point, put into warm jars then sterilize them in a water bath for 20 minutes for jars up to 1 litre (2 pints). Eat sauerkraut with plenty of plain creamy mashed potatoes and cold meats or use it in pork casseroles and with game.

PICKLED RED CABBAGE

A good old-fashioned pickle to eat with cheese and cold meats. It can be used soon after making and the vinegar keeps it crisp.

2 red cabbages
100g (4oz) salt
600ml (1pint) red wine vinegar
600ml (1pint) distilled malt vinegar
4 bay leaves
1 tablespoon juniper berries
4 whole dried chillies
1 tablespoon black peppercorns
Small piece fresh ginger
1 dessertspoon coriander seeds
5 blades mace

Quarter cabbages and remove stem and core. Shred very finely and put into a bowl, sprinkling layers with salt, and leave for 24 hours. Meanwhile put vinegars into a pan and add spices except bay leaves and juniper berries. Bring to the boil, simmer for 5 minutes then leave to get cold. Next day wash and drain cabbage and pack into jars with bay leaves and juniper berries. Pour in the strained vinegar and seal the lids.

■ *A sharp kitchen knife is the best way to shred red cabbage for the pickle pot (above). Red cabbage pickle should be eaten young while crisp and brilliantly coloured (right).*

COLD REMEDIES

There are many natural ways to help relieve the miserable symptoms of a cold. Peppermint tea sipped slowly or made into an inhalation rapidly helps clear the breathing, as does eucalyptus oil. Put a few drops in a bowl of hot water, put your head under a towel and inhale. Simply to make you feel better as you suffer, run a bath and add a few drops of essential oils before soaking. Try thyme, eucalyptus, lemon and rosemary. A few drops of these oils on a piece of muslin tucked under your pillow at night keep your head clear and make breathing easier.

At one time the stillroom produced all kinds of remedies and medicines for everyday ailments and soothing potions to alleviate the symptoms of winter colds and illnesses. Chilblains, tooth-ache, colds and coughs were all catered for, probably with varying degrees of success. Elizabethan households for example, seemed to have a vast range of delicious-sounding syrups and drinks, often based on flower infusions, which appear to have been no penance at all to swallow. In fact many of the recipes sound as if they were to be first and foremost a comfort or simply strong enough to make one no longer care about the symptoms. Little sweets called rose cakes made from damask rose petals and lemon syrup are one typical recipe for sore throats and honey often found its way into many of these recipes as it was sweet and soothing and considered a natural antiseptic. By Victorian times, medicines seemed to be somewhat harsher and children appear to have been dosed with frightening mixtures and purges, often as a preventative measure let alone a cure. While children today are no doubt relieved that they are not smeared with goose grease at the start of the winter and wrapped in flannel until the spring, or dosed with fish oils daily, they might take kindly to a gentle home-made cough mixture which can only help to soothe. Old recipes for cough treatments include candy made from the stems and leaves of coltsfoot, an early spring wild flower, and an alcoholic infusion of saffron which was thought to help a consumptive cough.

The warm comforting flavour and smell of cinnamon has been used for centuries in the kitchen and sick room where it was considered very important and curative. In a recipe dating from 1600 quite large amounts of this powdered spice were made into special sweets to help relieve the symptoms of a cold. Children were given the little sticks to take to church with them, presumably to try and soothe ticklish coughs through the sermon. Cinnamon was generally used in far greater quantities then and often provided much of the bulk of a recipe. Nowadays we are very restrained with it and use tiny amounts as a spice and flavouring. Compared with many spices it has always been quite plentiful and relatively cheap to buy. Cinnamon comes from the inner bark of a tree from the laurel family *Cinnamomum zeylanicum*, and is sold in little rolls of the bark or ground into a powder which loses its flavour quite quickly. It was often kept in a silver castor to shake onto hot buttered toast and muffins as a delicious tea-time food, a tradition well worth reviving.

Another old remedy for a child's troublesome cough was to make little balls of butter mixed with granulated honey which dissolved in the mouth and soothed the throat, while one of the best ways of ensuring a good night's sleep at the start of a bad cold is to drink a mixture of very hot lemon, honey and whisky, if you like it, last thing at night. The lemon and honey alone is fine while the whisky seems to make it all work faster. The classic cough mixture of lemon, honey and glycerine is still as good as ever and much more pleasing than many commercial remedies on offer at the chemists. Keep a bottle ready mixed in the late autumn or at least be sure to have the ingredients standing by for when you need them. The honey and glycerine soothe while the lemon adds a welcome sharpness and a good dose of Vitamin C which is needed in quantity during illness.

LEMON AND HONEY COUGH MIXTURE

Use honey which has been clarified and will not crystallize. Most shop-bought clear honey is fine. The honey will sooth a ticklish throat and the lemon juice provides a welcome boost of Vitamin C. Both adults and children can benefit from this mixture.

Two juicy lemons
150 ml (5 fl oz) clear honey
50 ml (2 fl oz) glycerine

Squeeze the juice from the two lemons and strain the juice to get it as clear as possible. Put the lemon juice, honey and glycerine into a jug and mix very thoroughly. Pour the mixture into a small medicine bottle and cork tightly.

■ *An old fashioned but soothing cough remedy made from ingredients that you have control over mixing and which actually taste good too (above).*

CINNAMON COUGH SWEETS

These little cough sweets are traditionally rolled into cigar shapes to mimic the real cinnamon quills.

Rosewater
Powdered gum arabic
Powdered cinnamon
Caster sugar

Gently warm about 2 tablespoons of rosewater and add enough gum arabic (approx 2 teaspoons) to make a sticky syrup. Now work in roughly equal amounts of caster sugar and powdered cinnamon until you have a solid paste. Press into a shallow tin and, as it dries, cut it into small sticks. Roll these slightly to make them round. Leave to dry completely.

■ *Little sticks of powdered cinnamon mimic actual curls of cinnamon bark and soothe a sore throat and ticklish cough (above).*

FOR AS long as there have been dried fruits and strong spirits the two have been combined to make ambrosial mixtures. The classic combinations such as prunes and armagnac are familiar to everyone but it is rewarding to experiment and try different versions. Recipes for rich fruit cakes often suggest soaking the dried fruits in brandy or other spirits to give them flavour and fatten them up. A jar of dried apricots in brandy or dates in rum are a useful storecupboard ingredient and can be added to puddings, especially ice creams, or a spoonful of the liqueur can be used as a flavouring or drunk on its own.

YELLOW SULTANAS IN BRANDY

Yellow sultanas are less common than the sweet brown kinds, but they are delicious when used in any recipe that calls for sultanas. They have a fresher, sharper flavour, much closer to a fresh grape, and if left to soak for a while in brandy they become deliciously plump and flavourful. Simply fill a wide-necked jar with the dried fruit, top up with brandy and leave for several weeks.

■ *Plump yellow sultanas soak up the flavour of brandy, ready to release it later in puddings and cakes or in surreptitious spoonfuls (above).*

CAKE TO LAST A YEAR

It is unlikely to do so once it has been cut of course but you can keep it and slowly feed it with brandy if you want to. It is simple and old fashioned but relies on the best ingredients. Find good dried fruit and use whole candied peel which you chop into pieces. You could use sultanas which have been soaked in brandy in which case substitute half the brandy in the recipe with orange juice.

350g (12oz) yellow sultanas
100g (4oz) candied peel, chopped
225g (8oz) currants
225g (8oz) raisins
150ml (5fl oz) brandy
225g (8oz) unbleached plain flour
1 teaspoon of each powdered: mace, nutmeg, cinnamon
225g (8oz) unsalted butter
225g (8oz) soft brown sugar
Grated rind of one orange and one lemon
5 eggs, beaten

A few hours before starting pour brandy over fruit and leave covered. Double line a round deep 23cm (9inch) cake tin with thick paper and non-stick parchment. Sift the flour and add the spices. Beat together the butter, sugar and grated rinds until light, then add the egg little by little, adding a little flour towards the end. Fold in the rest of the flour, then add the fruit. The mixture will be quite stiff. Spoon into the tin and smooth the top, making a slight hollow on the surface. Bake at 170°C (325°F) Gas Mark 3 for about 2½ hours. Test with a skewer towards the end of the baking time. Leave in the tin to cool for 30 minutes, then turn out on to a rack.

■ *A rich fruit cake that might keep a year if it is given the chance but most probably will be eaten at one large family gathering (right).*

THORNES

AUTUMN DEMANDS many hours' work in any garden, from clearing away bushels of leaves and pulling up spent summer bedding annuals to moving and splitting large clumps of herbaceous plants and planting new things such as trees and shrubs. Everyone has the very best intentions and starts work wearing gloves but somehow along the way they get put down and suddenly it's too late to save fingers from the soil and wet and cold winds. Certain soils seem to be more drying and some people have much tougher skin which doesn't seem to complain about rough treatment. The best thing to do is to use something preventative before you begin work, then at the end of the gardening session use a healing type of hand cream to repair the worst damage.

Old recipes seem to rely heavily on lard and animal fats and all kinds of ingredients which we are not likely to want to mix up these days, let alone put anywhere near our skin, but many of the old and more pleasant ingredients are incredibly effective. Making your own lotions and creams puts you in control of what goes into the mixture and most of them are quite delicious and can only do good.

Many chemists stock everything that you might need or can order ingredients especially for you. Certain ingredients such as almond oil are far cheaper bought at a straightforward chemist than at a specialist shop or herbalist. Build up a stock of containers to store your results in. Glass containers with screw top lids are normally the best solution for storing thick creams and lotions. Obviously creams which become quite solid when cool need to be put into wide-mouthed jars that are easy to reach into but liquids are safer in narrow-necked bottles.

GARDENERS' LAVENDER HANDCREAM

The lavender oil used here adds a very slight perfume and is also a powerful healer and antiseptic in its own right. The white wax is bleached bees' wax, once upon a time bleached outdoors in the sun, and is sometimes available as granules which dissolve faster than a large block. If you can only get a block of wax then grate it on the coarse blades of a food grater or shred slivers off the block with a sharp knife. Coconut oil is extracted from the dried flesh of the coconut and has been used for centuries in preparations to moisturize and condition the skin and hair. Almond oil is one of the oldest known cosmetics and is a very light but effective oil which has no scent of almonds. It is still used in many commercial cosmetics. The amounts needed in this recipe are measured in spoons so that you can choose the size of spoon according to how much you want to make.

4 spoons sweet almond oil
4 spoons coconut oil
3 spoons white wax
6 spoons glycerine
Lavender essential oil (about 6 drops if tablespoons are used as a measure)

Put the almond oil, coconut oil and white wax in a double saucepan or a basin over a pan of hot water and gently dissolve them. Stir the mixture to blend it together and when everything has melted add the glycerine drop by drop. Take it off the heat and stir until creamy. Finally add drops of lavender oil and mix well. Put into pots.

■ *Lavender handcream provides a slightly scented, soothing balm for gardeners' hands that get the roughest treatment clearing the autumn garden (left).*

BOX LEAF HAIR TONIC

While no one would dare claim this to be a cure for baldness, box leaves are supposed to be a great restorative to hair and to strengthen it while stimulating the scalp. The better known hair herb is of course rosemary. As the lotion is so simple to make it is probably well worth a try and whatever its effect on thinning hair is, it still makes a good astringent final rinse after hair washing.

4 handfuls of fresh box leaves
1.7 litres (3 pints) spring water
25 ml (1 fl oz) eau de cologne

Put box leaves in a large pan. Pour the water over and bring to the boil. Simmer with a lid on for 15 minutes. Leave to cool for at least two hours before straining the liquid and adding the eau de cologne. Pour through a funnel into bottles. Use as a lotion or final rinse after hair washing.

■ *Common or garden box leaves are used to make a hair tonic which is supposed to combat baldness, but still makes a refreshing hair rinse and tonic for all hair types (above).*

WINTER

horter days and longer evenings make us all turn inwards and try to forget what is happening outdoors. The garden can safely be left a while without working in it much until the weather improves, so time can be spent on comforting cooking sessions in a warm kitchen. This is a particularly pleasurable time, producing festive gifts and good things to re-fill the jars and bottles already being emptied of summer preserves.

■ *Pale grey and green squash in winter's washed out colours. These solid kinds, with a dry flesh, store right round until the next year in their natural state.*

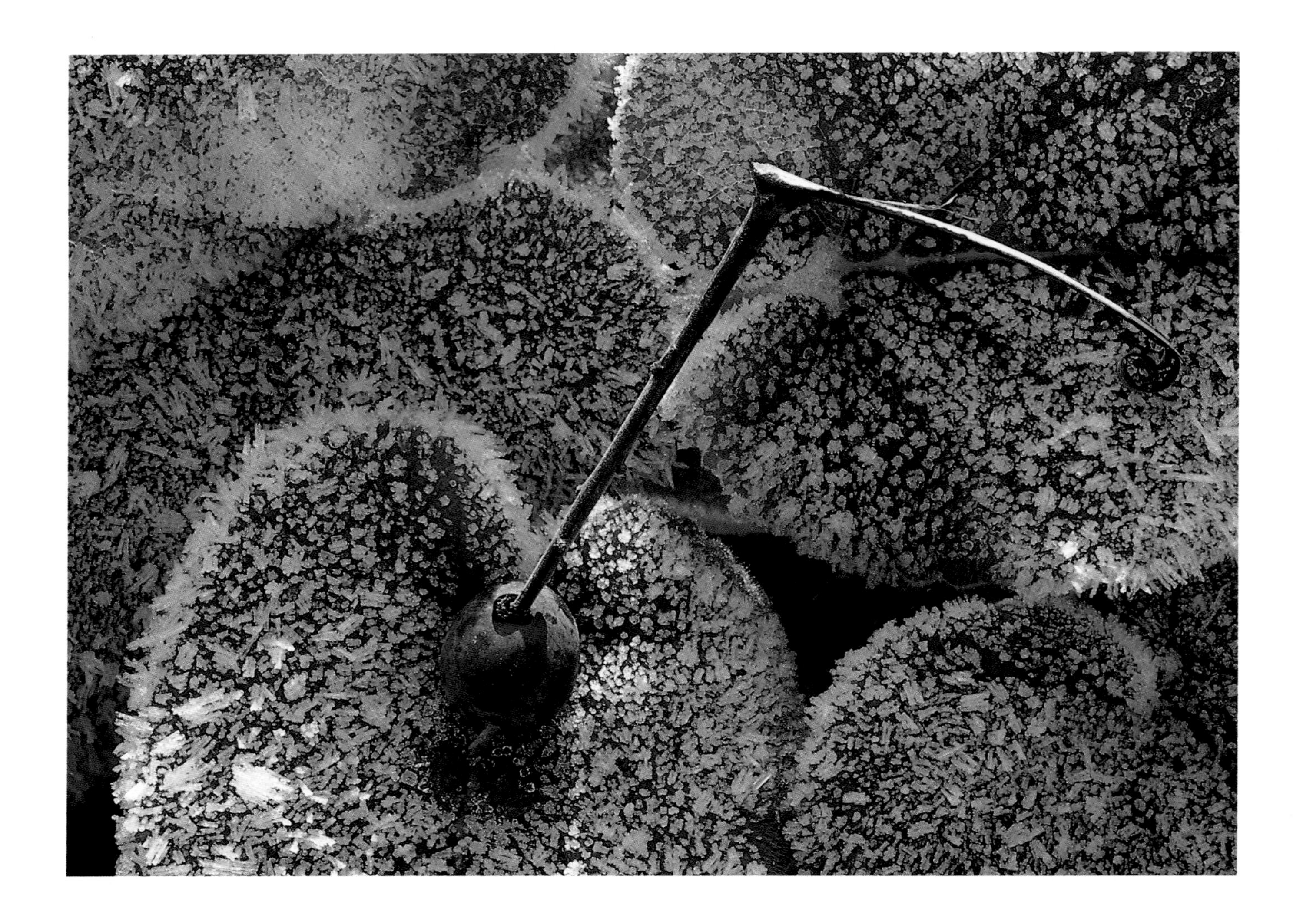

EARLY WINTER

'That which summer getts, winter eats.'
MS Proverbs c.1645

At this stage in the year few stillroom jobs are really pressing but for everyone who lives in the country there is one task which has to be done soon if the rewards of it are to be enjoyed next year. If you are lucky, a walk now along the hedgerows should produce a basketful of sloes. These tiny purplish-black fruits are a kind of wild plum. They contain a small round stone and mouth-puckeringly sour green flesh. The tough skins are coated with a fine silvery bloom and they perch amongst the by-now bare brown branches, all armed with treacherous thorns. The blossom of the sloe blooms early in spring on bare branches and the whole tree or shrub is known as blackthorn (*Prunus spinosa*). Those with a predilection for the superb liqueur that can be made from the fruits will have mapped out where the best bushes are likely to be well in advance of other pickers, though some years do provide a poor harvest. Sloe picking is supposed to be done after the first frost and the fruits are certainly very late to ripen, like their cousins, the wild bullace fruits. The bark of the sloe tree was used in medieval

■ *Traditionally each sloe used for sloe gin should be pricked with one of its own thorns (above).*

times to make a kind of ink and sloes were an old remedy for cow flux and mouth ulcers.

'Many sloes – many cold toes' is an old proverb which should perhaps be heeded. Sloe gin is certainly an excellent way to thaw out after the kind of cold winter walks which leave you feeling that you will never, ever get warm again. Wild fruits and hedgerow finds are the basis for many other different kind of potent ratafias and liqueurs. In the past drinks were made from the flowers of hawthorn steeped in brandy, from the hard fruits of the wild sorb, rowan berries, from elderflowers and elderberries and no doubt many other free pickings. In areas where beech trees were abundant a kind of noyau liqueur was made from the fresh young leaves. Broom flowers flavoured a wine and there were recipes for using cowslips, coltsfoot, primroses, violets and dandelions, though these were much gentler drinks – what we would now call country wines – rather than the stronger mixtures where a spirit was used as the base. Tree saps were made use of too, the best known being birch sap, and the trunks were tapped in early spring for just a short time with no damage done to the trees.

While many people are not willing to go to the effort of making country wines which can be a slightly hit and miss affair with often very disappointing results, all the spirit-based drinks are easy to make and always successful. Considering what they are made from, they are likely to be at least as good as the spirit which you start off with. The only equipment that you need is a supply of bottles with corks or stoppers, a large bowl or container for mixing, a strainer, a funnel and possibly a filter made from muslin or paper if you want a crystal clear drink. Bottles of home-made liqueur are one of the best gifts of all to give to friends though they are, of course, not cheap to make. The best base for many types is tasteless vodka, though brandy is the classic spirit to use with certain fruits such as cherries or apricots and soft summer fruits such as raspberries and blackcurrants. Gin does seem to be the ideal base for use with sloes or damsons, perhaps the juniper and herbal flavourings in it combine particularly well with the acid fruit. Liqueurs can be sweetened with a sugar syrup or simply sugar. The syrup is useful as it can be mixed in after the liqueur is made and adjusted to just the right degree of sweetness. Too much neat sugar at the start, however, cannot be removed after you have decided the drink tastes too sweet.

SLOE GIN

The fiddly part of this job is pricking all the fruits but it can be a soothing companionable task shared with friends or family round the kitchen table. You will need a wide-necked preserving jar with a lid for the first stage. These amounts give approximate proportions of fruit and sugar to spirit.

900g (2 lb) sloes
1.2 litres (2 pints) gin
225g (8 oz) white sugar

Prick each sloe several times with a needle or a sloe thorn. Put the fruit in the jar and add sugar then pour gin over to fill the jar. Seal the top and leave in a dark place for at least 4 months, turning and shaking occasionally. Strain liquid off fruit and bottle. Taste for sweetness and add more sugar if you choose. Keep until following winter.

■ *The result of the previous year's harvest should be savoured slowly and in comfort (above).*

SINCE IT was discovered that sugar preserved fruits, the art of crystallizing and candying has been refined to a high art. Recipe books from as early as 1600 such as *Delightes for Ladies* describe the art of preserving, conserving and candying with many recipes for this process using flowers and fruits, such as 'The most kindly waie to preserve plums', or how 'To candie orange pilles'.

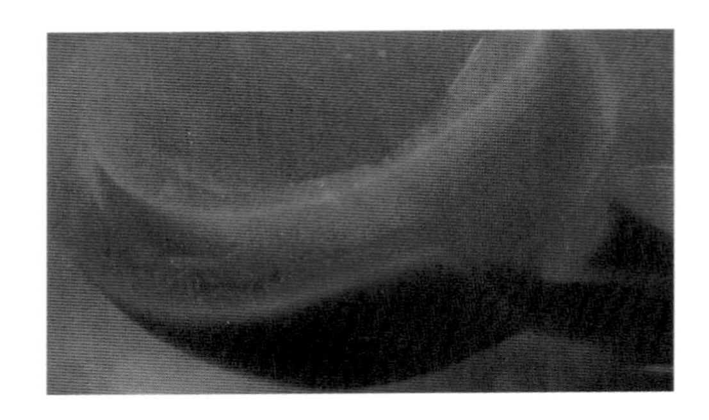

CANDYING FRUIT

The process is very simple in principle but takes time as the fruit is gradually steeped in sugar syrup of an increasing strength day by day until the flesh becomes translucent and completely candied. It is well worth making your own candied grapefruit, lemon and orange peels for cooking and also whole fruits such as apricots, pineapple or clementines. Always keep fruit submerged completely below syrup with a plate and weight. Discard any fruits or peel which do not seem to be taking up the sugar properly.

1. Cook whole fruit very gently in enough water to cover them. Cut unwaxed and preferably organic citrus peels into quarters, removing as much pith as possible. Bring peel to the boil in water once, discard the water, then cook as above in fresh water.
2. Take 300ml (10fl oz) of the water and add 225g (8oz) white sugar, dissolve, then add the drained fruit and cook for one minute.
3. Leave fruit submerged in the syrup for 3 days.
4. Strain the fruit, add 225g (8oz) sugar to syrup, dissolve and bring to boil. Pour over fruit. Leave for 24 hours.
5. Strain the fruit, add 50g (2oz) sugar to syrup, dissolve and bring to boil. Pour over fruit. Leave for 24 hours.
6. Repeat for 2 more days.
7. On the eighth day, drain the syrup and add 75g (3oz) sugar. Boil the syrup and pour over fruit. Leave for 4 days.
8. Drain fruit from heavy syrup and put on wire rack over a tray. Leave in a warm place to dry for several hours. Wrap in waxed paper to store.

Alternatively, to crystallize, dip the fruit in boiling water then roll in sugar. Re-dry. To glacé, make a fresh syrup of 50ml (2fl oz) water and 225g (8oz) sugar. Dip each fruit in syrup, then re-dry.

■ *Quarters of grapefruit peel take on a rich golden colour as they steep in sugar syrup (top).*

■ *An exuberant wrapping for glowing wedges of candied peel. Infinitely better tasting than bought peels, it is a way of re-cycling what is normally wasted (above).*

■ *Candied clementines, rich and sticky, are packed into plain white waxed boxes with a sprig of scented myrtle (right).*

MANY RECIPES for sweetmeats and desserts based on dried fruits, nuts and spices bear the suggestion of middle eastern origins. The rich flavours of almonds, dried apricots and dates, for example, thread in and out of our traditional winter festival-eating from medieval times onwards. The connection continues and foods made with these ingredients are luxurious enough to become delicious gifts or to be stored away for Christmas treats. Take trouble to find small pretty baskets and boxes to line with paper and fill with these delicacies if you are planning to give them away. Stand each sticky morsel in its own paper case to keep it well apart from its neighbour.

■ *A fireside indulgence of stuffed prunes, apricot sweetmeats and candied kumquats (above).*

STUFFED PRUNES

Try to find large Agen prunes if you can. The bigger the better for this recipe.

35 large prunes
cold tea
2 tablespoons Armagnac or brandy
Grated rind of one orange
Sugar syrup, optional

Soak prunes overnight in cold tea. Drain and stone them carefully. Keep 20 aside then process remaining ones with about 2 tablespoons of Armagnac or brandy. Add orange rind, mix and spoon this mixture into each prune to make a smooth fat shape. Put each one in a paper case and glaze with sugar syrup if you wish. There is no need for sugar in this recipe unless you have a very sweet tooth.

APRICOT SWEETMEATS

Easy enough for children to make, and a lot healthier than most sweets.

250g (9oz) dried apricots, chopped
75g (3oz) dried dates, chopped
75g (3oz) raisins
75g (3oz) ground almonds
50g (2oz) candied orange peel, chopped small
Grated rind and juice of one orange
Pinch of cinnamon and nutmeg

Put everything except the juice in a food processor and mix, adding enough orange juice to make a stiff paste. Spread paste into a shallow, paper-lined tin and leave to dry overnight. Cut into lozenge shapes and decorate with a sliver of candied peel or almond if liked. You can adapt this recipe by changing the proportions of dried fruits or using others such as figs and flavourings like rose water.

The idea of taking one dried fruit and stuffing it with a purée of its own flesh or of a different fruit is an old idea. These kinds of recipes are very easy to make and have no strict rules, allowing for a little creativity. Nut pastes made from almonds, pistachios or hazelnuts also make good fillings for dates, prunes or apricots. The simplicity of this kind of recipe demands the best marzipan which is usually one you have made yourself as the shop-bought kind is usually oversweet and artificially flavoured. Once made, a stock of it will keep well though to use for winter sweetmeats and baking.

Prunes are a much maligned yet delicious fruit which prove the point that preserving some foods can turn them into a completely new food in their own right. Children always find it hard to believe that a prune starts off life as a plum and from then on refuse to enjoy them. Perhaps the taste is actually rather sophisticated to a child's palate, though sophistication was never in the minds of institutional cooks who buried watery, stewed prunes under blankets of equally watery custard. Prunes need rich flavours such as Armagnac to bring out the best in them. Leave some to soak in brandy or Armagnac for a while and all will be revealed; even humble tea plumps them up nicely.

Dates are around in many forms, both fresh and dried, these days but only seem to crop up alongside walnuts in tea-breads or under a sticky coating at Christmas-time. Many are imported from the Middle East. They do make an instant reviver when you are hungry, being very high in natural sugars, and the dried and block kinds are useful in recipes such as the one for apricot sweetmeats where they are a natural sweetener. Fresh dates are delicious split and stuffed with savoury creamy mixtures such as Roquefort cheese mashed with a little crème fraîche for a dessert or to eat with aperitifs. The contrast of sweet and salt is pleasing in this case.

Dried apricots are an example of the flavour of the dried fruit being better than that of the fresh unless you can pick apricots ripe and warm from your own tree. The dried apricots with the best flavour are the small, dark orange and rather sour kinds, while other types are sometimes pale and large and very insipid tasting yet seem to be more commonly for sale these days than the first kind. Search out the best flavoured ones to use in recipes where you need to cook them, while the blander types are fine to eat straight from the packet.

TRADITIONAL HARD cheeses, such as Stilton and Cheddar, have always been made in tall cylinders or truckles which therefore have a large surface area of rind. Inevitably, as a whole cheese was cut and used over a period of time, there were plenty of scraps and broken pieces or areas of cheese which dried out near the rind to be used up in some way. Thrifty cooks made use of these odds and ends to pot into delicious cheese mixtures which could be stored in small jars and used when needed. The results are rich and best eaten in small quantities with very plain biscuits or oatcakes. Where the cheese and flavourings would once have been pounded by hand, we can now whizz them together quickly in a food processor if preferred.

Many old recipes suggest using port with Stilton potted cheese but the colour and taste it adds is not nearly as pleasing as using brandy or Madeira. Gorgonzola, Roquefort and other blue cheeses combine well with brandy or Armagnac.

POTTED HISTORY

There is a great history of potted foods. They were once served at homely high teas and suppers and as a savoury course during grand dinners. Potted beef, potted shrimps, potted tongue, potted cheese – they were all a clever way of stretching one ingredient with butter, seasonings, and the addition of spices, particularly mace, then sealed under clarified butter. Potted char, similar to salmon, was a speciality of England's Lake District where this fish comes from. Specially decorated china pots were made to hold the delicacy.

POTTED CHEESE

This recipe is for using Stilton but you could try other blue cheeses or a well-flavoured Cheddar or Double Gloucester. If you intend to eat the cheese immediately simply put into small pots. To keep it longer, pour melted clarified butter over the surface to seal the pot.

350g (12 oz) Stilton cheese, grated or crumbled
75g (3 oz) unsalted butter
½ teaspoon ground mace (½ teaspoon made mustard for Cheddar version)
Pinch of cayenne pepper
1 tablespoon brandy

Put the cheese into a bowl or food processor. Add the butter which should be at room temperature. Beat until smooth then, add spices and seasonings. Add brandy and continue mixing until well blended. Taste and adjust flavourings if necessary. Pack tightly into small ceramic or glass wide-necked jars. The flavours will develop over several hours. Eat with plain water biscuits or warm oat cakes.

■ *Small ceramic jars filled with potted cheese,-sealed with melted butter and covered with waxed paper lids (above and right).*

CENTERBE LIQUEUR

Of course this does not contain anything like a hundred different herbs but it is based on a version of an old Italian recipe. You can adapt the ingredients according to what you can obtain. In the summer there will be far more choice of fresh herbs and flowers but winter is still a good time to make this delicious digestif for parties and festivities.

570 ml (1 pint) vodka
350 g (12 oz) sugar
400 ml (15 fl oz) water
1 whole clementine or small orange, scrubbed
Peel of one lime
2 sticks cinnamon
6 cardamon pods
1 vanilla pod
4 juniper berries
Pinch of saffron
4 roasted coffee beans
Pinch of china tea
4 cloves
2 sprigs rosemary
2 bay leaves
3 lemon or orange leaves
1 tablespoon dried lime flowers
1 tablespoon dried lemon verbena
3 sage leaves
2 sprigs of thyme

Put all the dry ingredients except the sugar and water into a large wide-necked jar and add the vodka. Try to keep peel and fruit submerged under the liquid. Leave to infuse for about 1 month, then strain and add syrup made from the sugar dissolved in the water, then cooled. Return to the jar and leave for another month. Then filter through muslin or coffee filter papers, bottle and cork.

■ *A large glass apothecary's jar makes the perfect place to keep centerbe liqueur while it matures (right).*

THE INSPIRATION of southern Europe provides ideas for using dried fruits in an adventurous way, for example combining herbs with fruits which seems odd to us. If we simply think of herbs as providing flavour in the way that dried spices and seasonings do then there is no problem, say, about putting bay leaves with dried figs. We get very used to thinking of certain flavours joining with specific ingredients in classic combinations and rarely step out of line from the familiar.

The addition of fennel seeds to a fig cake, for example, has the effect of cutting across the sweetness of the dried fruit and should convert hardened fig-haters. Try dried figs split and stuffed with walnut halves or almonds or process them with other dried fruits and ground nuts to make little cakes or sweetmeats similar to Jewish Charozeth, flavoured with cinnamon or ginger. Display dried figs and delicacies made from them on fresh green leaves if you can, even during winter months. Bay leaves have a good glossy green colour which makes the potentially dull brown of the figs come alive.

Soaked in brandy or just orange juice to fatten them up, dried figs can be chopped and then scattered over ice-cream or creamy desserts where their crunch is a welcome contrast in texture or where they can be the main flavouring of an ice-cream in their own right with a little brandy added to make a really luxurious winter pudding. Figgy pudding remains immortalised in the Christmas carol and was probably a variation on a steamed or baked suet pudding, unless Christmas pudding once contained figs which are not now included in modern recipes. Eliza Acton who was writing in the middle of the nineteenth century has a pudding recipe for what she calls *Herodotus' Pudding (A Genuine Classical Receipt).* Her version substitutes sugar for honey as the sweetener and sherry for wine, but basically it is a steamed or boiled pudding dotted with chopped dried figs and cooked for an amazing fourteen hours.

More to our taste today would be simple puddings made with dried figs such as a compote made from the fruit poached in tea or vanilla-flavoured water, chilled and then served with thick yoghurt or soured cream. Or try cooking them gently in red wine flavoured with a sprig of thyme, some orange zest and a little honey to sweeten the syrup.

The best dried figs usually come from Turkey and they are sold packed tightly into cellophane or loose in bags with just a dusting of rice flour to keep each fruit separate.

FIG CAKE

Ideally this Provençal dried fig cake would be wrapped in fresh fig leaves or vine leaves which is only possible during summer months. Instead line a shallow 20cm (8in) round tin with non-stick paper to make it easier to turn the whole thing out. Not really a cake, this recipe produces a subtly flavoured layered sandwich of dried fig slices with the clean savoury taste of fennel seeds.

900g (2lb) dried figs
30 unblanched almonds
1 dessertspoon dried fennel seeds
Bay leaves
Runny honey

Slice each fig horizontally into rings. Layer the rings over the bottom of the tin. Sprinkle with almonds, a few fennel seeds and add a bay leaf. Continue making layers in this way until everything is used up. Cut a circle of non-stick paper to fit the top, then put a plate on this and a heavy weight. Leave in a cool place for several days, then remove the weight and paper and brush the surface with runny honey to add a gloss.

■ *Nuts and figs combine into a rich and subtle texture with bay and fennel to flavour them (above).*

MID-WINTER

'Yet in a little close, I find a patch of green,
Where robins, by the miser winter made
Domestic, flirt and perch upon the spade. . .'

JOHN CLARE
Winter in the Fens

THE HIGHLIGHT of the winter months in stillrooms and kitchens long ago must have been the arrival of the first crates of oranges and lemons of the season, bringing with them colour and fragrance to houses starved of sun and fresh foods. Now that we are used to citrus fruits all year round it is easy not to notice that the special bitter oranges from Seville are here for just a few short weeks and have to be made use of quickly to ensure a hoard of home-made marmalade. The only kind of oranges available in Europe at one time were sour with thick bitter skins. The Seville oranges which we use today for preserves are the last remnant of these types. Once sweet oranges from China and the east arrived, the demand for the sour types diminished. All early recipes for sour oranges make use of the peel in some way rather than the fruit or juice. Peel of both lemons and oranges was candied and preserved as a flavouring and sweetmeat, and *marmelado* from the Portuguese, meaning a preserve of quinces, became marmalade in English meaning a preserve of the peel and flesh of citrus fruits.

Marmalade is still often made at home and people who happily buy most of their food ready-made will nevertheless spend time each year making pots of marmalade. For some reason it maintains its traditional popularity as a breakfast food at a time when every other old-fashioned dish once served at this meal has been usurped by quicker, modern convenience foods.

OLD FASHIONED MARMALADE

This recipe differs from many traditional ones in that the fruit is cooked whole first. In some ways this makes it easier to deal with than slicing it raw and also makes for a slightly more relaxed time scale. The flavour is excellent however and very fresh tasting. Cut the orange peel to the thickness that you prefer. If you like a darker coloured and richer flavoured marmalade, you can include 2 tablespoons of black treacle when you add the sugar.

1.4g (3lb) Seville oranges
2.8 litres (5pints) water
2.8kg (6lb) granulated or preserving sugar
Juice of 2 lemons

Wash and scrub the oranges well and put in a large pan with 2.3 litres (4pints) of the water. Bring to the boil, cover with a lid and simmer gently for about 1½ hours or until the oranges are completely soft. Remove the fruit and save the water. Let the oranges cool a little, then cut each one in half and scoop out the pips and flesh into a small pan. Add the remaining 570ml (1pint) of water to the pan and simmer for about 10 minutes to extract all the pectin. Cut up all the peel and return to the original pan. Add the sugar, lemon juice and the strained juice from the flesh and pips. Stir over a low heat until the sugar has dissolved, then bring to a rapid boil and cook until you have a set – about 15 minutes. Take off the heat, let stand for about 15 minutes then pour into warmed, clean glass jars. Cover with waxed paper discs while hot and seal when cold.

■ *A satisfying row of gleaming jars of traditional home-made marmalade stocks the shelves ready for a new year (left).*

BLOOD ORANGE PRESERVE

Preserves are generally richer and much sweeter than jams and the fruit is kept as whole as possible, suspended in a lightly set jelly or syrup. They are meant to be eaten as a dessert with cream or soft cheeses. This recipe makes a beautiful scarlet syrup with orange rings suspended in it.

6 blood oranges
700g (1½lb) preserving sugar
150ml (5fl oz) brandy

Wash the oranges very well then slice them into rings, discarding the end pieces without flesh. Layer the slices in a shallow dish with the sugar and leave overnight. The next day put the orange slices and syrup into a large shallow pan. Bring gently to the boil then simmer until the slices are tender and translucent. Add the brandy, stir gently then remove pan from the heat and divide oranges and syrup between wide necked preserving jars. Seal while hot.

■ *The jewel colours of blood orange preserve glow behind glass jars (above), while sliced oranges are left in sugar to make the rich syrup (overleaf).*

FEED THE BIRDS

As well as providing bird food from the kitchen try to plan a garden which will offer other good things. Fruit left to ripen then drop from trees or vines will give rich pickings to many birds. Some crab apples and dessert apples are very late to mature so are excellent for birds once the weather gets cold and food is scarcer. Leave thistle-type plants to flower and resist cutting the dead blooms so that finches and other seed-eaters will harvest them. Cotoneaster and pyracantha shrubs hold their berries for a long time and are visited by birds in late winter after more perishable fruits have been eaten. Many small birds rely on over-wintering grubs and insects in tree bark so avoid pesticides and don't be too hasty to clear away old or dead branches.

As TRULY wild habitats for birds become fewer and farmland becomes neater and better managed than in the old days, gardens are increasingly important for the survival of many varieties of bird. Centuries ago many species would have lived through the winter months on the rich pickings found around farms and in the fields in the days when men and machinery were not as efficient as they are now, and grain and other scraps of food remained lying in rick-yards and at field edges months after the harvest had finished. Now crops are gathered speedily and precisely and stored away quickly into vast silos which are definitely scavenger-proof. Fields are ploughed as soon as one crop has been cleared leaving no time for opportunist gleaning by small mammals and birds. Species which once sheltered and lived along hedgerows are increasingly driven into town suburbs and villages and gardens where they rely upon humans for providing much of their food, even if it is often unwittingly done so on the part of the provider.

By planting fruit trees and shrubs and plants which produce berries and seed we are offering the means of survival through the winter to many species of bird and animal. Our feelings about winter visitors such as mice or birds sharing our habitation, or at least garden, is likely to be very different to the view of a medieval or Elizabethan householder who would have seen a threat to their winter supplies in any small visitor, furred or feathered. The domestic cat as predator was a necessary part of every household of whatever status, and elaborate measures were necessary then to protect stored grain, fruit, meat and vegetables which were the only means of survival through what might be a harsh winter, with no chance of replenishing supplies until the next harvest. Granary buildings were stood on rat-proof, mushroom-shaped staddle stones and grain and flour put safely into thick wooden bins. Hams and preserved sausages and meats were wrapped in muslin, coated with a kind of whitewash and hung high up in wide chimneys out of harm's way while fresh game, cheeses and other perishable foods were put in safes and larders secured against marauders with fine mesh. Liquids and moist foods were stored in earthenware jars and crocks and as a final precaution stood on little waisted ceramic or wooden cylinders which deterred mice from climbing up and breaking into the jars.

Small birds are generally seen as a beneficial thing for a garden, though flocks of sparrows and finches must have eaten through a large amount of stored winter grain once. Traditionally scraps of fat and halves of coconut have been hung up outside to attract and feed them through winter months and now we are likely to provide peanuts, seeds or special bird cakes as well. Resist throwing left-overs such as large crusts of bread out which simply attract rats but instead hang things which keep the birds busy and feed the most number of species. Try to cater for seed-eaters as well as omniverous types and remember that some are simply too shy or frightened to feed at a bird table but will scavenge on the small crumbs dropped below by other birds.

BIRD CAKES

This recipe can be endlessly adapted according to what ingredients you can get and for the kind of birds you are feeding. Fat is an important part of the cake as it is the binder for all the other bits and pieces as well as providing plenty of instant energy in cold weather for birds who need to eat huge quantities of food to provide enough fuel when the daylight foraging hours are short and the nights long and cold. You can add grated suet with the dry ingredients, too, if you wish. Either mould the cakes into discs to fit a wire feeder or make round balls to wrap in wire mesh and hang from a garden tree or bird table.

Approx 225 g (8 oz) solid white vegetable fat
1 cup oatmeal
1 cup chopped nuts
1 cup flaked maize
1 cup kibbled wheat
1 cup mixed wild bird seed
1 cup vine fruits chopped
or
6 cups ready-made wild bird seed mixture

In a large pan gently melt the fat. Put the dry ingredients into a large bowl and pour the fat over them. Stir the mixture until the fat is really well mixed with the dry ingredients. The amount of fat needed will depend on the dry ingredients you have used so add sufficient to get a mixture which holds together as the fat begins to cool. With damp hands, pat the mixture into small cakes or balls or put into shallow moulds. Leave in a cold place to set firm.

■ *It is sensible to tackle a session of birdfood-making in a place where making a mess won't matter. Heat the fat inside, then do the mixing in an outbuilding or shed (left).*

MID-WINTER may not seem the best time of year to make fragrant lotions and herbal rinses and yet in many ways it is just the kind of pleasing and gentle activity that one might feel like doing now, surrounding oneself in delicious scents that remind the senses of summer and banishing the season outside. Essential oils are available at any time of year and they can be the starting point for perfumes and colognes, either for yourself or to bottle up as gifts for birthdays and special occasions.

Some herbs are evergreen and as abundant in the winter as in summer months and although their pungency may be a little less than a hundred per cent, they are still fine for recipes such as the rosemary hair rinse. You will need water for these recipes so, unless your tap water is of a good quality, buy spring water or mineral water (not carbonated). Old recipes for perfumes often call for something called spirits of wine which was a kind of medicinal alcohol. This is no longer available so use a pure spirit such as an unflavoured vodka.

ROSEMARY HAIR RINSE

Rosemary has always been the herb connected with hair and the head. It is supposed to strengthen and stimulate the hair and scalp and also add a richness to dark brown or black hair. The essential oil from the rosemary plant is believed to stimulate the brain which is where it gets its memory-strengthening reputation from. It is also supposed to lift fatigue, aid the digestion and cure headaches. In this recipe the rosemary is simply made into an infusion to be used generously as a final rinse after washing the hair. It leaves the hair feeling and smelling good and the slightly acid balance of the liquid counteracts any residue of alkali from the shampoo.

Bunch of fresh rosemary, about 10 stems
2.3 litres (4 pints) spring water
150 ml (5 fl oz) cider vinegar
6 drops rosemary essential oil

Put rosemary broken into short lengths into a large bowl. Bring the water up to the boil then pour it over rosemary and leave for 4 hours. Strain the liquid and add the cider vinegar and drops of essential oil. Stir very well to mix, then pour into bottles and cork. Another version of this especially for blonde hair can be made with chamomile blossom. Instead of fresh rosemary use 2 cups of dried chamomile flowers and make in the same way. Use lemon essential oil or the original rosemary oil, whichever you prefer.

■ *A sprig of evergreen rosemary floating on an infusion of hair tonic (above left).*

■ *The kitchen can become your stillroom to make lotions and potions during winter. Only simple equipment is needed, such as a heat source, sink, funnels, sieves, bowls and bottles (left).*

EAU DE COLOGNE

This old fashioned lotion reminds people of grannies' handkerchiefs and dabbing wrists on hot days. The home-made version is light and refreshing. Neroli oil, an original ingredient, is too expensive to use these days so other oils have been substituted.

300 ml (10 fl oz) vodka
10 drops of these essential oils: citron, bergamot, rose geranium
6 drops of these essential oils: rosemary, orange
6 whole cardamon seeds
75 ml (3 fl oz) spring water

Put vodka into a jar and add oils and cardamon seeds. Stir, then cork and leave for 48 hours. Add water and stir well. Cork the bottle and leave for at least a week. Strain liquid through a filter paper and bottle.

■ *Eau-de-cologne and variations on it are far simpler to make than people imagine (above).*

ALMOND MACAROONS

Simple to make and excellent used in or with puddings or as a biscuit to eat with tea, macaroons store well in an airtight tin and are best a little chewy in the centre. They are nicer made quite small rather than the large size made commercially.

2 egg whites
110g (4oz) ground almonds
110g (4oz) castor sugar
Drop or two of pure almond essence
Almond halves

Line a baking sheet with non-stick paper. Beat egg whites till stiff and gently fold in ground almonds, sugar and essence. Drop small spoonfuls well apart on to sheet and decorate each one with an almond half. Bake for about 12 minutes in a moderate oven, 180°C (350°F) Gas Mark 4 until faintly tinged with brown. Cool on a wire rack.

■ *Delicate almond macaroons are old-fashioned and elegant to serve with tea (above).*

CANTUCCI

These hard little almond biscuits come from northern Italy where they are eaten dipped in a sweet wine, known as *vin santu*, at the end of a meal as a dessert. They store very well, but are also very more-ish!

110g (4oz) unblanched almonds
225g (8oz) plain flour
85g (3½oz) castor sugar
1 teaspoon bicarbonate of soda
2 eggs, beaten
1 egg white
½ teaspoon pure vanilla extract
Pinch of salt

Heat oven to 190°C (375°F) Gas Mark 5. Spread almonds on a baking tray and toast in oven for about 10 minutes. Let them cool, then coarsely chop half the quantity. Grind the rest in a food processor or blender. Mix flour, salt, sugar, bicarbonate of soda and ground nuts in a large bowl. Add eggs and stir to make a rough dough. Work in the chopped almonds and vanilla. Put the dough on to a board and divide into three parts. Roll each into a sausage shape about 2.5cm (1inch) thick. Put the rolls on a greased baking tray well apart from each other and brush over tops with slightly beaten egg white. Bake for about 20 minutes. Remove from the oven and cut the rolls at an angle into slices 1cm (½inch) thick. Lower the oven temperature to 140°C (275°F) Gas Mark 1 and put the slices back on the baking tray. Cook again for about 20 minutes. Cool on a wire rack and then store in an airtight container.

■ *English digestives, plain biscuits for cheese and Italian Cantucci are stored temptingly behind glass (right).*

ENGLISH DIGESTIVES

A good nutty flavour comes from the wholemeal flour and oatmeal. Another excellent keeping biscuit.

110g (4oz) wholemeal flour
110g (4oz) medium cut oatmeal
10g (½oz) demerara sugar
½ teaspoon bicarbonate of soda
75g (3oz) butter
Squeeze of lemon juice
15ml (½fl oz) milk
Pinch of salt

Put flour, oatmeal, bicarbonate of soda, sugar, salt and lemon juice into a large bowl. Rub in the butter until the mixture is crumbly. Add the milk and mix with a fork to get a manageable dough. Put it on to a large floured board and roll out to about 3mm (⅛inch) thick. Cut out circles with a metal cutter and prick all over biscuit surface with a fork. Transfer to greased baking trays and cook in an oven heated to 180°C (350°F) Gas Mark 4 for about 15 minutes until just very slightly browned. Cool on a rack.

BISCUITS FOR CHEESE

These very plain and simple biscuits are perfect to eat with soft and creamy types of cheese which demand a crisp contrast but not too assertive a flavour. Part of their charm is the way they bubble and puff up.

225g (8oz) plain white unbleached flour
25g (1oz) butter
Pinch of salt
Approx 150ml (5fl oz) hot milk

Put flour and salt into a large bowl and rub in the butter. Slowly pour in the hot milk, mixing as you go to make a firm, smooth dough. You may need to add more or less milk according to how absorbent the flour is. Put the dough on a board and knead it very well. Cut into about six lumps and roll each out very thinly which is hard work. When it is paper thin, cut out circles 4cm (1½inch) in diameter and put onto a greased baking tray. Bake in the oven at 220°C (425°F) Gas Mark 7 for 5 minutes until puffy and slightly browned in places. Cool on a wire rack and store in an airtight container.

LATE WINTER

'A thrifty housewife is better than a great income.'

C.H. SPURGEON

John Ploughman's Talk 1869

LEMONS ARE a mediterranean fruit growing best in the climates of countries like Italy and Spain where they are harvested in late winter and early spring. The trees have glossy evergreen leaves and deliciously scented white waxy blooms which break into flower alongside the ripening yellow fruits. Cooks simply hate to imagine life without the sharpness and flavour of fresh lemons which are used in so many dishes and nowadays we are spoilt in having them available all the year round. There used to be no very good way of preserving the fresh juice while it was in season, though it was sometimes bottled and covered with a thin layer of almond oil. Mixed with rum and bottled, the juice became the ration stored aboard ship and given to sailors after days of salted food to prevent them from getting scurvy.

In hotter tropical climates the lime takes over from the lemon and replaces it in many recipes, but it is altogether sharper and even more acidic than lemon with its own special flavour.

LIME CURD

This is made in exactly the same way as lemon curd. Take care not to grate any bitter pith with the peel.

4 limes
175g (6oz) castor sugar
4 eggs
110g (4oz) unsalted butter

Scrub the limes very well then grate the rind from two and squeeze the juice from all of them. Whisk together eggs and sugar then add the juice and rind. Put this into a double boiler or bowl over a pan of hot water and add butter cut into small pieces. Cook gently, stirring often, until the curd thickens (this may take up to 30 minutes). Put into sterilized pots, keep cool and eat within a month.

■ *Lime curd is delicious on good bread and butter (left). Its peel is easiest cut in rings (above).*

LEMON JELLY MARMALADE

A delicate preserve in contrast to the more robust breakfast orange marmalades.

1.4kg (3lb) lemons
3.4 litres (6 pints) water
1.4kg (3lb) preserving sugar

Scrub the lemons well then peel. Finely shred the peel and put in a pan with half the water. Simmer covered for 2 hours. Chop the fruit roughly and put in another pan with the rest of the water and simmer covered for 1½ hours. Strain the fruit mixture through a fine sieve or muslin and add this juice to the peel. Bring to the boil and cook for about 10 minutes, then add sugar and stir until dissolved. Boil rapidly until set then pour into jars.

■ *Sunshine yellow lemon marmalade makes for a rather special start to the day (above).*

GLASS HAS been around for centuries and used throughout the house and it has always needed special care if it is to keep the qualities which make it so desirable as a material. We get used to piling everyday drinking glasses into a dishwasher or a sinkful of detergent, but fine crystal and good glass still needs to be handled gently and cleaned carefully if it is not to cloud and lose its hard brightness. Before modern cleaners were invented, butlers and kitchen maids who had the task of looking after fine drinking glasses, decanters, dessert dishes, vases and even humble windows had all kinds of clever recipes designed to keep glass sparkling. Many of the old methods are still excellent today, it is just that most of us don't know that they exist and have never been shown how to use them.

The best way of cleaning windows is with a chamois leather wrung out in warm water with a spoonful of distilled vinegar in it. Polish the panes dry with a clean soft duster. Vases and decanters with awkward parts which can't be reached with brushes or fingers respond to being swilled round with a mixture made from crushed eggshells dissolved in lemon juice for forty-eight hours. Another method for removing stains from glassware is to drop some small pieces of raw potato inside and swish them around with a little cold water until clean.

■ *The humble potato becomes a magic cleaner for removing stains from glass (above).*

■ *Eggshells dissolved in acidic lemon juice produce a milky liquid which cleans cloudy decanters and bottles (right).*

LEATHER POLISH

Be very careful dissolving the wax and turpentine as they have a very low flash point and are inflammable. Keep this polish in a tightly stoppered bottle and shake it well before using it. A little goes a long way so it is very economical.

75g (3 oz) beeswax
25g (1 oz) white, bleached beeswax
570ml (1 pint) pure turpentine
570ml (1 pint) boiling water
25g (1 oz) pure soap flakes or castile soap

Either shred the waxes into the turpentine and leave until dissolved or warm the turpentine and wax in a double boiler or bowl fitted over a pan of hot water. Put the soap flakes or shredded soap into the boiling water and stir until dissolved. When cool add soap mixture to the melted wax and stir rapidly as it emulsifies. Pour into bottles and seal well.

AT ONE time leather as a material was important for all kinds of things which were used in the home and farm. When horses were the main means of transport the amount of harness and saddlery that was needed for them kept a leather craftsman busy in every village. To keep leather supple, waterproof and in good condition, all kinds of cleaners and polishes were necessary. A little of this tradition remains amongst those who still own and ride horses for pleasure and who know about the tins of saddle soap and special dressings still available for leather tack. Things are a little different in the average household, however, as few of us are likely to waterproof outdoor boots with a mixture of beeswax and mutton fat, nor polish brown shoes with the inside of a banana skin, but it is interesting to note that patent leather responds well to a polish made from one parts of linseed oil to two parts of cream.

Many modern leather finishes are designed to be given just a very occasional wipe over with silicone creams and spray polishes but try to avoid these treatments on old or very good leather which needs loving care to preserve it. Old fashioned polishes for leather, and similarly for wood or metal, always demanded sparing use of the polish itself but copious polishing or 'elbow grease' with a brush or duster. We tend to prefer an instant gleam from a bottle these days rather than a long session with a set of brushes, but there is a satisfaction in buffing up a pair of special shoes, a musty old leather-bound book or an ancient piece of leather luggage and seeing the colour come alive again under a good shine.

Many of the old recipes for hide food or polish are based on turpentine mixed with oils or waxes, but some of the old-fashioned ingredients are hard to find or simply not available. One recipe for waterproofing leather contained Burgundy pitch, linseed oil, turpentine and yellow wax which sounds as if it might work well but not have a very elegant look or smell. A good recipe for a modern leather polish has beeswax and turpentine as its main ingredients and is quite liquid and easy to use, especially on small pieces of leather or heavily detailed things. It is turned into a creamy emulsion by the addition of water and a little soap. Always use pure turpentine and never turpentine substitute in recipes for polishes.

■ *Skates need protection from water and should gleam as they flash across the ice (above).*

■ *A collection of old and beautiful leather has the shine of materials lovingly cared for (right).*

W. P. M

Truffles are the kind of special luxury that you will probably only have the good fortune to eat very occasionally in your life but it is well worth knowing what to do with them should you one day be presented with a gift of some fresh specimens. Newly dug from the ground with the earth still clinging to them, and looking like small potatoes or black stones, is of course the best way to have them. This is when you can smell their very special aroma and begin to understand some of the mystery surrounding them. Part of their strangeness is due to the fact that they are an underground fungus which does not show itself above ground in any way and is therefore very difficult to find. Oak woodland is home to the black truffle (*Tuber melanosporum*) or Perigord truffle. The white truffle (*Tuber magnatum*) or Piedmont truffle is used in somewhat different ways from the black variety.

TRUFFLE HUNTING

As the human nose is not sensitive enough to smell out truffles, traditionally animals have been used. The truffles can be hidden as much as a foot underground. In France and Italy hounds are employed more commonly than the truffle pigs who once rooted about in the oak forests. Dogs are less inclined to eat the treasure or at least can be stopped from doing so by training. The truffle season is fairly short, lasting only a couple of months.

There is an English truffle (*Tuber aestivum*) found only very locally in beechwoods but the English have never exploited this rare delicacy or built up so much tradition, secrecy and fuss as the French do about their truffle industry. At one time only nature could do whatever was necessary to produce truffles growing beneath an oak tree. Nowadays it is possible to have a little more control over where truffles may occur by planting young oaks in suitable sites and the hunting is then a little less hit-and-miss. Although truffles will never be grown commercially like other crops, it is now possible to find them in specially grown plantations rather than in wild oak forest.

Black truffles differ from many other fungi in that they appear in late winter and not during the warm, moist weather of early autumn. They need a quite precise mix of rain and certain other conditions for the crop to be successful, so there is always a gamble as to whether any will appear at all. Not surprisingly all this leads to high stakes in the truffle game and great intrigue in the small villages and towns in the areas where the truffle is common. Meanwhile, in Paris, restaurant chefs wait, hoping to be the first to be supplied with the fattest and most delicious truffles to be found that year.

Truffle to most people means the small specks of black to be found in some pâtés or the little shavings which are canned and lose much of their subtle taste and scent in the process. If you are ever fortunate enough to have a whole fresh black truffle, use it in a simple way to experience the taste properly. Truffles, like many other kinds of fungi, are delicious cooked with eggs and in rice dishes and they also have an affinity with chicken.

Truffles have the wonderful quality of imparting their scent and flavour to other foods that they are alongside so this can be exploited when it comes to using them in cooking. Traditionally a fresh truffle will be stored even for just a short time in a covered bowl or jar of fresh eggs where it will scent them with its truffle flavour, leaving them ready to use in a delectable omelette or scrambled egg dish. In the same way a spare truffle can be buried in a jar of Arborio rice to flavour the grains which can then be made into a creamy risotto or a stuffing for meat or poultry. Small truffles or scraps can be kept under brandy in a little jar and small spoonfuls of the resulting liquid can be added to special soups, gravies and sauces. Truffles can also be grated raw on to pasta and egg dishes.

TRUFFLE RISOTTO

Italian risotto is often served with shavings of white truffle, but rice flavoured with a black truffle is delicious too. Don't use parmesan which might disguise the flavour.

75g (3oz) unsalted butter
1 small mild onion, chopped small
225g (8oz) Italian risotto rice perfumed by a black truffle
150ml (5fl oz) dry white wine
About 570ml (1pint) chicken stock
Salt and black pepper

Over a low heat, melt half the butter and sweat the onion until soft. Add rice and stir until translucent. Pour in the wine and once absorbed add the stock, a small amount at a time, stirring until it has been absorbed. After about 20 minutes the risotto should be cooked. Add the rest of the butter, season and serve. It should be quite liquid and creamy. If you have some fresh truffle add small pieces half-way through cooking time.

■ *Clean white rice hides the mysterious flavouring of a small black truffle (above).*

TRUFFLED SCRAMBLED EGGS

A classically simple but rich way of serving eggs. Serve with small triangles of toast or crisp bread as contrast to the creaminess of the dish. The following ingredients are for one person.

2 beaten eggs that have been stored with a fresh truffle
Unsalted butter
1 dessertspoon of cream per 2 eggs
Fresh truffle, optional
Salt and pepper

If you are using some truffle in the scrambled eggs then slice it finely and put the pieces into the beaten egg and leave to stand for a little while to take up the flavour. When you are ready, melt some butter in a small heavy pan. When it is foaming put in the eggs and shake and stir gently until setting and creamy. Before it is too dry add the cream, stir again and serve immediately.

■ *French cooks make the truffle work extra hard by flavouring foods around it (above).*

THE IMPORTANCE of herbs and flowers as providers of scent and protection from insects in households was never as important at any other time than during the medieval period. Enough was known about the properties of different plants and the uses that they could be put to and gardens contained not just useful native wild flowers but plants from other parts of the world that could all be used in the house.

Your breath is sweeter than balm, sugar or liquorice . . .
And yourself as sweet as is the gillyflower
Or any lavender seeds strewn in a coffer to smell.

This poem from the late fourteenth century compares a woman with the sweet herbs which were commonly placed amongst stored linens and cloths in the solid chests and simple pieces of furniture which sparsely furnished the medieval house. Sweet fragrances were important in a time of plague, poor or non-existent sanitation and no running water, but certain herbs also had a very definite insecticidal effect. Tansy and southernwood were both used fresh and dried to repel moths from woollens and are still useful today with their pungent bitter scent. They were often mixed with lavender to give an extra bite to the fragrance. Lavender was the herb *par excellence* of the laundry and used to freshen linen and keep it sweet if it was to be stored for some time. In fine weather sheets and clothes were spread out over lavender bushes to dry in the sun and absorb some of the plant's essential oils in the warmth. Country people still did this until quite recently, which is probably the reason why lavender bushes or path edgings of lavender were commonly seen near doors leading to the kitchen, scullery and wash-house.

Sachets filled with herbs and powder mixtures are very easy to make and are a delight to stack amongst clothes or in an airing cupboard. Fresh herbs and flowers beat chemical concoctions any day so don't smother your washing in scented conditioners and detergents which fight with whatever scents you have used in the sachets. Very often the little bags filled with lavender or other herbs which one sees for sale commercially are small and mean and are easily lost amongst a drawer full of clothes. It is better by far to make really generous sachets even if you stuff some of the space with a filler material such as kapok or cottonwool. Large sachets are easy to slide between long rows of folded sheets, for example, and obviously have more effect.

LINEN-SCENTING SACHETS

You should be able to buy separate named dried herbs from herbalists or use your own harvested from the garden. Do try experimenting with amounts and proportions to get a scent which you like. The mixture is like a pot pourri but without the emphasis on it looking pretty as well as smelling sweet.

1 measure of dried thyme
1 measure dried rosemary
1 measure dried tansy
1 measure dried southernwood
3 measures dried lavender flowers
1 measure dried rose petals
1 measure broken cinnamon sticks
½ measure crushed cloves
½ measure orris root powder

Put all the leaves, herbs and petals in a large mixing bowl, breaking up any very large twigs or stems. Add the spices and orris root powder. Give everything a really good stir to spread the orris root evenly as it acts as a fixative for the other scents. Use in sachets.

■ *An old-fashioned print of medieval animals makes the perfect fabric for scenting sachets (above).*

Use very fine cotton fabrics such as lawn or muslin for the bag itself. The material can have an open weave if you intend to put leaves and petals in but for powders the fabric will have to be closer textured. Just make a square or rectangular bag by laying the two pieces right sides together and stitching round three sides. Turn the sachet the right way out and fill with your mixture, then sew the last side by hand. There is no need to make a sachet which can be opened to change or refresh the stuffing as it is really very quick to unstitch one short side again if you should ever need to. If you have difficulty finding the dried ingredients which you need, then try making sachets by dropping essential oils onto a wad of cottonwool and tucking it inside some stuffing such as terylene wadding which then slides inside the fabric sachet.

■ *An old-fashioned linen cupboard filled with clean folded linen, all scented and delicious, is a treat to open the door on (above).*

SPRING

At last there are signs of a fresh year getting under way as the first flowers of spring bravely bloom and the fickle weather warms us one minute and freezes us the next. This is a good time to make all kinds of things which don't need seasonal ingredients and to organise the rapidly emptying shelves and storecupboards which will soon begin to fill up again once spring really sets sail and the garden begins to produce its annual harvest.

■ *The purity of shape of the egg never fails to please. Piled into a bowl or basket in the kitchen they suggest the pleasures to come, of cakes, sauces and fruit curds.*

kg
0
100
200
300
400
kg. 1/2
600
700
800
900
kg. 1
500
2
500
3
500
4
500
5
500
6
500
7
500
8
500
9
500
10

EARLY SPRING

'Spring comes anew and brings each little pledge
That still, as wont, my childish heart deceives;
I stoop again for violets in the hedge,
Among the ivy and old withered leaves . . .'

JOHN CLARE
The Crab Tree

EGGS HAVE always been a token of spring. They were the first food to become more available as the days lengthened and the poultry, ducks and geese began to lay in earnest. To this day they remain a symbol of the season and the re-birth of the year and though we now buy our eggs all the year round, people who keep backyard hens still have a spring glut of fresh, delicious eggs to deal with.

At one time hens laid eggs mainly during the spring months, with geese and ducks laying only at that time, so many ways were devised to keep eggs for the barren months at the end of the year. Eggs were individually painted with grease or zinc ointment, or kept under limewater or water-glass. Special galvanised buckets with lids were available for this purpose, with a removable wire basket inside to hold the eggs. Another preserving method was simply to rub butter all over the shells or submerge them in a mixture of salt, water, slaked lime and cream of tartar. The aim of these processes was to block the porosity of the eggshell and therefore preserve what was inside.

Nowadays there is still no way to keep an egg perfectly fresh and even the freezer is no great help, except that one can separate the yolks from the whites and freeze them for later cake-making. Whole beaten eggs can also be frozen but again can only be used for baking or omelettes but never with the same success as fresh ones. It is better by far to use a glut of eggs in a quite different way by making special, slightly luxurious things which keep for a certain length of time and are always welcome in the storecupboard. Lemon and orange curd is one good example, the abundance of eggs coinciding perfectly with lemons in season. Other ideas include cakes or biscuits such as macaroons and meringues.

SPONGE FINGERS

These light and airy biscuits are excellent served with tea or coffee or alongside all kinds of creamy puddings and ices. They store very well in an airtight tin. Flavour them with a little grated lemon rind or use vanilla-flavoured sugar or a few drops of pure essence if you like. If it seems too fiddly to pipe the mixture then simply spoon small circles or rough finger shapes on to the baking tray. Don't worry if the biscuits remain quite flat – they will still taste quite delicious.

50g (2oz) plain flour
50g (2oz) caster sugar
2 eggs

Preheat the oven to 190°C (375°F) Gas Mark 5. Sift the flour and leave on one side. If you use an electric beater simply break the eggs into a mixing bowl and add the sugar. If you are whisking by hand put mixture of eggs and sugar in a bowl over a pan of hot water. Whisk until the mixture is thick and bulky then gently fold in the flour with a metal spoon. Spoon the mixture into a piping bag fitted with a 1cm (½inch) nozzle and pipe finger lengths on to a well-greased and floured baking tray. You should get about twenty biscuits. Sprinkle with a little caster sugar and then bake for about 7 – 8 minutes until just tinged brown around the edges. Remove carefully while hot to a wire rack to allow to cool completely. The biscuits will firm up and become slightly crisper when cold. Store in an airtight tin. It is sometimes more practical to make double this quantity at one time.

■ *The first pale primroses of spring decorate a kitchen shelf alongside a tin of sponge fingers made from the seasonal glut of fresh eggs (left).*

MULTI-COLOURED MERINGUES

3 egg whites
175g (6oz) caster sugar
25g (1oz) unsalted pistachio nuts, chopped
25g (1oz) crystallised violets
1 teaspoon rosewater
10g (½oz) crystallised rose petals

Preheat the oven to 140°C (275°C) Gas Mark 1. Line baking sheets with non-stick parchment. Whisk the egg whites until they form stiff peaks. Whisk in the sugar, a little at a time. Fold in the last few additions of sugar with a metal spoon. Divide the mixture into three and add to one the pistachio nuts, to the second the crystallised violets and to the last the rosewater and crystallised rose petals. Pipe the meringues on to baking sheets and cook for about one hour. Turn off the heat and leave meringues to cool with the oven door open.

■ *Pale, pastel meringues in different flavours are excellent storecupboard standbys (above).*

BEFORE THE days of stainless steel and easy-to-clean utensils and cookware, metal surfaces were difficult and time-consuming to keep shining and spotless. The earliest types of cleaning powders were just scouring pastes of some kind, often simply a fine sand or earth. Steel blades of knives, for example, were rubbed with brick dust or fine sand to make them bright and then they needed to be greased to avoid rusting or staining again. By Victorian times enormous patented machines were in use, consisting of rotating bristle brushes which had knife blades fed into them while the handle was cranked. By this time cutlery, apart from knives which needed to be kept sharp, was made from silver or silver plate in grand households and cheaper alloys in others. Tin which was used to line cooking pans could be cleaned with weathered limestone, which was also known as rottenstone, and colza oil, made from rapeseed. Any metal which might rust had to be kept near the fire, cooking range or heat source in the kitchen.

Copper and brass were the two metals commonly used for cooking utensils and more decorative items and both demanded time to be spent on them to keep them from tarnishing. Over the years all kinds of materials have been used to produce a perfect shine, from a mixture of wood ash, yeast, ginger and lemon juice to silver sand and vinegar.

For brass and copper which has become neglected, a mixture of salt and lemon or lemon and wood ash is still one of the best remedies or try vinegar and salt if you have no lemon. It is probably easier to use lemon as you can take a quarter of the fruit or just a piece of the rind and use it to get into awkward corners or details in the metal. A worn out toothbrush is another good device for attacking the difficult bits. Large quantities of old clean cloth are needed to rub the resulting blackness from the metal. Be sure to leave none of the acid mixture in crevices where it will develop a nice crusty crop of verdigris. This is a messy job at the best of times so it is sensible to collect everything together that needs the treatment and work outside in a garden or in an outbuilding.

■ *An assorted pile of ancient and dirt-encrusted copper implements waits to be given a new lease of life with simple, old fashioned ingredients and some hard polishing (left).*

GINGER IS the rhizome of a tall iris-like plant, native to tropical forests in south-east Asia but now grown in Africa, Australia and the West Indies too. Ginger stores and travels well so it was one of the first spices to reach the Mediterranean and then northern Europe by the first century AD. Its heat and flavour along with its digestive properties made it immediately attractive so it soon became as well used a seasoning as salt and pepper.

Every country has its special bread or cake made using dried ginger and increasingly these days it is used fresh or 'green' in Asian-inspired cookery. Fresh, it has a clean lemony taste as well as heat but dried and ground it is warmer and spicier. Ways of preserving it are numerous, from the red pickled ginger of Japan to the sweet sticky squares of crystallised ginger or stem ginger pieces preserved in syrup and at one time sold in beautifully decorated blue and white china jars.

■ *Fresh ginger roots store well covered with sherry and kept in a cool place. Always keep them submerged under liquid (above).*

GINGER SPICE CAKE

V This makes a shallow, quite sticky cake, or gingerbread as it is traditionally called in England. It keeps very well and the flavours develop and mellow with time so, if you have a strong sense of willpower, try to resist eating it for a few days after making it. If you prefer a plainer cake, omit the fruit and ginger pieces.

110 g (4 oz) butter
110 g (4 oz) dark molasses sugar
110 g (4 oz) golden syrup
110 g (4 oz) black treacle
100 ml (4 fl oz) warm milk
4 level teaspoons ground ginger
1 level teaspoon ground cinnamon
½ level teaspoon ground nutmeg
Pinch ground cloves
4 tablespoons sherry
3 eggs, beaten
225 g (8 oz) plain flour
1 teaspoon cream of tartar
Pinch of salt
Grated rind and juice of one orange
50 g (2 oz) yellow sultanas
50 g (2 oz) chopped preserved ginger
50 g (2 oz) candied lemon peel
1 level teaspoon bicarbonate of soda

Preheat oven to 170°C (350°F) Gas Mark 3. Cream butter and sugar together. Add syrups, milk, spices and sherry. Beat well then add alternate quantities of beaten egg and flour sifted with the cream of tartar and salt. Add orange juice and rind, sultanas, ginger and peel. Dissolve bicarbonate in a little water and add to mixture. Mix very well. Pour into a greased and lined tin about 30 × 23 × 7.5 cm (12 × 9 × 3 ins). Bake for about one hour. Leave to cool in the tin for about 15 minutes then turn on to a wire rack. When cool, cut into squares and store in a airtight container.

GINGER BISCUITS

These easy biscuits can also be cut into complicated shapes such as gingerbread men or stars, hearts, trees and so on for Christmas. It is very good natured dough which puts up with endless re-rolling and cutting out so is excellent for children to work with. In medieval times the cloves or other decorations would have been gilded especially for fair days and feast days.

2 tablespoons golden syrup
1 tablespoon black treacle
75 g (3 oz) caster sugar
1 tablespoon water
1 teaspoon ground cinnamon
1 teaspoon ground mixed spice
½ teaspoon ground nutmeg
1½ teaspoons ground ginger
Grated rind of one orange
75 g (3 oz) butter
½ teaspoon bicarbonate of soda
2 teaspoons orange juice
225 g (8 oz) plain flour

Gently melt syrups, sugar, water and spices in a large pan. Add the grated rind. Bring to the boil stirring well. Remove from the heat and add butter, bicarbonate of soda and orange juice. Add enough sifted flour to produce a stiffish dough. Leave on a board to cool. Heat oven to 180°C (350°F) Gas Mark 4. Roll out the dough to about 3 mm (⅛ inch) thick on a large board and cut into shapes with a knife or cutters. Decorate with a pistachio nut, clove or almond if you wish. Bake on greased trays for about 12 minutes. Leave for a few minutes, then transfer to wire rack to cool.

■ *Rich, sticky and full of spice, ginger cake improves with age (top left). The little biscuits are cut in lozenge shapes which somehow echo their medieval origins (bottom left).*

THERE WAS once a great belief in the power of the spring tonic. Something was considered necessary to wake up the body and get it moving again after the long sluggish days of winter. Lemons were very much part of this regime and home-made lemonade was no great penance for children to drink. At one time grandmothers and mothers always had their own methods for lemonade making it during the first days of spring when the sun at last had some warmth to it and people could happily be outside again. Rhubarb was also considered good for the system, appearing very early in the year before any fresh fruit was generally available. Other plants were made use of, too, to provide the first dose of fresh green food and vitamins. Sorrel leaves and nettle tops made soups and dandelion, chickweed and garden weeds such as fat hen added vital minerals to the daily diet. The sharpness and acidity of these foods were certainly welcome after weeks of stored and dried provisions.

Lemonade is a simple delight which is generally forgotten in place of commercial bottled and canned drinks. To make it to drink straight away, use the recipe below or make a *citron pressé* by just squeezing the juice of one lemon per person into a tall tumbler then adding sugar and water to taste. Stirring the mixture until the sugar dissolves is part of the pleasure of this drink.

HOME-MADE LEMONADE

Take three juicy lemons and cut off the peel but no pith. Put peel in a jug with three tablespoons of sugar and just cover with boiling water. Stir well then leave to cool. Squeeze the lemons and put the juice in the jug. Add cold water to taste. You may like a sharper or sweeter version which will depend on the lemons you use.

LEMONADE SYRUP

This is a concentrated syrup to make lemonade from. It can be bottled in sterilised bottles and sealed and should keep well in a cold place. Once opened use the syrup fairly quickly. Kept in the fridge, it is useful to make a quick refreshing glassful on a hot day. You can use soda water or carbonated mineral water to top up the glass and, of course, ice if you want. Add a sprig or two of mint, borage or lemon balm, if you have some, to each glass and a slice of fresh lemon.

5 small juicy lemons, scrubbed well
700 g (1½ lb) cane sugar
570 ml (1 pint) boiling water
25 g (1 oz) tartaric acid

Peel the lemons thinly with a sharp knife. Put the peel and sugar in a large jug or bowl. Add the boiling water and stir well. Squeeze the lemons and add juice and tartaric acid to the syrup. Leave to cool, then strain and bottle. Use about 2 tablespoons of syrup to each glass when mixing.

■ *A big crock of lemons about to be scrubbed and cleaned before making concentrated lemonade syrup (above). The result is a deliciously refreshing lemonade (right).*

THE PRODUCTS of the bee-hive have been made use of for centuries. Honey, of course, was the main product and it was used as a general sweetener of food and as an ingredient in drinks such as mead and metheglin, but other products of the hive were just as important. Beeswax was used for candles and still is to a small extent today, particularly for high quality slow-burning church candles. It was also a vital component of all kinds of polishes and finishes for wood, as well as an important ingredient for creams and skin lotions. Wax is a natural secretion produced by glands in the body of the bee and secreted in tiny scales which are chewed by the bee and then used to build a comb in which to lay eggs and store honey and pollen.

Beeswax is available in blocks simply made from melted down wax strained of any bits and pieces after the honey has been removed from the combs, and in this state it is a rich golden brown colour and has a lovely distinctive smell. For making beauty products you can buy a bleached wax, again in blocks or as easier-to-use granules which melt more quickly than a large chunk. When melting wax for any purpose you should always do it in a double boiler or in a bowl sitting over a pan of hot water. Beeswax has a very low melting point and is very inflammable so care should be taken particularly if you are mixing it with turpentine when making polish or something similar.

At one time wooden floors were always polished with a mixture of oils and beeswax. In thrifty households, all the old candle ends were kept to be melted down with turpentine to make the simplest polish of all. Over the years beeswax polish builds up into a wonderful gentle patina on woods of all kinds. If you miss a scent of lavender or something similar in the polish, then just add a few drops of lavender, lemon or rosemary essential oil to the mixture and stir very well to disperse it. Do this at the end of the recipe, just before pouring it into bottles or jars. If you have plenty of garden lavender growing and can spare the flowers, then you might like to make a strong infusion of fresh lavender flowers and use this as the water part of the recipe. Rosemary would work equally well but lavender is still the traditional herb favourite for cleaning and polishing.

Pure honey has been used for soothing skin preparations and as a healer for wounds and sore skin for centuries because its high potassium level means that bacteria cannot survive. It is still an important ingredient in many modern beauty treatments.

ALMOND AND HONEY HAND SALVE

Keep a jar of this ready to use after your hands have had rough treatment, such as a day's gardening or cleaning. Rub it in well or use larger amounts and then put cotton gloves on for a while or overnight. You can feel its benefits straight away. The benzoin tincture acts as a preservative and you can add a few drops of a scented essential oil to perfume the lotion if you wish. Rose geranium or lavender would be ideal.

2 handfuls of rolled oats
50g (2 oz) almonds, ground very fine
1 egg yolk
1 tablespoon pure clear honey
2 tablespoons sweet almond oil
8 drops tincture of benzoin

Beat all the ingredients together very thoroughly. Using a food processor is easiest, but by hand is fine though the result will be coarser. Pot into small jars and keep covered.

■ *Almond and honey handcream is very soothing and healing for rough or sore hands. Rub in well for instant relief (above).*

BEESWAX WOOD POLISH

This makes a thick cream which is excellent for fine wood furniture which should not be treated with modern silicone polishes. It is best used sparingly and the more buffing with a duster afterwards the better the shine.

50g (2 oz) beeswax
10g (½ oz) white wax
300ml (½ pint) pure turpentine
25g (1 oz) pure soap or soapflakes
150ml (¼ pint) boiling water
(Optional 5-6 drops of essential oil, see left)

In a double boiler slowly melt the waxes with the turpentine. Grate the soap into the boiling water and stir briskly to dissolve it. Let the soapy water cool to lukewarm then pour it into the melted wax stirring well as it makes an emulsion. Put in a small jar or container with a tight fitting lid. The polish keeps well for a long time.

■ *Good wood deserves fine polish which will not cover up the colour and grain (left). Beeswax, from pale bleached granules to hive 'foundation' rolled candles, is ideal for using in polishes (above).*

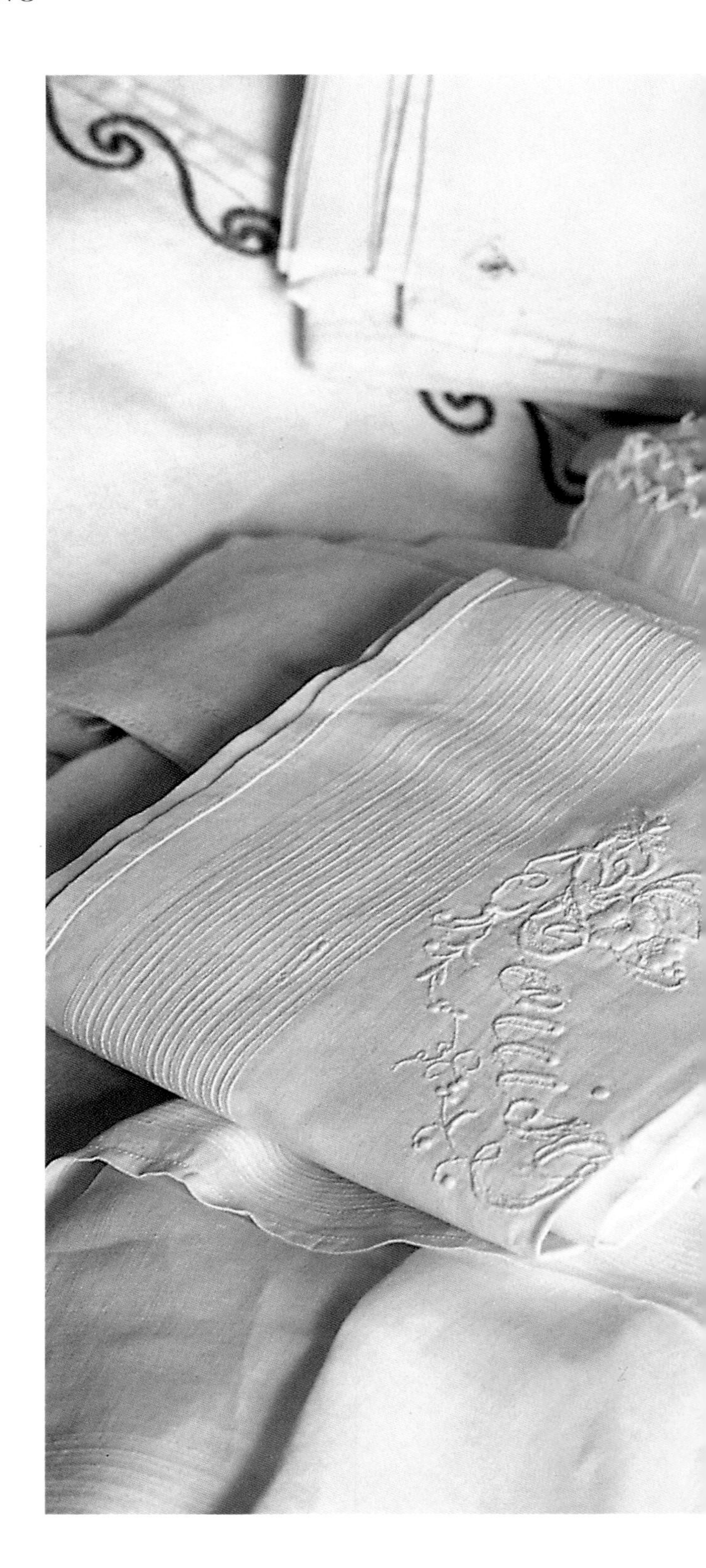

MID-SPRING

'To take away freckles . . . take one pint white wine vinegar and put it into a glass with six oaken apples and a few elder leaves. Set it in the sun and wash your face therewith.'

THOMAS NEWINGTON
Palladium of many Noble Familyes 1719

IN SPRING, when the days get longer and the light brighter, housekeepers traditionally gave furniture, floors and linens an extra clean and renovation. Summer clothes and delicate fabrics might have suffered in storage during winter months and so specific remedies for stains and damage would need to be made from household receipt books. Fabrics were all natural – linen, wool and cotton – but each demanded special treatment with pails of heated water and odd ingredients such as rice starch, lye, soda, bran and glue-like size to produce cleaned, sweetened and stiffened end results. Medieval launderers used size made from hoof parings to stiffen head dress veils and the elaborate neck ruffs worn in the sixteenth century were treated with starch then set between special heated goffering irons. Boiled and mashed ivy leaves cleaned black silks; potato water was used for pale coloured silks. Bran was boiled to clean chintz fabrics and grease stains were soaked in warm wine or rubbed with wet chicken feathers.

■ *The first daisies and early rhubarb appear now (above). Remove iron mould stains by soaking them in the juice from a stem of cooked rhubarb (right).*

Few of the thousands of recipes from the past for preserving and potting meat remain or are used today now that fresh meat is available all year round. At one time the only way to ensure meat was available to eat through the winter was to salt it in barrels, conserve it in fat or process it in some way, such as brining then smoking hams and bacon. Before canning and bottling jars had been invented, and people understood the effect of bacteria on food and the importance of sterilization, pieces of meat, game and poultry were cooked and kept from spoiling under a coating of their own fat in wood or earthenware containers. The process was slow and complicated and, to be safe, had to rely on a satisfactory exclusion of air and bacteria which would immediately spoil the result if allowed to get in. Food poisoning must have resulted quite often from careless cooking or from bad storage, but this was presumably an unavoidable risk.

In country areas of France, ducks and geese are still a very important food and the preserved dish known as confit is widely made at home. It is one remnant of this old type of preserved food which grew out of necessity but which is still worth producing today simply because it is so delicious and useful in its own right. The fat from the goose or duck is never wasted and used as a cooking medium for all kinds of dishes as well as the ones made of the duck or goose meat.

CONFIT OF DUCK

In France confit is usually made from the ducks and geese specially fattened to produce foie gras and in typical fashion nothing is wasted. This recipe can also be made from pieces of rabbit or pork. Cut a duck into four pieces, a goose into eight, rabbit into five and other meats into equal pieces. Lay the pieces of duck or other meat in a large shallow dish and rub coarse sea salt into them. Cut a few slits in the flesh and tuck in a few slivers of garlic. Grind some coarse black pepper over the duck and add some crumbled bay leaves, thyme or other herbs to add extra flavour. Leave in a cool place for up to 24 hours.

Meanwhile prepare some fat. A goose will have a fair amount of fat inside the carcass which can be removed before salting and a duck will have only a little. Ideally the fat should match the meat but you will probably have to supplement with pure pork fat (don't use vegetable fat). Wipe the duck pieces and remove any salt still sticking to them. Put them in a large shallow pan in a single layer and cover them completely in melted fat. Cook very slowly for about 1½–2 hours; the temperature of the fat should be about 80°C (175°F). Test the thickest part of a leg with a skewer to check that the juice runs clear and that the meat is properly cooked. It is very important that the duck is cooked through completely for it to keep well. When it is done, drain the duck pieces and pack them all into a large sterilized jar with a wide neck, or put just one or two pieces in smaller jars if you prefer.

Strain the fat and heat in a clean pan until it stops bubbling and all moisture has gone. Let it cool a little then pour over the duck to completely cover it. Tap the jar once or twice to settle everything and dislodge any air bubbles. When it is cold top up with fat if necessary and sprinkle with a thin layer of salt. Cover and seal. Keep in a very cool, dry larder or cellar or refrigerate.

To serve, slowly melt the confit and pour off the fat. Brown the pieces of meat until the skin is crisp or use as part of a cassoulet or other recipe. Traditionally the confit might be served with a potato galette or fried potatoes flavoured with garlic. If you use just part of the duck the rest can be re-covered with the fat and used later.

A sixteenth-century English way to preserve chicken to take on board ship for a long voyage is described by Dorothy Hartley in her book *Food in England*. The birds are salted and left for twenty four hours, then roasted and well drained of any juices. They are then packed into pots and surrounded by their own fat, heated with salted butter which has been well flavoured with mace, cloves, nutmeg and bay leaves. This same recipe was used by Dorothy Hartley's aunt in 1850 on a voyage to Africa. Often wooden containers called kits, made like a thin section of a beer barrel, were used for the preservation of meat in this way. They were closed and made airtight with a tight covering which created a vacuum on cooling just as jam pot cellophane lids do. Thick sailcloth was the final covering to protect the kits during long sea voyages.

■ *Traditional glazed earthenware jars used for storing preserved meats, fruits and vegetables surround a modern glass jar filled with duck confit (right).*

PORK RILLETTES

Rillettes are a kind of potted meat with more texture than pâté. Put 750g (1½lb) lean pork and 500g (1lb) belly pork, cubed, into a heavy pan. Add 150ml (5floz) water, 2 crushed garlic cloves, sprig of thyme, 2 teaspoons salt, ½ teaspoon ground mace, pinch of ground allspice, black pepper and a bay leaf. Bring to the boil then cook in oven at 150°C (300°F) Gas Mark 2 for up to 5 hours. Stir occasionally, adding water if it is sticking. Drain meat and reserve liquid. Discard the herbs, then shred the meat with two forks. Re-melt fat from the cooled liquid and add enough to meat to make a soft paste. Pack into jars and cover with a layer of fat. Store in refrigerator for up to two weeks.

■ *Spring clip jars are ideal for preserving confit (left).*

CRYSTALLISED SWEET VIOLETS

This is an easy modern way to make traditional crystallised violet flowers. Put a spoonful of powdered gum arabic in a small screw top jar. Just cover the powder with rosewater and leave to dissolve for several days. Pick purple and white sweet violets and carefully paint on the gum mixture with a fine brush, leaving no part of the petal uncovered. Sprinkle with caster sugar then leave to dry on a wire rack in a warm place. When crisp and dry, store in an airtight tin. Use to scatter over puddings and cakes.

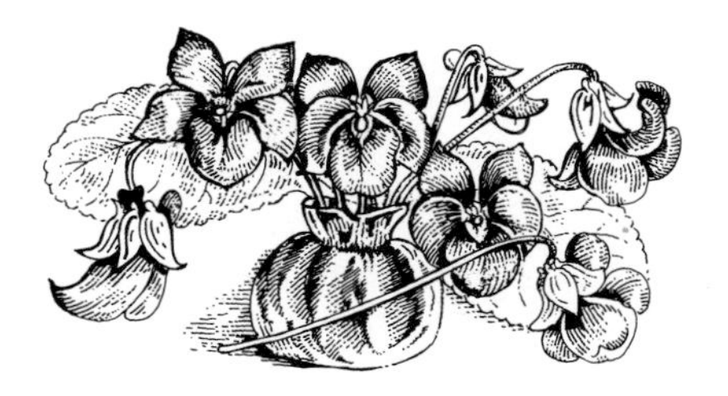

THE ANCIENT Greeks wore wreaths of violets and the Romans made the flowers into wine. Medieval gardeners planted flowery meads studded with white and purple violets on which to walk and Napoleon had Josephine's grave planted with a carpet of her favourite flowers. Not simply decorative, violets have been used medicinally and in the kitchen for as long as they have been grown. They were believed to cure sleeplessness, to assuage anger and to comfort the heart. In fact one member of the viola family once found growing commonly in arable fields is known as heartsease. Violets have had periods of great popularity throughout history reaching a climax in the nineteenth century in Queen Victoria's reign when it seemed every man and woman on the streets of London sported a buttonhole or posy of the sweet-smelling flowers when they were in season. Thousands of fragrant bunches were grown and exported from France each year and England had its own thriving violet industry, particularly in Devon, Cornwall and the west country.

■ *Sweet violets are unusual in that they drink through their flowers and leaves and relish a spray of water or even submersion to refresh them (above).*

■ *Violet-flavoured chocolates decorated with crystallised flowers are an old fashioned delight (left).*

Violets' perfume is subtle and gentle and the flowers themselves are small and secretive, often found growing low and hidden by their pretty heart-shaped foliage. Violet blooms were commonly used to decorate food and flavour spring salads, and soothing syrups and alcoholic drinks were made from them to store away for winter, keeping the violet colour if the liquid was not boiled. Vinegar was flavoured with the scent and a popular ingredient in the seventeenth century was violet pâté or violet-perfumed sugar.

Soaps and lotions are still scented with sweet violets. Little violet cachous or pastilles can be found in France, and one of the most popular fillings for chocolates is still violet cream. Parma violets are grown by only a few keen amateurs these days but at one time nurseries grew these strongly scented double flowers for the cut-flower trade and as little pot plants. They are not very hardy and are quite difficult to cultivate but well worth a revival in interest.

THE ROMANS used a fish sauce made from the fermented juice of salted fish in many of their dishes and at one time the Roman empire supported a huge industry making *liquamen* as it was called. Many countries still have their own specialised fish sauces and condiments and throughout the years there seem to have been recipes linking the Roman passion for fishy flavours through to the popular and insatiable taste for fish and other ketchups beloved by the Victorian male dining clubs. The strong fish sauces and ketchups were used to provide a very subtle hint of flavour to underpin the actual fish taste of a dish. They were seen as a condiment and often added to foods not containing fish of any kind.

Mrs Beeton included both anchovy essence and anchovy ketchup in her renowned cookery book which contained many weird and wonderfully named store sauces. These included Camp Vinegar, Benton Sauce, Carrack Sauce, Cherokee Sauce, the famous Harvey Sauce, Pontac Ketchup and Quin's Sauce. Many had fiery ingredients and powerful flavours which at that time were very much in vogue, with

spiced and vinegary foods and any pickled and hot recipes very popular. It is still possible to buy anchovy essence today and it is delicious added to egg mayonnaise for perfect egg sandwiches. You can, of course, buy Chinese oyster sauces but home-made sauces are better and extremely useful to add piquancy and flavour to all kinds of day-to-day foods.

■ *Glistening wet oysters straight from the sea are destined for a delicious sauce (above).*

OYSTER KETCHUP

This is well worth making for the storecupboard when oysters are at their best and cheapest.

12 oysters
50g (2 oz) anchovies, drained of oil
200ml (7fl oz) white wine
Juice and peel of one lemon
1/2 teaspoon mace
1/2 teaspoon cloves
1 tablespoon shallots, peeled and chopped

Open the oysters and keep their liquor. Put oysters, liquor, anchovies, wine, lemon peel and juice in a pan and simmer for 30 minutes. Add shallots and spices and boil for 15 minutes. Strain sauce through muslin and pour into clean bottles. Sterilize in a water bath for 15 minutes at 80°C (180°F). Seal.

YORKSHIRE SAUCE

A pungent sauce to be used with cold roast meats. Use salted dry anchovies if you can get them or drain off oil from tinned ones, wash and pat dry.

2 × 50g (2 oz) tins of anchovies
4 cloves garlic, peeled and chopped
4 shallots, peeled and chopped
1 tablespoon brown sugar
1 teaspoon ground mace
1/2 teaspoon ground allspice
3 tablespoons dark soy sauce
1 teaspoon cayenne pepper
1.1 litres (2 pints) malt vinegar
2 tablespoons mushroom ketchup, optional

Whizz everything except vinegar in food processor for a few seconds. Put into large jars, add vinegar and cover. Shake every day for a month. Strain through muslin and bottle.

SWEET GERANIUM MOUSSE

Use citrus or rose-scented geraniums.

1½ tablespoons gelatine
8 sweet geranium leaves
6 tablespoons water
2 large eggs, separated
60g (2 oz) caster sugar
150ml (5fl oz) thick Greek yoghurt
300ml (10fl oz) fromage frais
150ml (5fl oz) whipping cream

Dissolve gelatine in 4 tablespoons hot water. Pour 2 tablespoons boiling water over the geranium leaves and leave to cool. Beat yolks and sugar until light, add yoghurt. Whisk egg whites stiffly. Whip cream. Pour cool gelatine into egg yolk mixture and quickly fold in fromage frais, cream, water from leaves, and finally egg whites. Pour into a dampened mould and refrigerate for several hours. Turn out and decorate with frosted leaves.

■ *A row of scented geraniums on a windowsill was once a common sight in country cottages. They make good houseplants, though plenty of light is essential. Choose from some of the many different scents from balsam to rose, eucalyptus to lemon (top).*

■ *The prettiest leaves for frosting with sugar are from the pale green variegated scented geranium* Lady Plymouth. *Use the method described for crystallising violets on page 95 (above). A stock of them is good to keep for decorating cakes and puddings, such as geranium mousse (right).*

LATE SPRING

'Upon the small, soft, sweet grass,
That was with flowers sweet embroidered all,
Of such sweetness, and such odour overall . . .'

WILLIAM CHAUCER
Legend of Good Women

MOST OF us imagine that pot pourri is something which has been made for centuries, knowing, for example, that flowers and herbs were once strewn on floors and were important for many household uses. We imagine huge bowlfuls of sweet smelling mixtures standing on polished oak furniture in Elizabethan houses while in fact the use of such scents was far more discreet and practical. Dried herbs and flowers were generally ground into a fine powder which was then put into small bags and sachets and hung amongst clothes in closets or slipped between layers of cloth in a wooden coffer.

Recipes for moist pot pourris containing whole flowers and petals came into being around the end of the eighteenth century and this was the time when pot pourri containers were first produced as decorative items. Sweet bags of powdered ingredients were used firstly to repel insects such

■ *Sweet powder mixture being made. Whole and large spices will need to be ground to a powder (above).*

as clothes moths, beetles and bugs which might choose to make a home in fabric and fur or the walls and floors of houses. Buildings were, of course, less well ventilated and heated than they are today so linens and clothes quickly became musty or mildewed without careful storage.

There was always a fear of fleas, lice and bed bugs even in the grandest houses and the only means of repelling such creatures was by natural methods based on herbs, plants and spices. Certain herbs were discovered to be efficient at discouraging pests and other flowers and scents were used to provide a pleasant perfume. In medieval times fragrance in the garden and home was immensely important, possibly as a means to counteract the many bad smells which came from poor sanitation and ventilation, smokey fires, domestic animals living in close quarters to humans and lack of running water and cleaning agents. Sweet fragrance was considered to be God's breath and therefore sacred. This was also the time, and for several centuries onwards, when illness and disease were believed to be the result of foul odours and could be combated with sweet smells. By the sixteenth century Thomas Tusser, writing in his book *One Hundred Points of Good Husbandry*, describes twenty one different plants which were strewn on floors. Many of the aromatic herbs included in this list were later to become the ingredients of pot pourri recipes and were also important ingredients for sweet powder mixtures.

It was essential to try to hold the fleeting fragrance of flowers and leaves and this was done by using many different ingredients which had the ability to fix the scent. Sometimes these fixatives had their own perfume and sometimes not, but many were exotic and expensive. Musk came from glandular secretions of the male musk deer, and ambergris from the sperm whale, while civet came from the scent glands of the civet cat. Plant-based fixatives included labdanum, a resin produced from a shrub of the *Cistus* family which grows wild in the Middle East. There were other resins too, from *Liquidamber* and *Styrax* trees, many of which are still used today in the perfumery business, and a fixative which is now cheap and easy to obtain, orris root powder. This is the powdered rhizome of the plant *Iris Fiorentina* which has its own faint scent of violets but also has the ability to hold other scents. Gum benjamin or benzoin which comes from the tree *Styrax benzoin* is also easy to obtain but generally comes in small, hard, rocky lumps which have to be pounded down in a pestle and mortar.

SWEET POWDER MIXTURE

Make this in quantity and use to fill small muslin or cotton lawn bags. You can adapt the recipe according to the ingredients which you have and use a measure for the ingredients which suits your needs.

8 measures crushed coriander seeds
8 measures powdered orris root
1 measure ground cinnamon
1 measure ground nutmeg
1 measure ground cloves
½ measure white sugar
3 measures lavender flowers

Mix everything together really well in a large bowl then fill small bags with it. You can also add a small piece of cotton wool impregnated with a few drops of an essential oil such as rose, geranium, rosemary or citrus.

■ *Sachets of sweet powder mixture tucked between layers of linen to scent the cupboard (above).*

LATE SPRING sees the beginnings of new growth on the perennial herb plants such as thyme and sage in the kitchen garden and borders, and with luck bushes of rosemary will have been in an azure cloud of flower for weeks. The first shoots of mint and fresh grassy chive leaves appear all of a sudden, just when one is dying for the taste of spring again and it becomes a treat to make leafy salads and vegetable dishes which can be generously sprinkled with the bright green aromatic specks of chervil, parsley or marjoram. Annual herbs, unless brought on earlier under glass, are not really in fine form until a little later in the year but nowadays it seems possible to buy fresh herbs almost all the year round. It hardly seems necessary to dry one's own herbs or buy them because apart from a very few examples most lose all their flavour in the process. Dried bay leaves are good to have in the storecupboard and perhaps thyme and some of the mediterranean dried herb mixtures which really smell of hot sun-baked earth to add to grills and soups, but the over-use of dried herbs is to be avoided and nine times out of ten no herbs at all are preferable to using stale dried ones.

■ *The first stage of making a herb paste in a pestle and mortar (above).*

Of course fresh herbs need to be used quickly and there are not many ways to keep them successfully. If your garden suddenly produces a glut of one particular kind of herb it is probably best to try freezing some, or perhaps making small pots of sharp flavoured fruit jellies incorporating plenty of the herb. Try making some herb pastes which will keep in a fridge or cool place if they are well protected under a film of oil. Mixing mustards with fresh herbs is another good plan or making herb-based sauces such as pesto which use other ingredients along with the fresh herb.

Many cooks infuse oils and vinegars with fresh herbs and, although it so commonly recommended, it is an excellent way to prolong the scent and flavour of fresh herbs throughout the year. Even plain and rather tasteless vegetable oils can be greatly improved by being infused with a handful of savory, basil or thyme. If the oil is used for salad dressings, try to use olive oil for the best flavour but it doesn't have to be the most expensive. Vinegars are useful too, but one never needs them in great quantities. Use a light wine or cider vinegar for a base. Probably one of the best to make is tarragon, although rosemary is good too. If you feel truly creative you can try mixing your herbs and adding garlic, peppercorns, chillies for heat, lemon peel or other flavourings until you have a blend which you really like for salads or to zip up other dishes.

The process for both oils and vinegars is very simple. Put a handful of fresh herbs into a very clean bottle or jar with a screw lid. Top up the container with oil or vinegar and screw the lid on tightly. Leave on a windowsill or in a warmish place for several days or longer, giving it a good shake every day or so. Strain off the flavoured oil or vinegar into clean bottles to store.

Herb pastes are easy to make in a food processor or liquidiser or by hand in a pestle and mortar. Simply pound plenty of chopped fresh herbs, adding oil to make a thick paste. Put into small jars and cover surface completely with a layer of plain oil. Cover and store in a fridge or cold larder. Use spoonfuls in dressings, sauces and soups. You can season the pastes with salt, pepper or a little lemon juice or just leave them quite plain, using a tasteless oil such as groundnut or olive oil if you prefer.

It is very easy and immensely satisfying to try a little tea blending of your own. You will need to start with a basic tea to which you can then add flowers or other flavourings. Whether you choose a light China tea or a stronger Indian one will depend on your taste but as these flavoured teas are generally best drunk without milk, probably the best choice is a China tea such as Oolong.

FRAGRANT TEAS

Two classic flower perfumed teas are jasmine and rose petal, both very easy to make yourself and somehow much more delicious than when bought in a packet ready-mixed. For a rose-scented tea you will need dried red or deep pink rose petals which have come from a highly scented rose which holds its scent after drying. *Rosa gallica officinalis* is one such rose, used commercially for rose oil and rose perfume, or a deep red rose such as the modern climber *Guinée*. The small flowers of summer jasmine lose their fresh whiteness after drying but keep their rich, exotic scent and only a few are needed to flavour a small quantity of tea. You will need to experiment with the quantities of flowers to tea according to your taste but roughly a tablespoon of dried petals or flower heads to 110g (4oz) tea is about right.

Other flavourings to try are slivers of dried lemon, orange or lime peel made by carefully peeling off the outer rind without any pith and drying the strips in a warm place for a few days. When they are dry, chop or cut the peel into small pieces which are then mixed more easily into the tea than large curls of peel. Orange blossom makes a marvellous flavour but unless you have your own orange tree from which to raid some flowers it is harder to produce at home.

Other flowers to try are sweet violets which have an elusive but distinct scent. Up the proportions of petals to tea with these to say 2 tablespoons of flower heads to 110g (4oz) tea. In the summer months when there are fresh flowers and herbs to pick, try adding a handful of these to a normal tea brew to ring the changes on a drink we often take for granted. Remember that fresh herbs are not so concentrated in flavour as dried ones.

■ *A tapestry of greens and purples from a mass of different fresh herbs (left).*

■ *Little soft paper twists of scented teas can be stored in tins or given away as pleasing gifts (overleaf).*

DAIRY PRODUCTS by their very nature are not easy to preserve. Cheeses were invented as a way to store fresh milk long-term by reducing the water content and pressing the curds or milk solids into manageable shapes. In some cases the introduction of harmless bacillus gave special flavours or textures to the cheese and just by using different storage methods or wrappings for the finished cheese, thousands of varieties were produced from the same humble beginnings – liquid milk.

Cheese is made throughout the world from various milks including cow, buffalo, sheep, goat and even reindeer. After the initial processes of separating the curd from the whey for a hard, long-keeping cheese and then pressing and moulding the cheese into its own distinctive shape, little else is done. Much depends on the quality and constituents of the raw milk which is used, such as whether morning or evening milk is chosen or whether two different milkings are put together. Some cheeses have most character at certain times of year, when the animals are grazing on certain fodder for example. The size and shape of a cheese and how it is stored can also affect its taste and texture. Traditional cheeses such as English Cheshire or Wensleydale are all made using roughly the same process, but the breed of cattle local to one area and the particular grazing that the animal enjoyed determine the flavour and character of each type of cheese. Traditional hard cheeses keep well and need a long period of maturing to develop their flavour.

At one time soft cream and curd cheeses were commonly made in households to use up surplus soured milk, while the larger cheeses were generally made on farms in skilled dairies. The still room was not normally the place for cheese which needed to be made in hygienic surroundings in a separate room which could be used just for dairy work. Dairy work was considered very important in a large household or estate and good dairymaids were highly valued as the work was skilled and butter and cheese easily spoilt. A dairyworker would work only in the dairy while other kitchen servants might work at many different kinds of job throughout the house. Surfaces in the dairy had to be wood or stone, cold, clean and able to be vigorously scrubbed and doused in boiling water after every butter-, cream- or cheese-making session.

There seems to be a revival of interest in local traditional county cheeses, but alongside this is a great expansion of small scale cheese-making using goats' and sheep's milk.

GOAT CHEESES IN HERB OIL

Make up this basic oil and then put in about 4 or 5 small goat cheeses. Slices from a firm log of goat cheese can be used and when you have finished one batch, use the oil for some new cheeses.

570 ml (1 pint) olive oil
2 cloves garlic, peeled
1 sprig fresh rosemary
1 sprig fresh thyme
1 sprig fresh marjoram
2 fresh bay leaves
1 teaspoon mixed peppercorns, green, red and black
1 teaspoon coriander seeds
1 small dried red chilli
1 teaspoon whole allspice berries
1 teaspoon celery seed

Put the oil and all the flavourings into a wide necked jar with a cork or spring clip lid. Drop the cheeses in and be sure that each one is properly covered in oil. Leave for a few days before beginning to use them.

Goat cheeses are normally small and many types can either be eaten very young and fresh or left to harden and mature and develop a rind. A good way to store these small goat cheeses is to pick ones which are slightly aged with the beginnings of a rind and then keep them in flavoured oil. They are particularly useful to keep as a storecupboard standby either to grill quickly to eat as a first course or to accompany crisp green salads. Olive oil gives the best flavour and the choice of added flavourings is yours. Herbs, of course, should be added and garlic, pepper but not salt, spices if you want or even chillies for fiery heat. The cheeses must stay under the oil to avoid drying out and you can happily remove just one or two from a jar and leave the rest for another time. They do not need to be refrigerated but should be kept in a dark cool place, such as an old fashioned larder.

■ *French crottins are perfect for preserving in oil (left).*

■ *Use fresh herbs to put with the cheeses as they taste and look so much better than dried (below).*

■ *Buy, collect and re-use papers and cellophanes and keep a store ready for when you suddenly need them. File them in a shallow kitchen drawer or cardboard folder (above).*

Preserving food successfully has always relied on the use of clean, sound containers and safe coverings as well as good storage conditions. Materials have changed from the days of using wooden tubs with animal bladders stretched over them, but storage techniques remain very similar and have hardly been improved upon. In many cases it is important to exclude air from foods which would quickly spoil if airborne bacteria and yeasts were allowed to reach them. We now have special preserving jars with rubber rings and screw tops or spring clip fastenings. These work on a principle of air expanding under the lid when it is hot but shrinking when cool and therefore sucking the lid tightly into place with the help of the rubber washer ring. This seal will not come apart until it is forced open when you wish to use the contents. Bottled fruits and vegetables need to be treated in this way but jams and very sugary preserves are normally fine with just a cellophane lid.

It is possible to buy packs containing everything you need to cover jam pots or you can buy the components singly. However you buy them, you will need small waxed paper discs to put straight onto the very hot preserve after pouring it into glass jars, and larger cellophane discs which are wetted on the outer surface then put over the tops of the jar and held with a rubber band. As the cellophane dries it shrinks to a drum-tight fit.

Pickles and chutneys dry out quickly when exposed to air as the vinegar evaporates. They do not usually spoil or go mouldy though due to the powerful preservative qualities of

SEALING JARS

Bottles or jars with cork stoppers can be sealed and finished off with a coating of sealing wax dripped over them. Ordinary sticks of sealing wax are fine but if you can get these ingredients, try this old recipe for an excellent wax which makes a tight close seal on lids and stoppers.

In an old pot melt 110g (4oz) sealing wax, the same amount of black resin and a walnut-sized piece of beeswax. It froths up dramatically so should be stirred with a tallow candle. Paint over corks to seal.

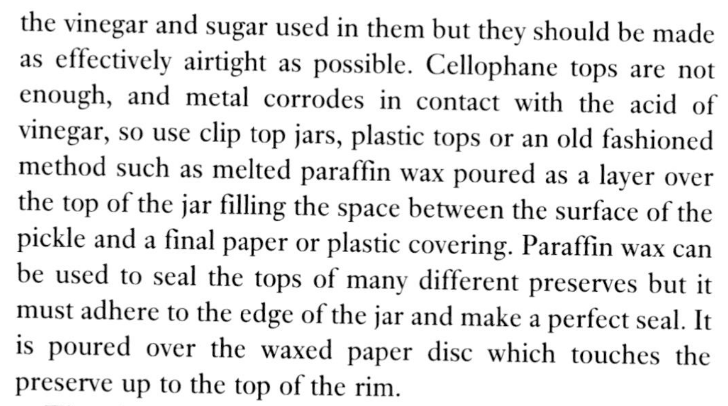

the vinegar and sugar used in them but they should be made as effectively airtight as possible. Cellophane tops are not enough, and metal corrodes in contact with the acid of vinegar, so use clip top jars, plastic tops or an old fashioned method such as melted paraffin wax poured as a layer over the top of the jar filling the space between the surface of the pickle and a final paper or plastic covering. Paraffin wax can be used to seal the tops of many different preserves but it must adhere to the edge of the jar and make a perfect seal. It is poured over the waxed paper disc which touches the preserve up to the top of the rim.

The choice of finishing off pots and jars of home-made preserves is often based on an aesthetic decision as well as a practical one. Old heavy glass jars look good lined up on the shelves and a covering of cellophane or waxed brown paper is far prettier than a clip-on plastic cover. One old trick to help inhibit mould growth on stored jams is to brush the surface with brandy or dip the waxed discs in brandy before placing them on the hot jam. Some people seem never to have a problem with keeping preserves in store while others, no matter how careful they are, end up with jars festering with mould. Always cover jam with waxed discs when it is boiling hot and either finish with cellophane at this stage or wait until the pots are completely cold. Covering them when lukewarm is often the cause of them not keeping well. Damp storage conditions are, of course, a major cause of preserves not keeping and even the use of over-ripe or sodden fruit during a wet summer season can encourage mould growth.

■ *Wholesome plain brown papers, simple labels and homely string still make the best wrappings and covers for finishing off pots and jars of homemade preserves and pickles (above).*

SUMMER

Roses fill the borders, vegetables flourish in the kitchen garden, and the scents of summer drift indoors. Capture them in all kinds of ways to last throughout the year. This is the time to harvest flowers and to make use of the far too fleeting crops of soft summer fruits. While meals are more relaxed and simple during hot weather, use the extra hours to store up delicious things for the bleaker months in the year ahead.

■ *A cabbage leaf put to use as a basket to collect the first plump raspberries. Fruits were often stored or displayed in a leaf, a practical and aesthetic choice.*

EARLY SUMMER

'Sweet as scarlet strawberry under wet leaves hidden,
Honeyed as the Damask rose, lavish as the moon,
Shedding lovely light on things forgotten, hope forbidden –
That's the way of June.'

NORA CHESSON

NOW IS THE right time to gather herbs and sweet scented leaves to dry for filling herb pillows and sachets. In early summer there is a strong flush of growth and the plant's energy is sent into making leaf rather than flower which will appear a little later. The foliage of sweet briar or Eglantine rose (*Rosa rubiginosa*) has the delicious scent of green apples which carries on the air, particularly if it is grown somewhere where the fragrance is confined. On warm humid days or when the air is moist after a shower of summer rain the smell fills the garden. The plant looks rather like a wild dog rose with small, pale pink single flowers, but the bright green, healthy-looking leaves should be harvested and dried quickly to retain their magical scent. Eglantine is a plant which crops up many times throughout early literature. Chaucer and Shakespeare mention it often and Thomas Hyll's gardening book of 1577, *The Gardener's Labyrinth*, suggests planting a deliciously scented hedge "either privet alone or sweet bryar and whitethorn interlaced together, and roses one, two or three sorts placed here and there amongst them".

The prefix sweet when associated with plants usually indicates that at one time they were gown for their special scent. Sweet woodruff (*Asperula odorata*) was a favourite medieval strewing herb and used to decorate churches on saints' days and festivals in garlands and ropes. Woodruff is not really scented when growing but the leaves develop a beautiful fragrance as they dry. They contain the substance coumarin which makes the sweet vernal grass of old-fashioned hay meadows smell delicious as it dries. In the past leaves of woodruff have been used to scent clothes and placed between book pages, made into lotions for the skin and, in Georgian times, tucked into a pocket watch to sniff when reading the time.

Other leaves which are suitable to dry to fill sachets and pillows are scented geraniums, lemon verbena (*Lippia citriodora*) and mint or mixtures of herb leaves or herbs and flower petals. Pick the herbs, flowers and plants on a dry day and pull the leaves off the stems. Scatter the leaves into a shallow basket or wire mesh tray and leave in a warm but airy place to dry. On a good sunny day they might dry rapidly in the garden or greenhouse, out of the wind. Dry them quickly to keep their best scent and colour. If you find it easier, rather than dealing with loose leaves, bunch the stems and hang them upside-down to air-dry over a stove or in an airing cupboard.

You can either fill pillows directly with the crumbled dried leaves or stuff the pillow first with kapok or terylene wadding, then fill a smaller sachet with the herbs and push this into the larger pillow. This makes it easier to replenish the herbs later when their scent has faded. If you need to remove the pillow cover frequently for washing try making an inner herb pillow to cover with an outer pillow case.

■ *Blue and white striped and checked covers are made amongst a carpet of flowering sweet woodruff which will be picked and dried later to fill the pillows (above).*

■ *The finished pillows lie amongst antique white lace cushions on a bed (right).*

The scented pillows do not have to have just a leaf mixture inside them – you could use other kinds of scents. Home-made pot pourris are an obvious choice or use favourite flower and herb essential oils dropped sparingly on to cotton wool which is then tucked inside the pillow stuffing. Other good scents include cedar wood raspings or sandalwood shavings for a less floral perfume and built-in insect repellent properties.

When making scented sachets or herb and leaf pillows, try to choose fabrics which are sympathetic to their contents. Fresh stripes and crisp checks somehow feel right with sharp, leafy, no-nonsense scents while softer flowery fragrances might suit prettier floral fabrics and richer, more luxurious textures. If your leaves or scented materials are at all prickly or dusty, you will need to use a fine and densely woven fabric to contain them, though the outer cover can be made from any material you choose. For many leaves, such as sweet woodruff, a fine lawn, muslin or inexpensive cheesecloth is perfectly suitable as the fabric sachet to hold them.

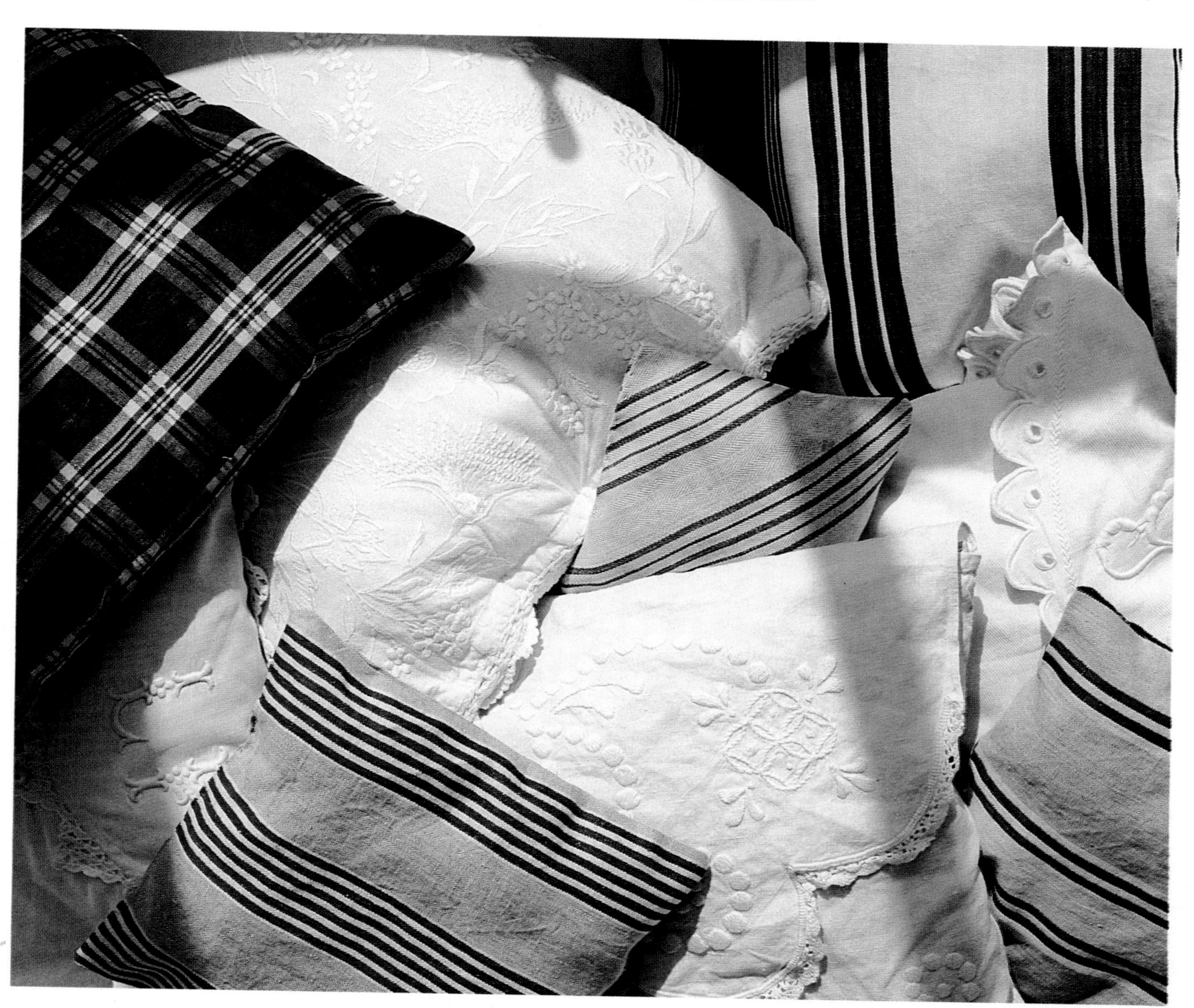

We are all spoilt for the taste of strawberries these days now that we seem to be able to eat them all the year round. Imagine how it was when they only appeared for a brief sweet season early in the summer, the first real soft fruit of the year, often cosseted and covered with cloches to bring the fruit to ripeness a week or two earlier than normal. In William Cobbett's day the list of strawberry varieties was vast, with names that seem strange and wonderful to us now that we only have a choice of growing a few over-large bloated garden varieties and even less choice of types to buy in shops. Strawberries are delicate and do not handle or keep well so new varieties have been bred for maximum shelf life rather than flavour. In 1829, in his *English Gardener*, Cobbett lists amongst others: Kew Pine, Chili, White Alpine, Red Alpine, Keen's Seedling and Hautbois.

Good strawberry jam is difficult to make successfully as it needs fresh ripe fruit which has had plenty of sun. A cold, damp growing season produces fruit which is bloated and tasteless, containing very little pectin. Strawberries are naturally low in the essential pectin needed to make jam set so they are often over-cooked and lose their fresh flavour. Strawberry preserves are probably a good case for using extra pectin, either of the artificial kind or from another compatible fruit such as redcurrants. However, it is worth persevering with as a good strawberry jam is still the classic preserve to eat at genteel teas, in airy sponge cakes or spread on scones with whipped or clotted cream. There are many old-fashioned recipes for making a preserve where the fruit is kept whole, the aim being to produce a clear scarlet jam with the whole strawberries suspended throughout it.

If you have a garden (and you need very little space for this) grow a few red or yellow alpine strawberry plants. Their flavour is incomparable and, for some reason, they are rarely taken by birds so are more rewarding to grow than the large varieties. From sowing seeds early in the year, you can be eating fruits the same year. Alpine strawberries make a delicious jam if you can grow enough to make it worthwhile, but otherwise they are lovely just to have to pick daily and scatter fresh over cereals and puddings.

As well as making delicious jams, preserves and puddings, strawberries have another quite different use as a skin conditioner and mild astringent. They also do a good job as a tooth cleaner, removing plaque and leaving teeth fresh and white. A mixture of creamy milk and strawberries liquidised together very thoroughly and stored in the fridge should be patted gently onto the face, left for a few seconds then rinsed off with cool water. It is mildly toning and leaves the skin with a finer texture. For a quick, reviving face pack, simply mash a few ripe strawberries and spread them on your face and lie down and relax for several minutes. This is not easy to do as gravity tends to take over as you spread the fruit over your skin! It's probably easiest and safest to do this while you are bathing than to attempt it while lying on the best carpet.

■ *Eat strawberries as soon as possible after picking and never put them near water which turns them soggy and tasteless. Here they wait for a jam-making session in the cool of the day (left).*

■ *Summer strawberries are a real treat for the skin as well as for the stomach and have been used for centuries for both cosmetic and beauty purposes (above).*

Gooseberries were traditionally eaten around Whitsuntide in Britain and provided some of the season's first fresh fruit in large enough quantity to begin to preserve and store in different ways. For centuries they have been eaten as sauces accompanying rich or oily savoury foods such as mackerel and goose, as well as making homely puddings and jams. Gooseberry bushes thrive in a cool northern climate and are useful because the fruit can be eaten in their tart young green state, although they demand powerful sweetening as a pudding, or left to ripen and become as large and sweet as plums later in the summer. Unlike the tempting red soft fruits which are always eaten by birds, gooseberries are rarely attacked while green and bristly but may be stolen when heavy and translucent and full of juice. Many country children remember being sent to sit in the garden to 'top and tail' a colander full of gooseberries for a Sunday pie and this fiddly process is a small drawback to the fruit, though it is quickly done with a pair of small scissors or just a pinch with sharp finger nails. In some regions gooseberry growing was taken very seriously at one time (and still is in a few places). There were weigh-ins and shows held to display the largest and heaviest fruits and record-sized gooseberries were grown weighing up to nearly two ounces each.

Gooseberry preserves were at one time dangerously cooked in brass pans to keep the green colour of the fruit. Boiled with sugar, the fresh green colour is lost to a warm, greeny-amber shade. Gooseberry jam can be a little dull and stodgy and is perhaps better made into a jelly flavoured with elderflower or used as it was in our household as a base for a delicious mint jelly to eat with lamb.

GOOSEBERRY MINT JELLY

Pot this up into small jars so it can be eaten at one sitting. It is delicious served with spring lamb.

900g (2 lb) green gooseberries
Sugar
A bunch of mint (not peppermint), about 16 stalks
Juice of 2 lemons

Put gooseberries in a large pan (don't bother to top and tail) and just cover with water. Bring to the boil and simmer until soft. Strain the fruit through a jelly bag and measure the juice. To every 570ml (1 pint) of juice add 450g (1 lb) sugar. Tie half the mint into a bundle and add to the pan with gooseberry juice, sugar and lemon juice. Heat until the sugar has dissolved then boil until a set is reached. Remove the mint. Chop the rest of the mint finely and add to the jelly before potting up.

■ *The pale green, translucent fruit ripen and grow over the summer and can then be eaten raw. At this stage, however, they are too sharp (left).*

GOOSEBERRY, ORANGE AND PISTACHIO JAM

This lifts the humble gooseberry out of the ordinary, the orange flavour working well with the gooseberries.

1.4 kg (3 lb) green gooseberries, topped and tailed
4 unwaxed oranges, grated and squeezed
1.4 kg (3 lb) sugar
175g (6 oz) unsalted, very fresh pistachio nuts

Put the gooseberries into a large preserving pan with the grated rind of the oranges plus 300ml (½ pint) water. Simmer the fruit gently for about 10 minutes, then add sugar and orange juice. Bring to a rapid boil and cook until set. This should not take long, so be careful not to overcook and make the jam too stiff. Take off the heat and add the coarsely chopped pistachio nuts. Stir well, leave to settle a little, then pour into pots and seal while very hot.

■ *Green gooseberries have always been an important fruit in the stillroom. They are plentiful and easy to grow (above).*

LIME TREES are quite late to flower and, when they do, the green blossoms are somewhat hidden amongst the mass of foliage. One is made aware of the flowering by the hum of bees working in the nectar rich blooms. Other trees, such as beech, flower in great profusion too and provide food for foraging bees, producing some of the best flavoured honey of all from single tree flowers.

Many tree flowers are useful to humans too, and two of the best known are elder (*Sambucus nigra*) and lime (*Tilia europaea*). At one time the almond-scented flowers of hawthorn (*Crataegus monogyna*) were often made into a kind of liqueur by macerating the tiny pink or white flowers with brandy and sugar and standing it in a sunny place for the blooms to flavour the liquid. Young ash keys, which are the stage on from flowers of the common ash (*Fraxinus excelsior*), were used to make a pickle in country homes similar to nasturtium seed pickle.

Lime or linden flowers are gathered in early summer and used fresh or dried to make a refreshing tisane, or what used to be called a 'grateful' drink. Elderflower, mint and sweet woodruff tisanes are good too and all can be drunk unsweetened or with a squeeze of lemon and a spoonful of honey added if you prefer.

■ *Creamy white elderflowers are endlessly useful for summer drinks, flavourings and lotions. In the autumn the berries give another rich harvest (left).*

■ *Refreshing lime flower tisane is a delicious drink when newly made from either fresh or dried flowers (above).*

THE DAYS lengthen and more time is spent outdoors under the clear blue skies we have longed for. Even with the greatest care it is easy to get sun- or wind-burned when active or working outside, particularly when you are on or near water. Once your skin reacts and turns red and sore it is too late to save the damage, but there are things which you can do to calm the irritation and burning and cool down the skin. These lotions can be made up and stored in the fridge for when you suddenly need them. They are good at any time, not specifically for damaged skin, and the elderflower water is excellent to use frequently or as a base for other infusions. Traditionally elderflowers had the properties to bleach and refine skin and perhaps as we all come to respect the sun's strength more and crave shade instead of blazing heat, we will want to return to a pale and creamy complexion. Many old recipes seem to have been designed specifically to bleach freckles and to achieve a perfect lily white skin. We might have different reasons now for making our own skin lotions but the old recipes were based on sound experiment and years of knowledge of common herbs and plants which means that they really work.

INSECT ALERT

Summer days mean biting insects. To repel them, try dabbing skin with an infusion of quassia chips or rub on lavender or citronella essential oil diluted in witch-hazel. Once bitten, try rubbing the bite with fresh marigold leaves (*Calendula officinalis*) or squeeze fresh parsley juice onto the skin.

SAGE LEAF LOTION

An infusion of sage leaves has always been recommended for sore throats and the same mixture is excellent dabbed onto sore skin that has had too much sun. Of course the sensible thing to do is cover up, wear a hat and good sunscreen in strong sun but there are always times when you get caught out and need some after-sun comfort.

Boil some spring water and pour about 300ml (½ pint) over a handful of fresh sage leaves stripped from their stems. Leave to infuse, and, when cool, strain the liquid and use. This is best made fresh when you need it as long as you have a good supply of sage in the garden. It doesn't much matter if the sage is the plain culinary type (*Salvia officinalis*) or a purple or variegated type.

■ *Sage, cucumber and elderflower lotions all help damaged sunburnt skin (above).*

■ *Rows of elegant old fashioned chemists' jars filled with summer skin lotions (right).*

CUCUMBER LOTION

Cucumber is soothing to skin and tired eyes and this lotion is a marvellous way to refresh hot summer skin. Cucumber has a natural pH of 5.48 which is very close to the skin's own 5.5.

Grate, chop or liquidise half an unpeeled cucumber, preferably one that has not been sprayed, and squeeze out the juice from the pulp, either through a sieve or muslin or just with your hands. Use this juice on sunburned skin just as it is or mix it with equal quantities of rose water and witch hazel as a more astringent toner.

ELDERFLOWER WATER

This is best made when elderflowers are in bloom but can also be made from dried flowerheads too. Pick flowers well away from roads or pesticide spray drift. Use as a soothing lotion any time.

Put 110g (4oz) fresh elderflowers in a bowl and bruise them with a pestle or wooden spoon. Pour over 300ml (½ pint) boiling spring water and stir for a few seconds. Leave to infuse and cool completely. Strain and add 2 tablespoons of eau-de-cologne if you want to store it for a little while. Bottle the water in clean jars.

MIDSUMMER

'Bring hither the pincke and purple cullambine,
With Gilleflowres;
Bring Coronations and Sops-in-wine,
Worn of paramours.'

EDMUND SPENSER
The Shepherd's Calendar 1578

By midsummer fruits and vegetables are in abundant supply and demand to be used in the kitchen and stillroom. They have a way of ripening all at once and are suddenly in great quantities, all demanding attention at the same time, but this lasts only for a few short weeks. A well grown mature bush of red, white or blackcurrants will provide as much fruit as a normal-sized household might need, while a double row of raspberry canes of say twenty plants will fill baskets and colanders daily for at least three weeks. Soft fruits such as raspberries and strawberries rarely become boring as their natural season is not very long but it is still important to capture something of their magical tastes for the months ahead. This is difficult to do successfully as the fruits are so delicious raw that cooking them somehow seems to be sacrilege. Follow tradition and pick or keep your fruits on a large cabbage leaf. This was believed to keep the fruit fresh longer.

RASPBERRY RATAFIA

A ratafia is a fruit-flavoured liqueur which is a perfect way of using just a few raspberries and making something memorable with them. You can adjust the sweetness to taste. You might like it with no sugar at all.

TO EACH 450G (1LB) FRESH RASPBERRIES:
110g (4oz) sugar
570ml (1pint) vodka, eau de vie or brandy
5 almonds or apricot kernels

Put the clean but unwashed fruit in a bowl and sprinkle the sugar over. Press gently with the back of a wooden spoon until the juice begins to run. Pour over the alcohol and add the almonds or apricot kernels. Put this mixture into a wide-necked jar and cover or seal the top. For the first week or so shake and turn the jar daily. After about a month, strain the fruit from the liquid and then filter the liquid through double muslin or a paper coffee filter until it is clear. Store in a dark place in a corked bottle.

■ *The rich, bubbling raspberry conserve fills the whole house with the smell of summer (left). One of the best colours of summer – the dull pinky red of raspberries (above).*

Red, white and particularly blackcurrants, though, are often more delicious cooked so that their rich flavours develop. The powerful taste of blackcurrants makes one of the best fruit jellies and you can almost feel the vitamin C oozing from the fruits doing you good. Redcurrants combine well with other soft summer fruits such as raspberries or even cherries to make mixed fruit jams and the high pectin in the currants makes jam- and jelly-making easy. A jelly of redcurrant alone is still the classic accompaniment to spring lamb and it's always worth making a few very small pots with just enough in each for one sitting so that you eat it at its very best.

Raspberries are well worth growing even a small garden as they need not take up too much room and never grow out of hand as the old canes are cut down each year, but they do have to be netted or protected from marauding birds in some way. The old intensely flavoured raspberries of years ago have given way to a new larger-than-life kind of fruit designed for the pick-your-own fruit farm market. Old varieties are no longer for sale as they are not virus-free so we have to grow what is on offer and make the best of them. Though the flavour is blander, the crop is usually magnificent and very much easier to pick than it once was, so raspberries are still one of the best fruits to make fine-tasting preserves. Some people find the pips in raspberries too irritating to eat so it is easy enough to make a jelly either of plain raspberries or one combined with redcurrants. Others are pleased to be able to eat the real pips after eating factory-produced horrors such as artificially coloured mixed fruit or vegetables masquerading as jam with, so the legend goes, wooden pips. Once you have tried homemade raspberry jam, it will be very difficult to revert to the shop-bought variety.

There are many recipes for a simple preserve made from raspberries which does not need long cooking. This means it has the freshest taste and maximum flavour possible. A mixture with a ratio of four to three, fruit to sugar, is left for a few hours for the sugar to begin to dissolve and the juices run. It is then heated until the sugar is completely dissolved and potted up. There are even methods which rely on the sun's heat on a warm day to dissolve the sugar into the fruit. Raspberries are high in pectin and so they set quickly, but a softer, runnier jam is far more delicious than one set solid. The method is very simple and the result is best kept in the fridge, frozen or eaten quickly.

OLIVADA

Stone ripe black olives and pound in a pestle and mortar or process in a food processor with a dribble of olive oil. Continue until you have a smooth paste. Add a turn or two of the black pepper mill, check the taste and then pot up into tiny jars. Float a film of olive oil over the surface and cover the jar with a lid. Use to spread on small pieces of toast or fried bread as an appetiser or add capers, anchovies and a dash of brandy to make tapenade.

Olives are one of the oldest foods known to man and have been eaten in the mediterranean area for centuries. Picked green in the autumn from ancient gnarled trees or later through the winter when they have ripened to black, they are then used whole or pressed to make oil which is the foundation for what we have come to think of as mediterranean cooking. There are many different types of olives ranging from the tiny pinkish-black olives from Nice to enormous pale green 'queen' olives from Spain. They can be bought loose or in cans and jars and will either have been brined to preserve them or, as with the ripe, wrinkled black varieties, simply shine in their glossy coating of oil. Olives come pitted or with stones, stuffed and flavoured with herbs and seasonings. They are essential to have in the storecupboard for summer, so that you can toss a handful into a salad or eat them lazily with an aperitif on summer evenings.

If you want your olives flavoured in some way, do it yourself by marinading green ones in olive oil flavoured with thyme, garlic and oregano or try them sprinkled with crushed coriander seeds. Olives kept under oil will store well for weeks and you can even use a bland vegetable oil which will absorb some of the olive taste itself and can be used in salad dressings later. You can mix your olive types too and layer them divided up by a handful of fresh bay leaves or rings of lemon. The spectacular result makes one of the quickest and easiest gifts to make providing you have the ingredients to hand and a jar with a wide neck that your hand will fit into. You can spend time arranging the olives in neat rings and rows but it looks just as good if they are spooned in anyhow. Use as many different colours and types of olive that you can find for the best visual effect. Be sure to keep the top layers well covered with oil to preserve what is below and check that this is still the case after you have used a layer or two of the olives. Use either a screw lid or just a circle of cellophane, fabric or paper to keep out dust.

Good olive oil with plenty of flavour is best savoured in simple salad dressings with lemon juice or wine vinegar. Oil without much flavour, say from a second pressing, is easily zipped up a bit by adding flavourings and left to develop for a few weeks. All kinds of flavourings can be experimented with, the best known being herbs. Basil-flavoured oil, which can only be made in summer when fresh basil is plentiful, is one of the best and most useful. This herb oil, as well as being used in dressings, can be drizzled over pizzas, vegetable dishes, baked tomatoes or mushrooms.

The preservative qualities of olive oil are well exploited in jars of vegetables submerged in the delicious liquid. Sweet peppers of all colours are excellent (see page 29) and so too are wild or cultivated mushrooms. You can either simmer the vegetables in wine vinegar and then put into the oil to make an Italian-inspired kind of antipasto or simply grill the ingredients, leave to cool and drain, then pack into the jars with flavourings. Baby globe artichokes or artichoke hearts are perfect for the first treatment and slices of aubergine, for example, are made even more delicious by the grilling method which brings out their smokey flavour. Once sealed, these preserves are probably best kept in a fridge for any length of time and once opened they should be eaten over a day or so.

■ *Glistening purple, black and green olives spread out on a tray waiting to be layered between fresh bay leaves and lemon slices (right).*

SICILIAN SPICED OLIVES

Serve as part of mixed hors d'oeuvres at a summer meal.

450g (1 lb) black olives in brine or oil
Peel of 1 unwaxed orange, cut into julienne strips
Peel of 1 unwaxed lemon, cut into julienne strips
1 tablespoon chopped fresh thyme
10 cloves of garlic, peeled and cut in half
1 tablespoon fennel seeds
Olive oil

Drain the olives and put in a bowl. Add rinds, thyme, garlic and fennel seeds. Mix well and put into preserving jars. Cover completely with olive oil and seal. Leave for at least one week before eating.

■ *Choose a tall, wide-necked jar for layering different coloured olives. Don't worry if the layers are not completely straight (above).*

PICKLED ROSE PETALS OR GILLYFLOWERS

Gillyflowers are what we now call carnations or pinks. The word carnation is a corruption of coronation and gillyflower comes from the French for clove, *girofle*, as the flowers have a clove-like scent. Pull the petals from the flower head and either nip out the white base of each petal or pickle the flower whole. Whole, small, red rosebuds can be used or loose petals.

Dry prepared roses or gillyflowers
Sugar
White wine vinegar

Weigh the flowers and measure an equal amount of white sugar. Now measure white wine vinegar in the proportions 25 ml (1 fl oz) to every 25 g (1 oz) of sugar. In a non-reactive pan, dissolve the sugar in the vinegar and remove from the heat as soon as it has done so. It does not need to boil. Leave the syrup to cool and pack the flowers into dark glass or opaque jars. The pickle must not have light getting in as this would spoil the colour. Pour the syrup over the flowers and seal.

IN ELIZABETHAN times great importance was given to the colour and decoration of food. There was great scope for elaborate and fanciful food in a time when the boundaries between courses was less distinct than now and when tastes as different as salt, sweet, spiced and pickled were combined in dishes served together. On the tables of the rich households multi-coloured pies and tarts were a great favourite of the period and every cook worth their salt was able to create a colourful and elaborate salad, even during the bleak winter months.

Much of the colour in these dishes was provided by the pickled or preserved flower heads made during the summer and stored away. The stillroom was kept busy through these long days, potting up fruit jellies and preserves in as many different colours as it was possible to create and making jars of pickled and candied rosebuds and carnations to stand on the larder shelves beside the spring versions of primrose, cowslips and violets.

Roses were by far the largest crop to be made use of and, if a garden did not produce enough of the raw material, it was possible to buy roses in the market for stillroom purposes. Rose petals were made into sweet waters and lotions, or dried, candied and made into sweetmeats and medicines. Honey was pounded with petals into a delicious paste known as melrosette and, of course, the dried petals were the basis of sweet powders and dried herb and flower mixtures for scenting the house, clothes and linens.

Strongly scented deep pink or red roses were required for all these recipes, often described as simply 'damask' roses in old recipe books. *Rosa gallica officinalis*, known as the Apothecary's rose, was probably the rose most commonly used and it is still available today. The scent is strong and lingering from the semi-double, light crimson flowers produced on a medium sized bush with bright green healthy foliage. In medieval times it was grown commercially around Provins in Northern France and the thickly textured petals retain their fragrance well when dried. *Rosa damascena*, which may be descended from *Rosa gallica*, is the rose grown in Bulgaria, Morocco and India to produce Attar of rose or rose essential oil.

■ *Deep crimson gillyflowers are made into a vibrantly coloured preserve to be stored for the winter months ahead (above).*

■ *The soft summer scents of roses are fleeting and subtle but they can be captured to last a little longer (right).*

TEINTURE
DE GAYAC

WHITE CURRANT AND NECTARINE JELLY

This is the kind of luxurious preserve to make in small quantities in summer to give as a present.

1.8 kg (4 lb) white currants
150 ml (5 fl oz) water
Preserving sugar
Juice of two lemons
3 nectarines

Put white currants in a large pan with the water. Don't bother to strip them off their stems. Bring to the boil and simmer very gently until soft. Tip the mixture into a jelly bag and leave to drain overnight. Next day measure the juice. To each 570 ml (1 pint) liquid measure 350 g (12 oz) preserving sugar and put this with the juice in a preserving pan. Add the lemon juice. Skin, stone, and slice the nectarines and keep them in slightly acidulated water to stop them turning brown. Boil the jelly until a set is reached, take off heat and leave to cool a little, then add the nectarines. Pot up just as it is setting to keep fruit suspended in jelly. Seal while hot.

■ *Ripe white currants are particularly beautiful fruits. Use them as you would redcurrants and enjoy their subtly different taste (above).*

APRICOT CHUTNEY

This tastes fresh and delicious and is good with spiced foods or cheese.

1.4 kg (3 lb) fresh apricots, stoned and chopped
350 g (12 oz) onions, chopped small
2 cloves of garlic, crushed
Small chunk of fresh ginger, grated
570 ml (1 pint) cider vinegar
225 g (8 oz) demerara sugar
1 dessertspoon salt
1 dessertspoon mustard seeds
1 teaspoon each of ground cinnamon and mace
½ teaspoonful ground cayenne

Put everything in a large non-reactive pan and simmer gently until soft and thick. Pot and seal.

PEACH AND WALNUT CONFITURE

900 g (2 lb) ripe peaches, skinned and stoned
Juice of 2 lemons
450 g (1 lb) sugar
225 g (8 oz) walnut pieces

Chop the peaches into cubes and put in a bowl with the sugar and the lemon juice. Leave overnight. Next day put the contents of bowl into a preserving pan and bring to the boil. Cook until the peach begins to turn translucent (about 20 minutes). Now remove the fruit from the syrup with a slotted spoon and put into a bowl. Rapidly boil the syrup until thick, add the walnuts and peach pieces. Stir well then remove from heat and leave to cool slightly before putting into pots.

■ *Peach and walnut confiture is very rich but the crispness of the walnuts cuts through the sweetness well (right).*

A LIST OF peach varieties from the early nineteenth century includes at least 29 named types, including Old Newington, Gallande, Red Magdalen, French Mignonne, Persique and Incomparable. Peaches were taken seriously in those days and graced the dessert dishes of any person with pretensions to good taste. The fruit trees were generally trained against warm south-facing walls in well protected kitchen gardens, but it does make one wonder whether peaches were hardier then or if summer weather was kinder than it is today. Later glasshouses were widely used as a means of protection, and by the Victorian period every large garden had its special peach house to produce fruit out of season – peaches at Christmas were not unheard of. At one time the county of Gloucestershire supported a thriving peach industry, growing mostly the delicate white fleshed types rather than the coarser flavoured yellow ones we see these days.

Nectarines are a hybrid fruit with the richness of a peach but a slightly sharper edge to the taste, with a smooth skin rather than the fur of the peach. Recipes for the fruits are interchangeable and there are many for jams, conserves and chutneys or simply spiced to eat with cold meats.

Apricots are an altogether different fruit though the trees are similar, not least that the pale pink flowers bloom early on the bare branches and risk late frosts and cold wet weather at pollination time. At one time apricots were picked small and green and used like green gooseberries. This was partly done to thin over-abundant fruit and it improved the quality of what was left.

■ *Perfectly ripe nectarines piled on a dish glow in the late evening summer light (overleaf).*

LATE SUMMER

'Make use of time, let not advantage slip;
Beauty within itself should not be wasted;
Fair flowers that are not gather'd in their prime,
Rot and consume themselves in little time.'

WILLIAM SHAKESPEARE
Venus and Adonis 1593

MUSTARD BELONGS to a large genus of plants known as *brassicas*, part of the cabbage family. The white seeded kind (*Brassica alba*) was once commonly grown as a seedling crop alongside cress to make the familiar salad used in sandwiches and as a food decoration. In England black mustard, and now the brown seeded mustard, has long been a field crop and in medieval times was grown in gardens to provide the fiery spice. The volatile oil in ground mustard was considered a digestive and was used medicinally in poultices and hot baths prescribed for colds and chills.

Its use now is as a condiment traditionally eaten with a list of specific foods, such as herrings, roast beef and meat brawns. English mustard is made from mustard flour mixed with water while the French make a less fiery version with wine or vinegar. Mustard is a storecupboard ingredient with great potential and by starting with a classic plain mustard you can add other ingredients to make your own mustard *maison*, invaluable for salad dressings and cooked dishes.

■ *By adding chillies, dill, lemon juice, honey and beer create your own smooth and grainy mustards (left). Mustard mixtures await an inventive cook (above).*

MARIGOLD PETAL CHEESE

Untreated milk turns sour naturally and can just be hung up to drain. Pasteurized milk is most people's option and needs rennet or buttermilk to curdle it.

570 ml (1 pint) creamy milk
1 tablespoon fresh or dried marigold petals
Few drops of rennet (check manufacturers' instructions for quantity needed for 570 ml milk)
Pinch of grated nutmeg
Salt

Warm milk to 16°C (60–65°F). Bruise marigold petals and add to milk. Put in a few drops of rennet and when it has curdled spoon into a double thickness square of cheesecloth and hang to drain in a cool place. After about 6 hours, take it out and sprinkle with a little salt and nutmeg. Shape into small rounds and decorate with more chopped fresh marigold petals. Keep in the fridge.

Late summer sees the garden full of the bright colours and simple shapes of annual flowers. Often scorned by sophisticated gardeners, they are some of the prettiest and most cheerful plants to have around. Many of the hardy and half-hardy annuals we grow are not native and their brash colours and artless style can look alien in a muted garden, but sometimes their splash of brilliant colour is welcome and in many cases they have edible and decorative petals and leaves. Nasturtiums (*Tropaeolum majus*) have been grown in every type of garden from the days when they were brought back from South America. Their peppery spicy leaves contain powerful amounts of vitamin C and the flowers taste good too, their bright orange, gold and red petals contrasting deliciously with green salad leaves.

Marigolds have been bred and improved from the days when they grew as a widespread native plant over much of Europe. Today's varieties now have large heavy heads, laden with orange petals. At one time the plant was much simpler with a big central eye and a single layer of petals around it and it is still possible to buy seeds of this version which is known as pot marigold (*Calendula officinalis*). It was originally one of the important medieval pot herbs, or flowers used in the kitchen, providing welcome colouring and flavouring to cheer the interminable winter dishes of bland and stodgy foods.

The orange petals dry easily and keep well so were an important ingredient in the storecupboard and used in place of costly spices such as saffron. They can be used fresh or dried in cooking and keep their colour well in the dried state, particularly if they are stored out of the light. To dry the petals, pick marigolds on a sunny day when they are completely open but still young. Either snip off the heads from the stalk and dry these whole or pull off the petals when fresh and dry these loose. Put the petals or heads in a basket or colander and leave in a warm, airy place for several days until dry and crisp. Store in brown glass jars or tins to exclude the light. Marigold petals were once used as a form of mild rennet to curdle milk for soft cheeses but the recipe on the left is for a soft cheese which is simply flavoured by the flowers.

■ *Brilliant orange marigolds look both exotic and homely when arranged in a simple kitchen jug (above).*

■ *The stillness and calm of the dairy captured in the shape of a cheesecloth quietly hanging to drip its whey (right).*

MELONS ARE exactly the right fruit for hot weather. Their cool juiciness is sometimes the only kind of refreshment you have the energy to eat, providing food and drink in one deliciously scented mouthful. Naturally revelling in hot climates, melon plants have always been nurtured and cosseted to produce fruits in northern cooler climates too. In the eighteenth century the hot bed system of gardening which was commonly used to grow tender fruits and vegetables and to force them into earlier production, provided many households with baskets of melons through the summer months. Any spare fruits would be made into melon pickle.

SPICED MELON PICKLE

Orange-fleshed melons such as cantaloupes make the best version of this recipe. Be very careful to blanch the fruit no longer than necessary or it may turn to a stringy pulp and lose its chunkiness. This pickle is delicious with smoked meats and strongly spiced dishes of all kinds. Pack it into wide necked jars in order to be able to spear a chunk to remove it easily.

1.7 kg (3 lb) cubed melon flesh
[you will need about 3 melons each weighing 900 g (2 lb) each]
300 ml (1/2 pint) white wine vinegar
450 g (1 lb) white sugar
1 lemon, sliced
1 cinnamon stick
1 dried red chilli
1 teaspoon allspice
4 cloves

Blanch the cubes of melon in a large pan of boiling salted water for no more than 2 minutes. This is made easier using a wire blanching basket suspended in the water. Remove and refresh in very cold water. Drain and gently pat dry if necessary, then pack into preserving jars. Heat the vinegar, sugar, lemon and spices in another pan stirring until the sugar is dissolved, then bring to the boil. Simmer for about 20 minutes then strain to remove lemon and spices (or leave a few whole spices in the syrup) and pour over melon in jars. Seal while still hot. Leave for a few weeks to mature before eating and use quite quickly once opened.

■ *The dull green netted skin, once cut, reveals glowing orange flesh (above left).*

■ *The taste and scent of late summer melons captured in a jar of glowing spiced pickle (right).*

At one time beds of earth were raised on a layer of decomposing material such as horse manure which produced heat underneath the melon plants and forced them into quick growth and fooled them into thinking they were in more tropical conditions. Melons plants grow in long trailing vines which were usually grown up strings or a complicated system of wires. Each melon was cradled in it own little net to protect it as it ripened and keep it off the earth.

No still life painting of this period was complete without wonderful craggy melons often cut open to reveal the orange or green flesh inside. The fruit of the many different melon varieties is generally eaten fresh and raw, but there is one way to capture their texture and taste for longer than their natural fruiting season and this is in a melon pickle. Ideally slightly under-ripe fruits are best for this but they should be ripe enough to have developed some flavour. Very ripe fruit is too soft and disintegrates during the brief cooking that it requires. This recipe is good for using chunks of any melon – Charantais, Cantaloupe, Honeydew and Ogen – but do not try to use watermelon. Orange-fleshed types of melon make the most colourful version of the recipe. There is also a famous water melon pickle made in countries where it is commonly grown, but this is made from the strip of flesh between the rind and the inner pink flesh.

FEW PEOPLE can resist the distinctive and astringent smell of lavender, fresh or dried. A bush of lavender in flower simply invites you to pick a stem and crush the flower head to release the volatile oil and fragrance. Lavender has always been the household herb of most importance, giving its scent to freshen both newly washed linen and clothes in store. Pots of lavender or bunches of the herb were put near windows to scent the room and repel insects. The essential oil is healing to burns and wounds and has a calming yet restorative effect on the senses. It is used as a bath herb, as a fragrance for sweet waters and is a classic and important ingredient for pot pourri mixtures.

Second only to rose petals in its usefulness, the larger growing old fashioned varieties of lavender bloom quite late in the summer and attract bees and insects to their pale mauve flowers. To dry and use home-grown lavender, pick the flower heads on a fine day when the petals are just open amongst the bracts. Hang whole stems to dry in bundles then rub off the dried flowers and store in jars for sweet bags and pot pourris.

■ *An old carpet bag filled with treasures kept sweet and scented by fragrant lavender pot pourri (above).*

LAVENDER POT POURRI

You can add all kinds of decorative dried petals to the basic mixture such as cornflower, mallow, larkspur, etc, to make it look pretty, but plain lavender is subtle and attractive on its own or can also be used in sachets for linen scenting.

4 cups dried lavender
3 tablespoons ground orris root powder
1 tablespoon each of ground cinnamon, mace and allspice
6 drops lavender essential oil

Put all the dry ingredients in a large bowl and mix really well to distribute orris root powder. Add the drops of oil and mix again thoroughly. Put the mixture into paper bags, loosely close the top and store away in a cool dark place for six weeks to cure. Use as required, adding whole spices, leaves, flower heads, etc, for decoration.

SUMMER POT POURRI

A fresh lemony variation on lavender pot pourri in a pretty green and mauve colouring.

2 cups lavender flowers
1 cup lemon verbena leaves
½ cup sweet gale leaves
½ cup jasmine flowers
3 tablespoons ground orris root powder
1 tablespoon each of ground coriander and cinnamon
3 drops lavender essential oil
3 drops lemon verbena essential oil

Use the same method as lavender pot pourri.

■ *Dusky mauve dried lavender flowers in a bundle can be used just as they are for scenting cupboards or for decorations (right).*

A THINNING JAM

To achieve a perfect bunch of grapes, a careful gardener snips out some of the fruit to allow the rest to swell. The grape thinnings were once made into a delicious summer jam. Simply simmer the small fruits without water until soft. Try to skim off some of the skins as they rise to the top. Add equal quantities of sugar to fruit and boil until a set is reached. Pot as usual.

THERE IS a point in the late summer when time seems to stand still for a while just before a headlong rush into the profusion and plenty of early autumn. The great harvesting of summer fruits and crops is not quite under way so there is a lazy lull. Things are just ripening now, not really growing, so there is a sense of marking time and a relaxed holiday atmosphere everywhere.

One crop which is ready now is hot house grapes. Outdoor vines will not have ripe fruit until the autumn but the heavy clustered bunches of indoor varieties hang bloomy and delicious amongst drips of condensation. In Victorian times bunches of grapes were picked, their stems kept in water in special grape glasses and stored in cool dark sheds. In this way a perfect bunch of dessert grapes could grace a dinner table throughout the winter months.

■ *Swags of vine leaves and heavy bunches of fruit crowd an old glasshouse roof. Careful pruning and thinning of fruit produce perfect grapes (left).*

INDEX

Page numbers in *italic* refer to the illustrations

THE GREAT

ANTIQUES TREASURE HUNT

Test Your Knowledge of Antiques and Collectables and Learn While You Search

COMPILED BY
PAUL ATTERBURY

TIGER BOOKS INTERNATIONAL

A Marshall Edition
Conceived, edited and designed by
Marshall Editions
170 Piccadilly, London W1V 9DD

This edition published in 1997 by
Tiger Books International PLC,
Twickenham

ISBN 1-85501-956-6

Film supplied by Dorchester Typesetting
Group Ltd
Origination by Global Color, Malaysia
Printed and bound in Italy by Mondadori,
Verona

Valuation is an imprecise art and prices can
vary for many reasons including the
condition of a piece, fashion and national
and regional interest. Prices given in this
book are approximate and based on likely
auction values. *Insurance* values reflect the
retail replacement price and as such are
liable to be higher.

The publishers would like to thank John C.
Benjamin of Phillips auctioneers for his
invaluable help with the jewellery section
on pages 16–19.

Contents

Introducing
The Great Antiques Treasure Hunt

Antique collecting is all about hunting – the tracking down of that rare and elusive object, the searching for the vital background information that will confirm the attribution, and the moment of triumph when the object is finally captured. And, as every collector knows, so much is a matter of luck.

For a true collector, the excitement of stepping into a crowded antique shop and scanning the cluttered shelves is one that never dies. Every shop or market stall is a new thrill, full of possibilities and promise, and a challenge to the eye and the memory. The pages of this book are a series of splendid and richly stocked antique shops, packed with hidden treasures.

Every object tells a story, but some have more to say than others, and the challenge is to pick these out. Each page is a treasure trove of secrets waiting to be discovered – the only clues are a set of questions and brief descriptions. The rest is up to you, your eye, your memory and your imagination. All the excitement of the chase is here, in areas both familiar and unfamiliar, and there are plenty of opportunities to test your knowledge – and your luck.

Here are a thousand ways of building in your imagination some of the best collections in the world, with all the pleasures of the hunt but with none of the worries about display, storage, insurance, condition and, above all else, the cost. As these pages fill your mind with all those things you might one day acquire, enjoy the knowledge gained along the route. Remember, when it comes to the antiques trail, knowledge is power. Good hunting.

Paul Atterbury

The Treasure Hunt Begins Here

Set before you on these pages is a mass of objects from each of twelve major collecting areas – from all types of furniture to glass, and from militaria to china. Accompanying each collage is a series of questions to test your wits.

To help you answer the questions a 'decoder' gives a brief definition of each piece, explaining what it is, when it was made and its probable worth. It also highlights any special features that may help you in your quest.

When your eye has finished roaming each delightful collection, and you think you have the solution, turn to the back of the book, where you will find the answers given in full.

Rhapsody in Blue

1 Find something for the desk, for the bathroom, for bulbs and for flavouring.

2 Where is an edible Japanese delicacy?

3 Where was the famous willow pattern invented? Search out examples, and find the odd one out.

4 Which is the most valuable piece and how much would it cost?

5 Locate and find uses for a garniture and some lambrequins.

6 Find something inspired by the art of a lost Italian city and a Meissen imposter.

7 Find receptacles to capture the spirit of Scotland and the fire of France.

8 Which piece is associated with some well-known baggage?

9 Locate two north African beasts of burden.

10 Find a lady taking tea and a gentleman teeing off.

LG
ROYAL WORCESTER ENGLAND
WITH J.W. HARRISON'S COMPLIMENTS
LIVERPOOL
1879
BONE CHINA
ROYAL WORCESTER
MADE IN ENGLAND
780
大明萬曆年製
TO COMMEMORATE THE CORONATION OF KING GEORGE V AND QUEEN MARY
SEVRES 1848
786
MINTON
STOKE
TRENT

Rhapsody in Blue

1 Staffordshire meat dish with pattern 'Chinese Juvenile Sports' and floral border **(1a)**. 1825. 19in. ***(B)***
2 Pickle dish from Limehouse in London; the first factory producing English blue and white porcelain. 1748. 4¼in. ***(E)***
3 Three Chinese dinner plates **(3a,b)** from the vast quantity made for export to Europe during the 18th century. Typical designs **(3c–e)**. 1750–75. 7–9in. Each ***(A)***
4 Japanese Hirado porcelain rat on a radish. 1860–80. 7in. ***(C)***
5 'Kraak' dish with bird centrepiece **(5a)** and painted border **(5b,c)**. Kraak is the earliest exported Chinese porcelain and takes its name from the carrack it sailed in. *c.*1620. 14in. ***(C)***
6 Spill vase or brush pot made in China. 1880. 11in. ***(B)***
7 Japanese Arita dish copied from a Chinese 'Kraak' original; the design is obscured by the glaze **(7a–c)**. 1660–80. 14in. ***(E)***
8 Chinese jar painted with rambling prunus flowers **(8b,c)** on a blue 'cracked ice' ground. It has a decorated knop **(8a)** and neck **(8d)**. Late 1900s. 13in high. ***(C)***
9 Hanau faience ginger jar and cover. Made in Holland to resemble Chinese porcelain. *c.*1710. 12in. ***(G)***
10 Chinese plate painted with typical motifs and patterned border detail **(10a–e)**. 1770. 8½in. ***(A)***
11 Ming tea bowl, bearing the mark of Emperor Yung-lo. *c.*1403–24. 3¾in. ***(G)***
12 Liverpool painted tile depicting English rural landscape. Other design **(12a)**. 1800s. 6in. ***(B)***
13 Dynasty marks from Chinese porcelain: Ch'ing emperor Yung-cheng, 1723–35 **(13)**; Ming emperor Ch'eng-hua, 1465–87 **(13a,e)**; Ming emperor Hsüan-te, 1426–35 **(13b,d)**; Ch'ing emperor K'ang-hsi, 1662–1722 **(13c)**.
14 Transfer-printed Staffordshire pearlware punch bowl. 1820. 11in. ***(B)***
15 Chinese jar with dramatic dragon and phoenix designs in vivid blue **(15a,b)**. 1425–50. 5in. ***(G)***
16 Transfer-printed Staffordshire bowl with picturesque scene from English country life. Interior **(16a)** 1840. 9in. ***(A)***
17 Classic willow pattern plate by Dillwyn and Co. of Swansea, Wales. Many misleading legends have been attributed to the motifs **(17a–f)** which are purely artistic. 1820–30. 10in. ***(A)***
18 Delftware bowl decorated with a view of the Tower of London. Called after the Dutch town of Delft where it was copied from Chinese exports. Detail **(18a)**. 1600. 11in. ***(G)***
19 Two Chinese meat dishes with gilded edges **(19b,c)** from a dinner service. Detail **(19a)**. 1760–80. 14in and 13in. ***(C)***
20 Meissen cream pot in experimental underglaze blue; this technique was not a success for the German company and so pieces are rare. Knop on cover **(20a)**. 1730. 5in. ***(E)***
21 Japanese tea or punch pot from Arita. 1720. 7in. ***(F)***
22 Date marks from English Worcester china pieces: 1903 **(22)**; 1937 **(22a)**; 1873 **(22b)**; 1890 **(22c)**.
23 W&R Ridgway meat dish with a printed lotus pattern **(23a)** and unusual 'lobed' edge **(23b)**. 1830. 15in. ***(B)***
24 Florian ware vases by English designer William Moorcroft, in his 'Pompeii' shape **(24a,b)**. 1903. 4in. ***(D)***
25 Pearlware 'bell' custard cup by English potters Spode, used for desserts. 1810. 2in. ***(A)***
26 French St. Cloud cup and saucer with undulating reeding **(26a)**. 1730. Saucer 5in. ***(B)***
27 Staffordshire meat dish with unusual pattern based on a textile design **(27a–h)**. 1820. 20½in. ***(C)***
28 Chamber pot **(28b,d)** and covered dishes **(28a,c)** from an earthenware bedroom set by Thomas Lawrence of Longton, England. 1925. ***(A)***

55b

PRICE GUIDE: ***A*** less than £100 ($150) ***B*** £100–250 ($150–400) ***C*** £250–500 ($400–800) ***D*** £500–1000 ($800–1600) ***E*** £1000–2000 ($1600–3200) ***F*** £2000–3000 ($3200–4800) ***G*** over £3000 ($4800)

57a

29 Date marks from Minton china and earthenware: 1891–1912 **(29)**; 1845–72 **(29a)**; 1800–15 **(29b)**; 1860–69 **(29c)**; 1850s **(29d)**; pattern number from 1812 **(29e)**.
30 Chinese salt dish or 'salt'. 1770. 3in. ***(A)***
31 Beaker vase made in the 'Transitional' period, at the end of the Ming dynasty, with typical shape, figures and purplish tone of blue **(31a)**. 1620–44. 16½in. ***(G)***
32 Commemorative plate showing the popular Prime Minister William Gladstone (1809–98) **(32a)**. 1880s. 10in. ***(A)***
33 Meat dish with crest and initials. 1780s. 18in. ***(C)***
34 Chinese teapot with floral pattern in underglaze blue. Details of lid **(34a)** and spout **(34b)**. Mid-17th C. 4in. ***(B)***
35 Chinese 'Kraak' porcelain dish with segmented border **(35a)** and traditional knot motifs **(35c–e)** surrounding a central scene of flowers and birds **(35b)**. 1600. 19in. ***(F)***
36 Novelty gift plate with calendar in lavender underglaze for Liverpool company J.W. Harrison **(36a,b)**. 1878. 8in. ***(A)***
37 Date marks from French Sèvres porcelain: 1845–48 **(37)**; painter's mark of Dodin 1754–1802 **(37a)**; 1756 **(37b)**; 1778 **(37c)**; painter's mark of Le Guay 1778–1840 **(37d)**.
38 Giant willow pattern cup, with a mercury-gilt rim **(38a)** and ornate ring-handle **(38b)**. 1880. 4½in high. ***(A)***
39 Chinese pen tray made in the reign of the Ming Emperor Wan-li. Date mark **(39a–d)**. 1573–1619. 7½in. ***(G)***
40 Set of Chinese soup and sauce tureens made for export. Decoration **(40a)**. Mid-18th C. Largest one 16 x 12in. ***(C)***
41 Sauce tureen, one of a pair, made in China as part of a complete dinner service. Late 19th C. 9in. ***(E)***
42 Set of four willow patterned spirit decanters made in England. Other decanters **(42a–c)**. Early 19th C. 8in. Set ***(C)***
43 Shallow 'Kraak' bowl with traditional aster and fan symbols **(43a)** on the border panels. 1640. 11in. ***(E)***
44 English Delftware copy of Ming dish. 1635. 12in. ***(F)***
45 Staffordshire meat dish decorated with Chinese mythical beasts **(45a–d)**. 1825. 19in. ***(C)***
46 Pearlware ribbon plate with pierced border for a ribbon. Detail of centrepiece design **(46a)**. 1795. 7½in. ***(B)***
47 Chinese export dish with temple landscape featuring a pagoda, bridge and boats **(47a)**. 1770. 16 x 12½in. ***(C)***
48 Bow plate from London with knapped border **(48a–c)** and golfer and caddy design **(48d–g)** based on a Chinese original of a sage and his servant. *c.*1755–60. 8in. ***(E)***
49 Chinese vase from a matching group of five; different shapes **(49a,d)** enable them to sit closely together **(49b)**. Decorative panels **(49c)**. 1780. 12in. ***(C)***
50 Earthenware plate commissioned to commemorate the coronation of King George V. 1911. 9in. ***(A)***
51 Breakfast service by Wood and Baggaley in 'Flo' blue with gilding. Tea cup **(51a)**. Jug **(51b)**. Early 19th C. ***(A)***
52 Japanese Fukagawa vase with mountain landscape in underglaze blue. 1900s. 11in. ***(D)***
53 Bridge, bird **(53a)** and boat **(53b)** motifs from a willow pattern plate. 18th C.
54 Chinese teapot based on a silver design, with gilding on body and spout **(54a)** added later in England. *c.*1790. 5in. ***(C)***
55 Underglaze blue teapot with neo-classical shape and picture of the owner taking tea in her garden. Spout **(55a)**. Obverse side **(55b)**. 1781. 5½in. ***(D)***
56 Top of ewer by English makers Doulton with blue and white narcissi and gilt leaves. Ewer **(56a)**. 1895. 12in. ***(B/C)***
57 Wedgwood candlestick dipped in jasper, a stoneware fired at a high temperature. Pair **(57a)**. 1840. 9in. Pair ***(B/C)***
58 Quintal vase, so called because of the five joined vases surrounding its central stem **(58a)**. 1870. 9in. ***(C)***
59 Pearlware plate with oriental scene of figures, rafts and pagodas **(59a,b)**. 1800. 9½in. ***(A)***
60 Rare shield-shaped flask from 17th-century China depicting a warrior in underglaze blue **(60a)**. 1650. 7in. ***(C)***
61 Butter dish in the shape of a shell. 1750. 5in. Pair ***(D)***
62 Powder blue panel vases by William Moorcroft. The slip-trailed decoration is inspired by oriental ceramics **(62a)**. 1915. 12in. Pair ***(E)***
63 Miniature cup and saucer by Minton. Detail **(63a)**. 1860. 2in. ***(A)***
64 Ewer and basin by English makers Gater, Hall & Co. with gilt borders. 1914. 14in. ***(A)***
65 Spode earthenware plate with exotic, North African scene. 1815. 9in. ***(A)***
66 Wedgwood pearlware jug with printed flowers and gilded details. 1805. 7½in. ***(C)***
67 Chinese dish with mountain scene and border of painted prunus. 1890. 16in. ***(B)***
68 Oriental dish with wand patterns imported into Europe. 18th C. 15in. ***(B)***
69 Florian ware vase with slip-trailed design in shades of blue **(69a,c,d)** and triangular handles **(69b)**. 1904. 12in. ***(E)***
70 Tureen from a Sèvres dessert service decorated by the celebrated flower painter Michaud. 1790. 4in high ***(C)***
71 Maker's mark of leaf within two circles from an 18th-century Chinese dish.
72 Mark of German makers Sitzendorf intended to resemble Meissen. A more individual mark **(72a)**.
73 Bee design from fine Chelsea porcelain plate. Further examples **(73a,b)**. 1755–60.
74 Flower and bird **(74a)** details from Derby chestnut basket. *c.*1760.

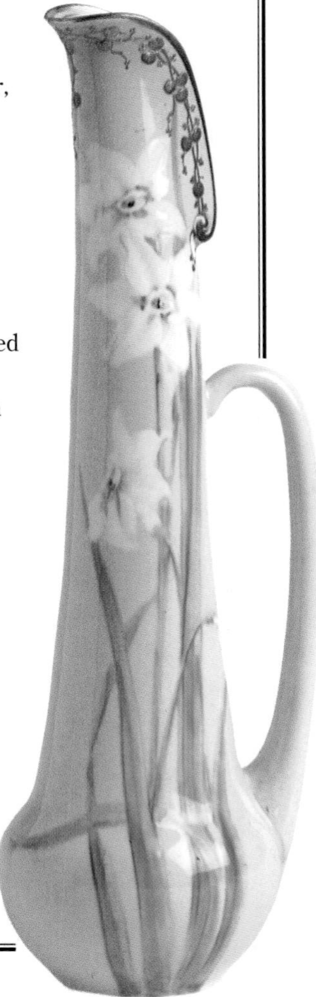

56a

PRICE GUIDE: ***A*** less than £100 ($150) ***B*** £100–250 ($150–400) ***C*** £250–500 ($400–800) ***D*** £500–1000 ($800–1600) ***E*** £1000–2000 ($1600–3200) ***F*** £2000–3000 ($3200–4800) ***G*** over £3000 ($4800)

Country Style

1 Which boxes or coffers are used to store blankets, a chamber pot and baker's dough?

2 Name three popular woods used for country-made furniture, and find an example of each.

3 What would you do with a canterbury?

4 Samplers are now in great demand, but of what were they a sample, and which of the three shown remains true to that aim?

5 'Religion in Wood.' Which three pieces of furniture reflect the pious ideals of one American community?

6 The wood for one of the chairs shown here came from the sea. Which one is it and what is kept in the drawer?

7 Which Windsor chair was made farthest from the Royal Berkshire town?

Country Style

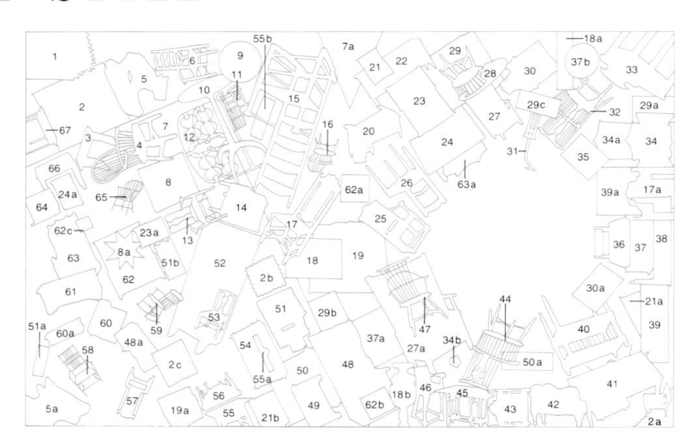

1 English patchwork quilt with cloth sections joined in a diamond mosaic pattern typical of the period. 1838. ***(E)***
2 'Sunshine and Shadows' quilt worked by the Amish community in Ohio, USA. Details of geometric pattern **(2a,b)** and whole quilt **(2c)**. 1910. 6ft 6in x 7ft 8in. ***(D)***
3 Single bench from Austria, used in churches or orphanages in place of dining chairs. 1890. 21in high. ***(A)***
4 Windsor-type chair with arms and back made in a hoop construction known as a 'comb-back'. 1830. 3ft. ***(E)***
5 Primitive Staffordshire pottery bear decorated in underglaze ochre, brown and yellow. The muzzled bear **(5a)** this piece was modelled on was either baited or forced to dance for popular entertainment. Late 18th C. 8in. ***(F)***
6 Traditional English ladder-back chair with simply turned uprights and stretchers (leg braces), shaped horizontal rails and rush seat. 1700–10. 3ft 6in high. ***(C)***
7 Amish 'sunshine' quilt. Detail **(7a)**. *c.*1900. 7ft x 7ft. ***(D)***
8 Amish 'Harvest Sun' patchwork quilt from Pennsylvania, USA, using bold colours and repeating geometric shapes **(8a)**. 1880. 7ft 10in x 7ft 10in. ***(D)***
9 Interlocking section from an American 'Wedding Ring' quilt, made either as a wedding gift or by the bride herself. Detail of pattern **(9a)**. 1920. 5ft 8in x 6ft 2in. ***(B)***
10 Elegant cherrywood round table made by the Shaker community in America. 1820. 2ft 1in. ***(G)***
11 Yew wood rocking chair with flatly turned uprights, legs and stretchers. Early 19th C. 4ft. ***(E)***
12 Cottage-style cast iron bedstead with central plaques in the bedhead and foot panel. 1870. 4ft 6in wide. ***(D)***
13 Oak armchair from England with vase-shaped back or 'splat', crest rail and padded feet. 1700–10. 3ft 7in high. ***(C)***
14 Stripped pine commode with simulated mahogany grain. 1840. 2ft 5in high. ***(C)***
15 Shaker rocking chair with rush seat and turned uprights and legs. Made from cherrywood. *c.*1820. 3ft 9in. ***(G)***
16 Child's Windsor chair made from yew and beech with curved crinoline stretcher (leg brace). 1840. 20in. ***(C/D)***
17 English oak chair used in the entrance hall or dining room of a manor house. The long raised panel gives the back a slender appearance **(17a)**. 1670–1700. 3ft 6in. ***(E)***
18 Carved door from a reproduction court cupboard **(18c)**, used as a piece of dining room furniture in the 16th and 17th centuries. Period details include inlaid panel **(18a)** and cup and cover carved columns **(18b)**. 1920s. 4ft 5in high. ***(E)***
19 Functional pine dresser and cupboard combined, for a kitchen or dairy. Dresser **(19a)**. 1825. 3ft 10in wide. ***(C)***
20 Oak crib on rockers with initials and date carved in the foot panel and a removable head cover. 1700. 3ft long. ***(E)***
21 Irish farmhouse dresser made from pine with generous shelving, scalloped canopy **(21a)** and diagonally constructed door panels **(21b)**. 1870s. 6ft 8in high. ***(F)***
22 English pine coffer imitating an earlier 17th-century piece and used for storing household linen. 1820. 3ft 2in wide. ***(C)***
23 Glass-fronted Irish dresser in pine with darker elm panels on the cupboard doors. Dresser **(23a)**. 1890. 7ft 6in. ***(E)***
24 Standing corner cupboard divided into two sections **(24a)**. Made in Lincolnshire, England. 1810. 6ft. ***(B)***
25 Oak armchair with tapering 'gun barrel' front supports and elaborately carved crest rail. 1660. 3ft 8in high. ***(E)***
26 Elegant Austrian side chair made in Linz and held together with simple peg joints. 1850. 3ft high. ***(A/B)***
27 Unusual Orkney chair from northern Scotland, with plaited straw seat **(27a)**. Late 19th C. 4ft 2in high. ***(D)***
28 Painted Windsor chair with unusual writing desk extension. Made in America. 1780–90. 2ft 4in. ***(G)***

18c

PRICE GUIDE: ***A*** less than £100 ($150) ***B*** £100–250 ($150–400) ***C*** £250–500 ($400–800) ***D*** £500–1000 ($800–1600) ***E*** £1000–2000 ($1600–3200) ***F*** £2000–3000 ($3200–4800) ***G*** over £3000 ($4800)

29 17th-century-style hall bench in oak with lift-up seat and heavily carved panelled backrest **(29a–c)**. Assembled in the mid-19th century using parts from a 17th-century chest; the top rail is genuine. 1850. 4ft. ***(D)***
30 Mirror-backed sideboard from Ireland. The spindled gallery and incised decoration were inspired by the 1870s Aesthetic Movement, but the flower heads are a typically Irish motif **(30a)**. 1890s. 6ft high. ***(D)***
31 Carved support from a mahogany Art Nouveau cradle, used to drape a swathe of muslin or other fabric over a sleeping child. Cradle **(31a)**. 1900. 6ft high. ***(G)***
32 Beech and elm Windsor-type chair with shaped centre splat and unusual cabriole legs. 1750s. 4ft. ***(G)***
33 Painted Hepplewhite bedside table with backboard and single drawer. Made in America. *c.*1825–40. 3ft. ***(F)***
34 Austrian hanging cupboard from the Tyrol. There are traces of the original decoration on the doors **(34a)**. Carved centrepiece **(34b)**. 1820. 4ft 1in high. ***(D)***
35 Sewer's sampler worked in a variety of stitches by an English child, Elizabeth Forth, aged eight. 1821. 16in. ***(C/D)***
36 Large box decorated with carved geometric patterns. Each leg has a turned baluster. 1675. 3ft 6in long. ***(D)***
37 Oak trousseau box for bridal possessions prior to a wedding. Resembling a miniature chest, with original lock and key **(37a)**, it is decorated with carved roundels **(37b)**. Early 17th C. 8in high x 21in wide. ***(D)***
38 Country oak dresser with mahogany cross-banding on the drawer fronts. 1740. 2ft 10in high. ***(G)***
39 Sampler with pulled thread work **(39a)**. 17th C. 14in. ***(C)***
40 English 'canterbury' made of pine with fine turned baluster supports. 1890. 21in high. ***(C)***
41 Dolls' house country kitchen. 1890–1940. 5in long. ***(B)***
42 Child's sofa; homemade with primitive decorative carving and classified as 'folk art'. 1870. 22in long. ***(A)***
43 Oak bedstead from northern France with traditional Breton spindles and carved pediments. 1870. 5ft wide. ***(E)***
44 High back chair of yew and beechwood with a fine pierced centre splat. 1770. 4ft high. ***(F)***
45 Early English gate-leg table made from oak. This well constructed piece has a single drawer. 1680. 2ft 4in long. ***(F)***
46 Child's oak high chair with scrolled arms and turned legs joined by square stretchers. 1660–85. 32in. ***(G)***
47 American fan-backed elbow chair developed from a basic Windsor design. Late 18th C. 3ft 6in. ***(G)***
48 Tall-backed box chair with cheek-shaped panels added to protect the sitter from draughts **(48a)**. 1780–90. 4ft 5in. ***(E)***
49 Panelled oak chest with original locks and hinges and embellished with fine carving. 1640. 3ft 6in long. ***(F)***
50 Early oak chest with carved drawer fronts **(50a)** possibly dating from the reign of James I. The handles and feet are replacements. 1603–25. 3ft 3in long. ***(E/F)***
51 Lincolnshire chest of drawers with chamfered (sloped) edges to the drawers **(51a)** and surfaces. The mirror is supported by stands with bull's eye decoration over trinket drawers **(51b)**. 1880. 2ft 11in wide. ***(C)***
52 Simply designed Shaker cabinet in pine with cupboard and drawers. The cupboard door has a simple catch. Made in New York or New England, America. *c.*1810–80. 5ft. ***(F)***
53 Simple oak chair with solid splat back, one of six used in a dining room. 1760. 3ft high. Set ***(E)***
54 Panelled oak chest with architectural mouldings typical of its period. The front panels have been converted into doors. Mid-17th C. 4ft long. ***(D)***
55 Arts and Crafts Movement pine pantry table with a single drawer and sturdy splayed legs. The incised design **(55a)** and cross-hatching **(55b)** on the drawer give a rural character to this piece. 1860. 18in. ***(C)***
56 Fruitwood table with wide overhanging top and roughly carved cabriole legs. 1750. 4ft 2in wide. ***(E)***
57 Oak panelled back chair with an arched crest rail and bobbin-turned front stretcher. 1680. 3ft high. ***(C)***
58 Stained ash chair with rush seat and back made of three rows of turned spindles. 1820. 3ft 9in. ***(C)***
59 Child's rocking chair made from turned wood and replicating a full size 'gandfather' chair. 1880. 2ft high. ***(C)***
60 Austrian deed or Bible box with wrought iron hinges and candle box inside. Original paintwork **(60a)**. 1840. 2ft 8in. ***(C)***
61 Miniature pine chest used by a chemist or ironmonger to store their wares. 1800. 2ft 6in wide. ***(B)***
62 Welsh dresser, made of oak, with traditional arrangement of well-constructed shelves, drawers and cupboards **(62a)**. The kite-shaped ivory escutcheons **(62b,c)** indicate that it was made in the Anglesey area. 1830. 7ft high. ***(G)***
63 Child's commode chair with a lift-up seat. A 'paper scroll' decoration adorns the back with some carved initials and a date **(63a)**. 1758. 2ft 3in high. ***(F)***
64 Fire screen with needlework sampler. The oak frame was made in 1920 and the sampler in 1845. The latter bears the name of its maker. 2ft 4in. ***(B/C)***
65 Hoop-backed chair for a child made of elm and yew, with turned beech arm supports. 1840. 2ft 1in. ***(C)***
66 Pine washstand with splash board to keep the wall from getting wet. 1860. 3ft 2in wide. ***(B)***
67 Danish kitchen table made of pine, with tapered square legs and overhanging top. 1870. 3ft wide. ***(C)***

9a

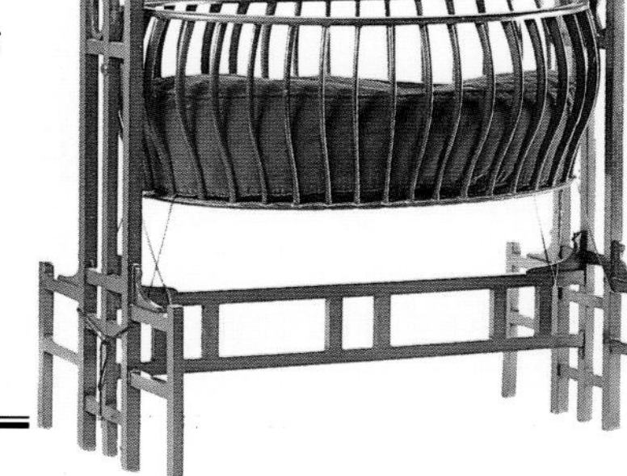
31a

PRICE GUIDE: ***A*** less than £100 ($150) ***B*** £100–250 ($150–400) ***C*** £250–500 ($400–800) ***D*** £500–1000 ($800–1600) ***E*** £1000–2000 ($1600–3200) ***F*** £2000–3000 ($3200–4800) ***G*** over £3000 ($4800)

1 The East exerted a strong artistic influence worldwide. Find English, French and American examples.

2 Find textiles made in three oriental countries.

3 Identify three examples of inlay work using different materials. What are the names of the techniques?

4 Find an inro, a netsuke and an okimono. What was each used for in everyday life?

5 Which three *objets d'art* were made or decorated in the East to satisfy western tastes?

6 Eastern craftsmen incorporated many animal products. Find three examples, crafted from four different natural materials.

7 Birds exert a special fascination for eastern craftsmen. Find a crane, a goose and an eagle.

8 Which piece is the most valuable?

9 Find a games player.

Mysteries of The East

1a

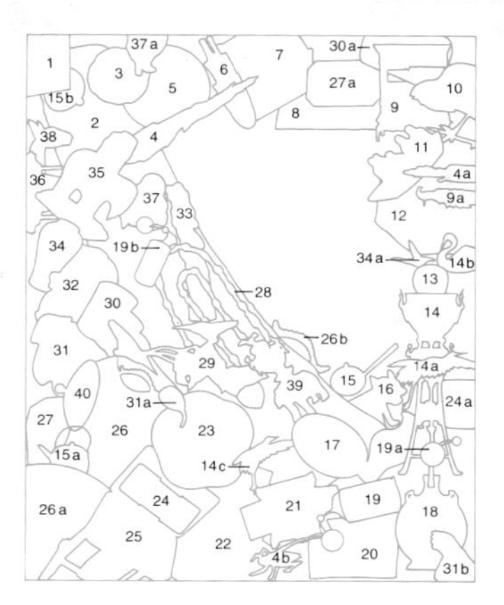

1 Door from a miniature Japanese cabinet **(1a)** made from sheets of ivory and lacquered in gold and black. *c.*1880. 7in. ***(F)***
2 Chinese fisherman carved in ivory with detailing in black; represents an 'immortal' or minor Buddhist deity. 19th C. 19in. ***(C)***
3 Armorial plate made in China with an unusual waved border. 1740. 8¼in. ***(E)***
4 Chinese lettuce, radish **(4a)** and grasshopper **(4b)** carved in ivory and coloured with vegetable dyes. 1920. 8in. ***(D)***
5 Armorial charger, or serving plate, made in China. *c.*1760. 17in wide. ***(G)***
6 Japanese wooden toggle in the shape of a bearded sage holding a basket. 1750. 4in high. ***(B)***
7 Fall-front bureau made in the East from rosewood; the rippling effect is a Dutch influence. *c.*1760. 5ft high. ***(G)***
8 Indian bridge cloth with a wide chain-stitched border sewn on to a velvet background. 1850–60. 3ft 3in. ***(C)***
9 Japanese display cabinet or 'shodana' containing asymetrically arranged cupboards and drawers, and decorated with fine lacquerwork **(9a)**. *c.*1900. 3ft 8in wide. ***(G)***
10 Bronze pheasant from Japan with dark patination and details picked out in copper and gold. 1890. 12in. ***(E)***
11 Small ivory carving of five peasants on a boat journey. Deliberately aged by staining it with sepia. 1900. 2in. ***(C)***
12 Japanese wall hanging in fine floss silks on a satin ground with birds, flowers and maples. *c.*1910. 4 x 5ft. ***(C)***
13 Peasant's head with comical expression from an early Japanese ivory sculpture. The complete figure depicts a struggle with an oversized radish – a popular subject in Japanese humour. 1800. 1½in high. ***(C)***
14 Jardinière, or flower stand, in the Japanese style with gilt bronze celestial clouds and wave and crane motifs **(14a–c)**, supported by a mock bamboo pedestal. 1874. 5ft 3in. ***(G)***
15 Fine Japanese-style tea set made of iron and decorated with flowers and sea creatures in gold and silver alloys. Kettle **(15a)**. Sugar bowl **(15b)**. 1883. ***(E)***
16 Porcelain tiger from China. 1850s. 6in. ***(C)***
17 Colourful vase and bowl set decorated with dragons, the Chinese symbol for regeneration. 1930s. Bowl 11in wide. Vase 13in tall. ***(B)***
18 Japanese-style moonflask decorated in a traditional oriental pattern of wild flowers in blue and green enamel. 1870s. 11in. ***(D)***
19 Japanese kimono accessories, consisting of two multi-layered boxes for small daily items lacquered in gold and held together by a toggle **(19a)**. **(19)** 1850. 4in. ***(C)***; **(19b)** 1820. 4in. ***(D)***
20 Embroidered panel depicting two Turkish gentlemen; worked in silk and metal threads. 1780–1820. 21in. ***(C)***
21 Japanese miniature chest of drawers or 'kodansu' made by Komai, who specialized at inlaying gold into iron. 1900. 3in high. ***(F)***
22 Japanese cabinet decorated with inlaid woods. The raised lid shows Mount Fuji in lacquerwork. Late 19th C. 17in. ***(B)***
23 Chinese cinnabar lacquer box. Early 19th C. 10in. ***(D)***
24 Watch case lacquered in Japan and depicting a galloping samurai warrior **(24a)**. 1920s. 3in. ***(D)***
25 Chinese-made work table with lacquer finish in two tones of gold with a work bag beneath. 1830–50. 2ft 5in. ***(F)***
26 Japanese moonflask showing a carp turning into a dragon as it leaps a waterfall **(26a)**, symbolic of a student passing exams. Handle **(26b)**. 1860s. 13in. ***(D)***
27 Lady's ivory work box, made in China, with fitments for winding silks and sewing **(27a)**. 1850s. 12in. ***(E)***
28 Japanese damascene necklace, inlaid with gold and decorated with good luck symbols. 1910. 16in. ***(A)***
29 Three ivory kingfishers on a lotus pad made from a stag's antler by the Japanese carver Kofu. 1900. 11in. ***(G)***
30 Three Chinese brush pots. Detail **(30a)**. 1900. 4–6in. ***(A)***
31 Japanese figurine of Daikoku, god of farming, with silver, mother-of-pearl and lacquer. Details **(31a,b)**. 1870. 1in. ***(E)***
32 'The Sack of Happiness' carving in wood from Japan, signed Kanshu. Opens to reveal Hotei, god of happiness, playing Go with a small boy. 1765. 1in. ***(D)***
33 Walrus ivory fisherman with Raiden, god of thunder. Made by the Tamayuki studio in Japan. 1900. 12in. ***(C)***
34 Japanese bronze vase with a flying bird emblem **(34a)** inlaid in gold and silver alloy. 1900. 9in. ***(B)***
35 Pottery money box in the shape of an elephant and castle. *c.*1790. 8in. high ***(G)***
36 Indian worktable in elaborately carved and pierced rosewood. 1830–60. 20in. ***(E)***
37 Miniature figure in ivory of a Japanese drum seller. Detail **(37a)**. 1890. 2in. ***(B)***
38 Dragon-shaped handle from a Japanese ornamental ewer in enamel and gilt. Complete ewer **(38a)**. 1832. 8in. ***(G)***
39 Oriental elephant in ebony with inlaid silver mounted casket. *c.*1900. 14in. ***(G)***
40 Enamel cup cover. 1920s. 7in. With cup ***(C)***

38a

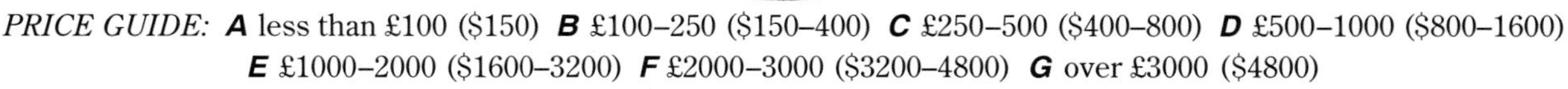

PRICE GUIDE: ***A*** less than £100 ($150) ***B*** £100–250 ($150–400) ***C*** £250–500 ($400–800) ***D*** £500–1000 ($800–1600) ***E*** £1000–2000 ($1600–3200) ***F*** £2000–3000 ($3200–4800) ***G*** over £3000 ($4800)

Jewellery Box

1 Find a dragonfly which is not a fairy; a lion; and a dove looking at a cross.

2 Which gemstone is reminiscent of the seas and oceans? Find three examples.

3 Locate a pair of cufflinks made by a famous Russian goldsmith.

4 Find two pieces depicting the god Apollo drawing the chariot of the sun. What are they made of?

5 Which reptile carries a pearl on his back, and to which pendant does he give his backing?

6 Which brooch has been plucked from a chicken?

JEWELLERY BOX

109

1 Gold brooch set with a diamond and two rubies in a star design **(1a)**, flanked by beadwork. 1885. ***(A)***
2 Sapphire and diamond flower brooch. 1880. ***(F)***
3 Art Deco diamond plaque pendant set with ruby flowers and emerald leaves. Diamond link **(3a)**. 1920. ***(G)***
4 English gold seal hanging from an elongated oval link and embossed hooplike chain. 1865. ***(D)***
5 Diamond 16-ray star brooch set with a sapphire. 1885. ***(F)***
6 Agate cameo portrait brooch in Etruscan-style gold mount **(6a)**. Details of cameo **(6b,c)**. 1880. ***(D)***
7 Victorian music brooch made by Hunt and Roskell, Queen Victoria's jewellers. Complete with case **(7a)**. 1870. ***(C/D)***
8 Maltese gold locket with a rose-cut diamond flower spray centrepiece **(8a)**. Attachment **(8b)**. 1860s. ***(D)***
9 French or Swiss gold and enamel pendant. 1890. ***(C)***
10 Art Nouveau maiden brooch in gold, with gem encrusted and *plique à jour* enamel wings. 1900. ***(G)***
11 Tortoiseshell *piqué* pendant set with gold and mother-of-pearl designs. Hanging support **(11a)**. 1880. ***(A)***
12 Gold beadwork brooch with a single diamond. 1880. ***(C)***
13 Carved ivory hand clenching a hardstone and gold baton with seal. Made in England. 1845. ***(F)***
14 Frosted 15ct gold bracelet with banded agates set in a neo-classical shell design border. Banded agate **(14a,c)**; in setting **(14b)**. 1900. ***(D)***
15 Fabergé enamel, sapphire and gold torpedo cufflink with *guilloché* enamelling. Other cufflink **(15a)**. 1895. ***(G)***
16 Diamond and ruby brooch. 1915. ***(E)***
17 Gold pendant, inset with portrait miniature. 1905. ***(A)***
18 Bracelet with carved lava plaques **(18a)** mounted in gold. 1850. ***(C/D)***
19 Mourning brooch with a lock of hair **(19a)** held by a seed pearl clasp. 1865. ***(B)***
20 Passion flower brooch made of paste to simulate emeralds, amethysts, topaz and diamonds. 1760. ***(E)***
21 Gem and clasp from a garnet **(21a)** and gold bracelet by John Brogden **(21c)**. Linking gold baton **(21b)**. 1865. ***(F)***
22 Gold tablet-section serpent necklace, set with various semi-precious stones. 1875. ***(F)***
23 Onyx cameo of Apollo Belvedere. 1870. ***(D)***
24 Hollow-link gold bracelet with a tiny padlock **(24a)** and set with semi-precious stones. 1900s. ***(B/C)***
25 Shell cameo engraved with biblical scene. 1880–90. ***(B)***
26 Italian cameo set in a gold mount. 1860–80. ***(C)***
27 Hinged gold bangle with micro-mosaic classical scene and the motto ROMA. 1880. ***(G)***
28 Italian brooch with classical-style cameo scene held in a gold mount inset with turquoise **(28a–c)**. 1830. ***(E)***
29 Victorian chased-gold panel bracelet set with amethysts, aquamarines and citrines. 1875. ***(E)***
30 Victorian gold teardrop fringe necklace. 1880. ***(F)***
31 Transfer-printed porcelain plaque set in a gilt brooch mount. 1880–90. ***(A/B)***
32 Victorian diamond 12-ray star brooch. 1875. ***(F)***
33 Bakelite bangle in translucent red. 1940–45. ***(A)***
34 Diamond, sapphire and ruby peacock brooch. 1950. ***(G)***
35 Ruby and diamond *pavé* cluster clip. 1930. ***(G)***
36 Garnet cabochon and gold hinged bangle. 1865. ***(E)***
37 Gold wishbone brooch, with ruby **(37a)**, diamond and sapphire **(37b)**. Made in South Africa. 1880. ***(C)***
38 Art Nouveau style 9ct gold pendant, set with half pearls and garnets **(38a,b)**. 1900–10. ***(B)***
39 Red enamel and gold Imperial Order. 1880. ***(C)***
40 Opal and diamond ring. Detail **(40a)**. 1920. ***(C)***
41 Burmese ruby and diamond ring. Ruby **(41a)**. 1985. ***(G)***
42 Van Cleef & Arpels calibre ruby brooch in the shape of a leaf. 1930. ***(G)***
43 Glass bead necklace. 1940. ***(A)***

51a

77b

PRICE GUIDE: ***A*** less than £100 ($150) ***B*** £100–250 ($150–400) ***C*** £250–500 ($400–800) ***D*** £500–1000 ($800–1600) ***E*** £1000–2000 ($1600–3200) ***F*** £2000–3000 ($3200–4800) ***G*** over £3000 ($4800)

7a

44 Unmounted Burmese ruby and obverse **(44a)**. 1985. ***(G)***
45 Wooden sailor brooch with leather sail **(45a)**. Made in America. 1940. ***(A)***
46 Coral grotesque brooch. 1865. ***(D)***
47 Celluloid fox head buckle. 1940. ***(A)***
48 Gold crossover ring with diamonds and rubies. 1912. ***(C)***
49 Gold pendant with amphora drop and centre set with seed pearls. 1880. ***(D)***
50 Emerald and diamond arrow *sûreté* pin. 1910. ***(E)***
51 Spider from a bar brooch **(51a)** featuring a spider and fly inset with a pearl and pink tourmaline. 1900. ***(A/B)***
52 Diamond and onyx coronet brooch. 1910. ***(E)***
53 Gold brooch with vari-colour agate cameo. 1790. ***(E)***
54 Platinum and diamond brooch and detail **(54a)**. 1950. ***(G)***
55 Pearl and diamond ear-clip. Other clip **(55a)**. 1965. ***(F)***
56 Diamond ring between diamond shoulders. 1985. ***(G)***
57 Dragon buckle in carved and pierced white bakelite and diamanté. Dragon's wing **(57a)**. 1940. ***(A)***
58 Brilliant- and baguette-cut diamond coil and cascade brooch. Central motif **(58a)**. 1955. ***(E)***
59 Geometric platinum and diamond bracelet. 1950. ***(G)***
60 Step-cut line bracelet in Burmese rubies. 1935. ***(G)***
61 Etruscan-style bangle with micro-mosaic panels **(61b,c)** and *salve* (salvation) in gold on the reverse **(61a)**. 1870. ***(E)***
62 Half-hoop opal and diamond ring in retailer's box. Hand-carved gold mount **(62a)**. 1911. ***(B)***
63 Diamond, ruby and emerald bracelet. 1925. ***(G)***
64 Diamond Saint Esprit brooch with emerald drop. 1865. ***(E)***
65 Articulated diamond dragonfly brooch with flat-cut peridot wings. 1895. ***(G)***
66 Diamond and emerald bee brooch with ruby eyes in gold and silver mount. Thorax **(66a)**. Wing **(66b)**. 1860. ***(G)***
67 Heart-shaped locket with raised diamond and pearl centre **(67a)** and green enamel surround. 1900. ***(D)***
68 Hinged gold bangle with wirework design. 1885. ***(D)***
69 Art Deco style diamond, emerald and onyx ring. 1985. ***(F)***
70 Maltese 18ct gold bangle with mosaics of country people in local costume **(70a,b)** set in malachite. 1870. ***(E)***
71 Emerald dorp earring with diamond surround. Other earring **(71a)**. 1950. Pair ***(E)***
72 Peridot and gold pendant. 1875. ***(G)***
73 Green enamel, gold and ruby frog brooch. 1960. ***(D)***
74 Crescent-shaped gold brooch set with diamonds and opals. 1900. ***(C)***
75 Brooch with *pavé* and baguette diamonds and drop-shaped sapphires. 1950. ***(G)***
76 'Albert' watch chain with tassles. 1860. ***(E)***
77 Centrepiece of a bar brooch with die-stamped surround **(77a,b)**. 1904. ***(A)***
78 Gold brooch set with rose-cut diamonds **(78a,b)**. Border **(78c)**. 1880. ***(B)***
79 Edwardian bar brooch with half pearls and overlaid with a diamond and ruby scroll. 1905. ***(B)***
80 Diamond strap bracelet set with multi-coloured gems. 1935. ***(G)***
81 Amethyst and gold hinged panel bracelet. 1865. ***(G)***
82 Art Deco opal and diamond clip. 1910. ***(F)***
83 Boat-shaped sapphire and diamond cluster ring in a platinum mount. Sapphires **(83a–c)**. 1915. ***(D)***
84 Gold and turquoise padlock locket clasp. 1845. ***(D)***
85 Gold cufflinks with enamelled racehorses **(85a)**. 1930. ***(D)***
86 Gold turtle brooch with baroque pearl body. 1890. ***(C)***
87 Pliny's Doves micro-mosaic brooch. Detail **(87a)**. 1850. ***(F)***
88 Art Deco sapphire and diamond cufflink. Other cufflink **(88a)**. Details of face design **(88b–d)**. 1935. ***(G)***
89 Blue glass earrings imitating lapis lazuli. 1920s. ***(A)***
90 Sapphire cabochon and diamond dress ring. 1920. ***(E)***
91 Sapphire dress ring with diamond shoulders. 1965. ***(G)***
92 Art Nouveau enamelled silver pendant. 1909. ***(B)***
93 Star sapphire and diamond pendant. 1930. ***(G)***
94 Gold serpent necklace with blue enamel, diamond and ruby head and articulated body. 1845. ***(F)***
95 Aquamarine pendant earrings **(95a)**. 1950. ***(G)***
96 Enamelled silver butterfly brooch. Wing **(96a)**. 1920s. ***(A)***
97 Gold *pavé* turquoise coiled serpent bangle. 1845. ***(F)***
98 Aquamarine and diamond plaque brooch. 1950. ***(G)***
99 Art Nouveau enamelled pendant with integral chain by Charles Horner. Detail **(99a)**. 1909. ***(B)***
100 Aquamarine **(100a)** and diamond pendant. 1950. ***(G)***
101 Gold *pavé* turquoise serpent bracelet. 1845. ***(F)***
102 Aquamarine **(102a)** and diamond dress ring. 1950s. ***(G)***
103 Cluster ring with sapphire and diamonds. 1965. ***(G)***
104 Sapphire and diamond dress ring. 1965. ***(G)***
105 Gold bracelet folding into miniature book, the spine set with turquoise **(105a,b)**. 1850. ***(F)***
106 Ring mounted with a sapphire and diamonds. 1985. ***(G)***
107 Mourning ring enamelled in turquoise blue. 1808. ***(B)***
108 Georgian diamond ring set in silver and gold. *c.*1790. ***(D)***
109 Diamond and calibre ruby wristwatch. 1925. ***(F)***
110 Florentine plaque brooch made from *pietra dura* in 15ct gold mount **(110c)**. Details **(110a,b)**. 1850. ***(C)***
111 French diamond collar with detachable centrepiece **(111a)**. 1930. ***(G)***
112 Embossed gold pendant set with mother-of-pearl cameo of a lion. 1780. ***(D)***
113 Brooch with basket of flowers of multi-coloured gemstones. 1950. ***(G)***

110c

21c

PRICE GUIDE: ***A*** less than £100 ($150) ***B*** £100–250 ($150–400) ***C*** £250–500 ($400–800) ***D*** £500–1000 ($800–1600) ***E*** £1000–2000 ($1600–3200) ***F*** £2000–3000 ($3200–4800) ***G*** over £3000 ($4800)

1 Many instruments shown here enlarge images; but which one is capable of both enlarging and reducing?

2 Which devices would help you to find your way at sea, in outer space and underground?

3 Locate two early devices used to receive important messages.

4 Which two instruments, one navigational and one climatic, have polar associations?

5 Which instruments measure direction, distance, weight and temperature?

6 Not all these instruments have a practical purpose. Which three are devised purely for pleasure and entertainment?

7 What do a banjo, stick, aneroid and wheel have in common: what do they predict?

8 Find an instrument with a peaceful purpose in time of war.

Wonders of Science

1 Block instrument used by signalmen of the Great Central Railway to determine if a line was clear. When the handle was pulled **(1a,b)** a telegraphic signal indicated one of three possibilities on a coloured dial **(1c)**. 1900. 2ft 6in. ***(A/B)***
2 Jupiter and moons section from a rare orrery, or model of the solar system, by William and Samuel Jones of London. Complete orrery **(2a)**. 1810. 5in high. ***(G)***
3 Exotic singing bird automata mounted in a gilded cage with Art Nouveau designs **(3a)**. Made in France. *c.*1900. 20in high. ***(E)***
4 Pocket set of compass **(4a)**, thermometer **(4b)** and aneroid barometer **(4c)** in a crocodile-skin case. This English-made device was used by walkers. 1885–90. Case 3 x 4in. ***(C)***
5 Thermometer from a priceless collection of scientific instruments used to record extreme weather conditions. Other items include a sundial **(5a)**, compass **(5b)**, altitude scale **(5c)** and aneroid barometer **(5d)**. 1910. ***(G)***
6 Nautical refracting telescope with leather-bound tube, brass draw and inset plate of pendants and flags from the merchant service **(6b)**. Further example inset with flags of the world print **(6a)** and a good quality brass eyepiece and draw tube **(6c)**. Mid-19th C. 2ft 6in. Each telescope ***(C/D)***
7 Stick barometer named after the British hydrographer and meteorologist Admiral Fitzroy. The case is made of ash with gothic-style inspired back panel. 1880s. 3ft. ***(C/D)***
8 Traditional Victorian banjo, or wheel barometer, made in England from rosewood. 19th C. 2ft 10in. ***(B)***
9 Gould-type microscope made of lacquered brass with a mahogany storage box doubling as stand. The adjustable specimen platform allows the compound lens in the eyepiece **(9a)** to be focused. Mid-19th C. 12in. ***(B)***
10 Set of shop balance scales, complete with porcelain slab **(10a)** and brass weights **(10b)**. 1860. 2ft 6in high. ***(C)***
11 French-made opera glasses with telescopic mother-of-pearl handle. 1910. 5½in across. ***(B)***
12 Brass sextant for determining latitude and longitude, fitted with small telescope **(12a)** for taking accurate sightings of stars and the sun. Detail **(12b)**. 1850s. 8in. ***(C/D)***
13 English-made brass refracting telescope in its original case; designed for use on a tripod. Mid-19th C. 2ft 8in. ***(C)***
14 Rare pantograph with hinged sections enabling drawings and maps to be copied. Made by Benjamin Martin of Fleet Street, London. Case **(14a)**. Mid-18th C. 18in. ***(E)***

2a

15 American Edison Gem phonograph with horn and cylindrical record featuring the inventor **(15a)**. 1880s. Horn 21in. ***(C)***
16 'Ticka Spy Camera' disguised as a pocket watch and made in England from chrome-plated brass **(16a)**. 1910. 2½in. ***(B)***
17 Mahogany stick barometer with detachable thermometer and ornate mercury reservoir **(17a,b)**. Made by the English firm J. B. Dancer. 1840. 3ft 1in. ***(E)***
18 Brass balance beam scale with scoop for weighing dry goods. 1870. 20in. ***(B)***
19 Military surgeon's kit by J. Weiss & Son. The three metal trays housing the instruments can be immersed in boiling water for easy sterilization. 1917. 2ft. ***(C)***
20 Surveyor's dial made of lacquered brass and used for surveying the direction and angle of tunnels. 1880. 10in. ***(C)***
21 Mother-of-pearl opera glasses and case, owned by popular English actress Ellen Terry (1847–1928). The maker's name is etched around the eyepieces **(21a)**. 1905. 3in. ***(C)***

31a

22 Stick barometer with integrated bulb and cistern to store the 30 inches of mercury required. 19th C. 3ft long. ***(D)***
23 Ebony and brass octant made by Troughton & Simms of London, in its original oak box. Used by explorers in waters off the North American continent. 1820. 11in. ***(C/D)***
24 Georgian ivory draughtsman's rule made by Cary of London. Late 18th C. 12in. ***(A/B)***
25 Culpeper microscope and protective carrying case. A tray in the base contains accessories. 18th C. 16in. ***(C/D)***
26 Precision scale model of a 'swift' or industrial machine for winding yarn or thread. Made in Britain. 1900s. 10in. ***(D)***
27 Monocular microscope, with six eyepieces of different powers, and other bench accessories. 1880s. 14in. ***(C)***
28 Leather-bound telescope with Turk's head knot added by the original owner. Late 19th C. 2ft 6in long. ***(A)***
29 Versatile chest microscope whose box is also a stand and container for assorted lenses, bone slides **(29a,b)** and specimen receptacles. 1790. 12in. ***(D)***
30 Chronometer made in Germany by A. Kittel **(30a)** with a balance to compensate for temperature. 1890. 6in. ***(G)***
31 Brass binocular microscope eyepiece. Complete microscope in mahogany case **(31a)**. Late 19th C. 15in. ***(G)***

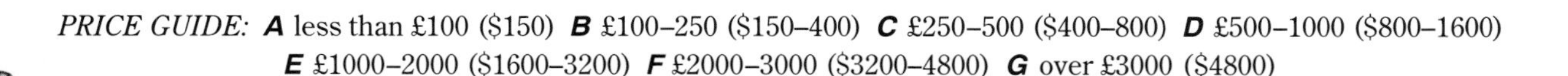
PRICE GUIDE: ***A*** less than £100 ($150) ***B*** £100–250 ($150–400) ***C*** £250–500 ($400–800) ***D*** £500–1000 ($800–1600) ***E*** £1000–2000 ($1600–3200) ***F*** £2000–3000 ($3200–4800) ***G*** over £3000 ($4800)

Take a Seat

1 Chippendale, gothic, Federal and Hepplewhite are four classic chair styles. Find a representative of each.

2 Find one table which is not made of wood. What would it have been used for?

3 Name three games associated with tables shown here.

4 Which three tables have liquid links?

5 Most chairs shown here have a formal character: find two of a more intimate nature.

6 Which piece of furniture has musical associations?

7 What sets 19th-century upholstery apart from that of the previous century?

8 Which chair was made to take outside?

TAKE A SEAT

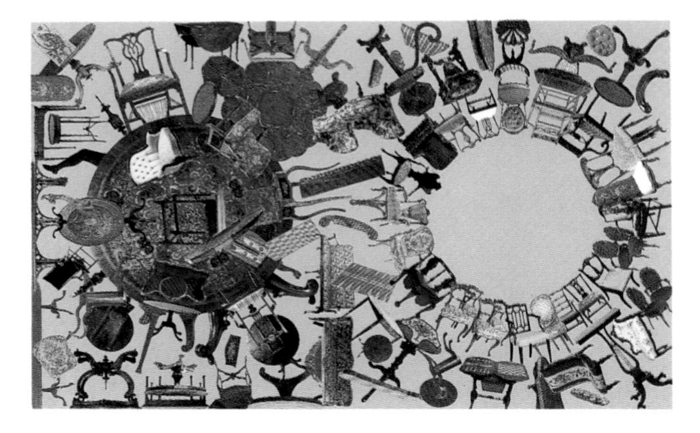

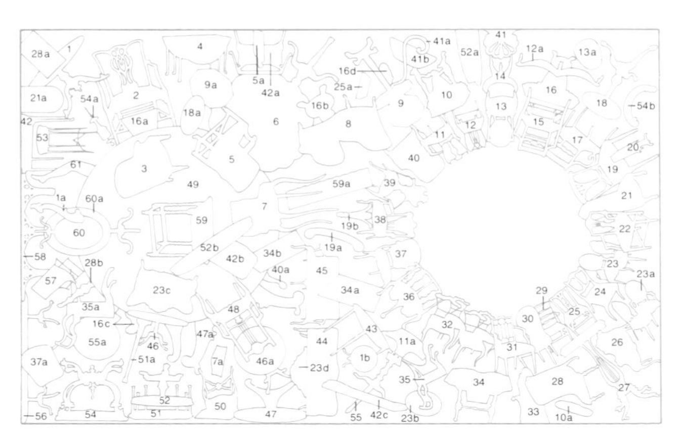

1 Rosewood table with elaborately scrolled legs **(1a)** and pedestal. The top **(1b)** tilts to 90 degrees. 1850. 4ft 2in. ***(F)***
2 Chippendale-style mahogany chair with shaped crest rail and pierced, interlaced splat. 1760–65. 3ft. ***(D)***
3 Victorian rosewood-framed armchair with scroll arms, baluster legs and buttoning on the back. 1865. 3ft. ***(E)***
4 George II oval drop-leaf table with shaped frieze and turned, tapering legs terminating in pad feet. 1735–60. 4ft. ***(E)***
5 George III library chair with padded arms **(5a)** ending in a wooden scroll; known as a 'Gainsborough' since the artist often seated his models in such chairs. 18th C. 3ft. ***(F)***
6 Mahogany table with ornate Georgian-style carving added later. Mid-18th C. 2ft 7in wide. ***(D)***
7 French-style teapoy decorated with figured veneers, marquetry panels **(7a)** and ormolu mounts. 1870. 2ft 5in. ***(F)***
8 English settee with swivel ends, known as a 'confidante'; the machine-turned legs indicate its period. 1875. 5ft. ***(E/F)***
9 Satinwood work table; the painting **(9a)** on the inside of the lid was added later. Late 18th C. 14in diameter. ***(E)***
10 Papier mâché sewing table and desk. The great era of papier mâché was *c.*1820–40, but the shape and decoration **(10a)** of this piece are typical of its period. 1865. 2ft. ***(F)***
11 Edwardian mahogany parlour chair with stylized shield back and Renaissance-inspired inlay **(11a)** on the shaped cresting and splat. 1910. 2ft 11in high. ***(C)***
12 One of four gothic-style mahogany dining chairs, with a carved drapery crest rail **(12a)**. 1775. 2ft 11in. Set ***(G)***
13 Low, walnut-framed drawing room chair with a padded button back **(13a)**. 1870. 2ft 6in. ***(C)***
14 Edwardian piano stool in a mixture of revival styles – Egyptian, Roman and rococo. *c.*1910. 2ft 2in. ***(C)***
15 Birch or maple Federal period armchair, with painted decoration. *c.*1800–20. 3ft. ***(G)***
16 Rosewood work table with a silk-lined work bag **(16a)** beneath for sewing materials. The base **(16b)** has realistically carved feet **(16c)** and unusually carved supporting scrolls **(16d)**. 1830s. 2ft 6in high. ***(F)***
17 Typical Regency mahogany dining chair with curved, veneered top rail, horizontal central splat with a lyre motif, drop-in seat, scrolled arms and sabre legs. 1815. 2ft 9in. ***(D)***
18 Mahogany kettle stand or wine table with scrolled legs and baluster. Detail of table top **(18a)**. 1745. 2ft high. ***(G)***
19 Rosewood chair. The shape of the back is Regency-inspired with well-carved top rail **(19a)** and splat **(19b)**, but the style of the legs and seat is later. 1845. 2ft 9in high. ***(C)***
20 Victorian Sutherland foldaway table, made for smaller rooms and easy storage. Open table **(20a)**. 2ft 6in. 1860. ***(D)***
21 Partially gilded low-seated walnut side chair known as a 'prie-dieu', or prayer chair – the tall back **(21a)** supports the arms of the person kneeling on the seat. 1860. 4ft high. ***(E)***
22 Hepplewhite-style chair in mahogany with shield back in the wheat-ear design. One of a set of six with original green hide coverings. Early 19th C. 3ft 10in high. Set ***(F/G)***
23 Dutch mahogany parlour set of two spoon-backed armchairs, two side chairs and a settee **(23c)**, all button backed **(23b)** and covered in plush. Matching centre table **(23d)**. Arm and side chair **(23a)**. 1840. Chair 3ft. Set ***(G)***
24 Mahogany dining chair, one of a set of six, probably Danish. The smooth curves are like the Regency Trafalgar style, but the back shape and stylized drapery decoration are not typically English. 1815–25. 2ft 8in high. Set ***(F)***
25 One of a pair of side chairs with a pierced back and carved top rail and seat **(25a)** upholstered in green brocade. 1760. 3ft high. Pair ***(F)***
26 Boudoir chair in flamboyant *tous les Louis* style. The cabriole legs are decorated with rococo scrolls and foliage. 1880–90. 3ft 6in across. ***(E)***
27 Regency occasional table in rosewood veneer and original brass castors. 1815. 2ft 5in high. ***(G)***

33a

PRICE GUIDE: ***A*** less than £100 ($150) ***B*** £100–250 ($150–400) ***C*** £250–500 ($400–800) ***D*** £500–1000 ($800–1600) ***E*** £1000–2000 ($1600–3200) ***F*** £2000–3000 ($3200–4800) ***G*** over £3000 ($4800)

61a

28 Nursing chair of ebonized wood with incised and gilded design. The original upholstery shows a beadwork squirrel **(28a)**; the castors **(28b)** are porcelain. 1870s. ***(C/D)***
29 One of a pair of ladder-back chairs in Chippendale or Late Georgian style. 1770. 3ft 4in. Pair ***(G)***
30 Walnut parlour chair, one of a set of four, bearing the stamp of English makers Gillow. 1880. 3ft. Set ***(G)***
31 One of eight Federal inlaid mahogany dining chairs branded 'Anderson'. New York. 1790–1810. 3ft. Set ***(G)***
32 Four of a set of six English rosewood chairs. The backs show a strong French influence. 1845. 3ft 9in. ***(G)***
33 Large mahogany table on a turned central pedestal supported by four elaborately carved splay legs **(33a)**. The top has a moulded edge with shaped apron. 1840. 4ft 3in. ***(G)***
34 Gaming and work table in burr walnut. The swivel top opens out to reveal gaming boards **(34a,b)**. *c.*1860. 2ft. ***(E)***
35 Mahogany side chair with stylized animal legs at the front and raised sides to hold a fitted cushion. 1810. 2ft 8in. ***(C)***
36 American mahogany and cherrywood corner chair in Chippendale style. Made in New York. *c.*1760–70. 2ft 6in. ***(D)***
37 Painted and partially gilded armchair in Louis XV style, possibly Italian. It has padded arms, an upholstered seat **(37a)** and cartouche-shaped back. 18th C. 3ft high. ***(D)***
38 Upholstered salon chair in a mixture of design styles, from rococo and Adam to classical. Early 20th C. 3ft. ***(C)***
39 Mahogany chair in early 18th-century style, with late 18th-century type of painted decoration. 1890. 2ft 6in wide. ***(E)***
40 Wing armchair with mahogany legs ending in ball and claw feet **(40a)**. 1725. 2ft 10in wide. ***(G)***
41 The horizontal bar splat from a Regency Trafalgar-style dining chair, one of six, features the anthemion or honeysuckle motif. Arms on the carvers **(41a)** curve from a solid top rail through to sabre legs. The brocade seat **(41b)** would originally have been covered in leather. Two complete chairs **(41c)**. *c.*1815. 2ft 8in high. Set ***(G)***
42 George II laburnum fold-over card table. The concertina mechanism **(42a)** provides support. The brass hinge **(42b)** in each half of the top is fastened with screws and works on two small pins. *c.*1730. 2ft 5in high x 3ft 11in wide. ***(G)***
43 Fine satinwood Pembroke table painted with garlands around the top and on the drawer. 1785. 2ft 8in wide. ***(G)***
44 Well-carved walnut framed settee with scrolled arms and turned baluster legs in the curvilinear French revival style. 1865. 5ft 6in. ***(E/F)***

41c

45 Walnut settee with cabriole legs and pad feet. The arm rests have eagle-headed terminals. 1720. 6ft 4in across. ***(G)***
46 Oak tilt-top pedestal table in a sophisticated design usually associated with mahogany. It has a 'gun-barrel' pedestal and a four-splay base **(46a)**. 1795. 4ft 3in. ***(G)***
47 Triform base table with bands of marquetry in the centre and on the edge of the top and legs. 1865. 4ft 3in. ***(E)***
48 Edwardian open armchair. The crest rail has a central roundel inlaid with ivory and boxwood. 1910. 3ft 5in. ***(B)***
49 Circular pedestal table with rosewood top and elaborate revived rococo-style marquetry. 1840. 2ft 6in high. ***(G)***
50 Swivel-top rosewood card table with cabriole legs and a top made up of four triangles inlaid in ivory and beech. 1895. 2ft 5in high. ***(D)***
51 Chippendale revival side table with crisp carving and fluted legs **(51a)** with sharply defined outer edges. 1920. 6ft long. ***(G)***
52 Rosewood table with 16 sides. The edge of the top **(52a,b)** is deeply carved. 1840. 4ft 4in wide. ***(F)***
53 Edwardian Sheraton-style occasional table with satinwood cross-banding. 1895–1910. 18in wide. ***(E)***

20a

54 Fold-over card table decorated with highly figured walnut veneers and an unusual curvilinear supporting framework **(54a,b)**. 1850. 2ft 7in high. ***(F)***
55 Early oak tripod table with a plain top and a birdcage mechanism **(55a)** which allows the table to rotate as well as tilt. *c.*1740. 2ft 6in high. ***(G)***
56 Early George III-style mahogany dining table with three pedestal supports. 1790. 10ft long. ***(G)***
57 Victorian folding chair; the ratchet adjustment is made on a cast iron fitting under the arms. *c.*1895. 3ft 2in high. ***(B)***
58 Long refectory table in Victorian gothic style with three carved pedestals. Made in oak. Mid-19th C. 10ft long. ***(G)***
59 The joined frame, bobbin turning and perfect dovetailing of this oak side table show fine craftsmanship. The drawer **(59a)** has a carved bottom edge. 1670s. 2ft 6in wide. ***(G)***
60 Mahogany tilt-top table in Chippendale style. The top is inlaid with contrasting veneer and marquetry and the feet and columns are carved **(60a)**. 1780–90. 2ft 6in high. ***(G)***
61 One of the tripod legs on a mahogany tea table **(61a)**, carved to represent that of an 18th-century gentleman. Such tables are known as Manxman tables, since the Isle of Man flag bears a three-legged emblem. 1750. 2ft 4in high. ***(E)***

PRICE GUIDE: ***A*** less than £100 ($150) ***B*** £100–250 ($150–400) ***C*** £250–500 ($400–800) ***D*** £500–1000 ($800–1600) ***E*** £1000–2000 ($1600–3200) ***F*** £2000–3000 ($3200–4800) ***G*** over £3000 ($4800)

1 Glass-making techniques have created four objects normally associated with other materials: which are they?

2 Glass was decorated in many ways, often adapting techniques from other mediums. Find examples of overlay, cameo and enamel work.

3 Which piece would have been sought after during the decalcomania craze of the late 19th century?

4 Find an Italian copy of a French original.

5 Two types of popular American glass are 'frigger' and 'carnival'. Find examples and explain their names.

6 Find four styles of early glass made for particular drinks.

7 Which of the five pieces of Tiffany glass is most sought after?

The Glass Menagerie

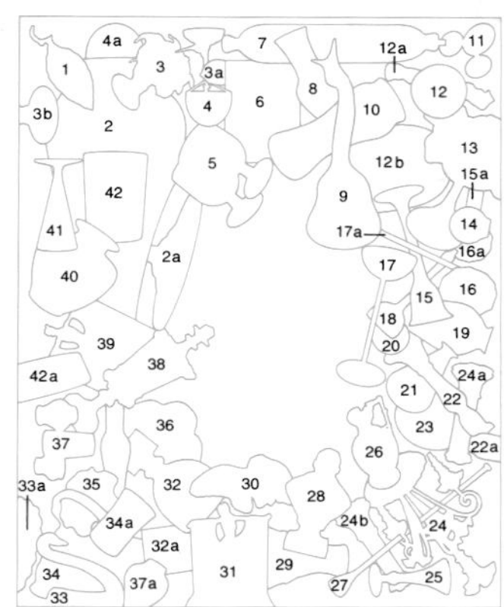

1 Opaque pressed glass scent bottle moulded to resemble a bunch of grapes. 1875. 3in long. ***(A/B)***
2 Favrile vase by American makers Tiffany with iridescent gold finish. The body tapers to a narrow stem and stand **(2a)**. 1900s. 11in. ***(G)***
3 Italian Art Deco lamp in the form of a lemon tree. Each fruit conceals a bulb **(3a)**. Ornamental glass base **(3b)**. 1920s. 14in high. ***(A/B)***
4 Layered glass lampshade made by Müller Frères of the Luneville Glassworks in France. 1900–10. 16in. Table lamp ***(F)***
5 Pair of English engraved glasses, known as 'rummers', depicting a local feat of civil engineering, the Sunderland Bridge. 1840. 6in. Pair ***(C)***
6 Mosaic of sulphur-crested cockatoos on a flowering shrub in iridescent and opaque glass. Attributed to Joseph Briggs of the Tiffany mosaic studio. *c.*1905. 2ft 7in high. ***(G)***
7 Glass rolling pin. The interior is pasted with colourful transfers and sealed with a paint wash. 1880s. 12in. ***(C)***
8 Tiffany aquamarine glass vase, with fish, sea urchins and seaweed embedded in green-tinted 'sea water'. 1913. 8in. ***(G)***
9 Art Nouveau gooseneck vase by Austrian makers Loetz, using cobalt iridescent 'papillon' art glass (a purely decorative glass). 1900. 10in high. ***(G)***
10 Loetz vase in amethyst iridescent 'papillon' glass with a silver decoration applied by electrolysis. 1900. 8in. ***(D/E)***
11 'Fountain dumpies' made in England from waste glass and used as paperweights. 1860s. 5½ and 3½in. Set ***(B)***
12 Millefiori mushroom paperweight made in St. Louis, France. Millefiori, little flowers, are created by melting rods of coloured glass together **(12a,b)**. 1848. 2¾in. ***(E)***
13 American glass sweet dish. 1890s. 7½in. ***(A)***
14 Stopper from a two-colour Bohemian ship's decanter. Complete decanter **(14a)**. 1920. 9in. ***(A)***
15 Cordial glass with colour-twist stem **(15a)** made by William Beilby of Newcastle, England. 1760–70. 6in. ***(E/F)***
16 Iridescent glass dishes with crimped decoration around the rims **(16a)**. 1910–30. 5–6in. ***(A)***
17 Wine glass by Otto Prutscher for the Austrian company NEFF with secessionist pattern **(17a)**. 1905. 8in. ***(E)***
18 Favrile vase by Tiffany, loosely based on a Turkish rosewater sprinkler and painted with soft gold and peacock blue on a black glass. 1908. 12in. ***(G)***
19 Pod-shaped Art Nouveau vase in magenta, electric and peacock iridescent blues. Made by Tiffany. 1906. 7in. ***(G)***
20 Millefiori paperweight made in England. Mid-19th C. 1¼in. ***(A)***
21 Cypriotware vase from Tiffany with a pitted, lustrous surface achieved by coating the surface with minute glass chips and lustring with metallic oxides. 1908. 4in. ***(G)***
22 Candlestick made by mixing end-of-day coloured glass. Detail **(22a)**. 1870s. 8in. ***(A)***
23 Small rose design paperweight from either China or Bohemia. 1900s. 1½in. ***(A)***
24 Cranberry glass 'epergne' or centrepiece with six trumpet-shaped flower holders and two matching vases **(24a,b)**. 1870. 22in. ***(D)***
25 Goblet with a folded foot and trumpet-shaped bowl. 1730–40. 8in. ***(E)***
26 Claret decanter with attractive rococo-style silver shell and coral shaped mounts. 1882. 10in. ***(F)***
27 Working glass trumpet with a drawn and twisted stem; made to show the glassmaker's skill. *c.*1840. 2ft 1in. ***(B/C)***
28 Bust of Emperor Napoleon III (1808–73) made in St. Louis, France. 1873. 8in. ***(B/C)***
29 Vase imitating the style of Lalique. *c.*1920. 8in. ***(A)***
30 Condiment set in pressed glass. *c.*1900. 5in long. ***(A)***
31 Clear and frosted glass figurine of 'Suzanne' by glass and jewellery designer René Lalique (1860–1945) with bronze illuminated base depicting peacocks. 1930s. 8in. ***(G)***
32 Rummer engraved with sailing ships and a message of friendship, with lemon squeezer base **(32a)**. *c.*1780. 5in. ***(C)***
33 Fine press-moulded swan-shaped tureen cover and dish **(33a)**. Complete piece **(33b)**. 1910. 8in long. ***(A)***
34 Glass lemonade jug and beaker **(34a)**, crafted to resemble cut glass, with design of lilies. 1910–20. 12in. ***(A)***
35 Mass-produced pressed glass dish in the shade of orange popular until WWII. 1910. 6in. ***(A)***
36 Rare layered glass lampshade made at the Daum Frères glassworks in Nancy, France. 1900. 18in. ***(G)***
37 Tiffany lava glass vases which simulate the effect of flowing lava **(37a)**. 1908. 4–8in high. ***(G)***
38 Bohemian ruby glass vase and cover, engraved with a woodland scene. 1850. 18in. ***(F)***
39 Moulded opalescent figurine by the Marius Sabino glassworks in Italy. 1930s. 8in. ***(E)***
40 Millefiori vase with trailing foliage and flower heads embedded in the glass. 1902. 8in. ***(C)***
41 Drinking glass with typical engraved images of hops and barley, associated with its contents. 1770. 5in. ***(A)***
42 German souvenir beaker with view of health spa near Dresden or Leipzig and floral decoration in enamel **(42a)**. 1812. 4in. ***(G)***

14a

33b

PRICE GUIDE: ***A*** less than £100 ($150) ***B*** £100–250 ($150–400) ***C*** £250–500 ($400–800) ***D*** £500–1000 ($800–1600) ***E*** £1000–2000 ($1600–3200) ***F*** £2000–3000 ($3200–4800) ***G*** over £3000 ($4800)

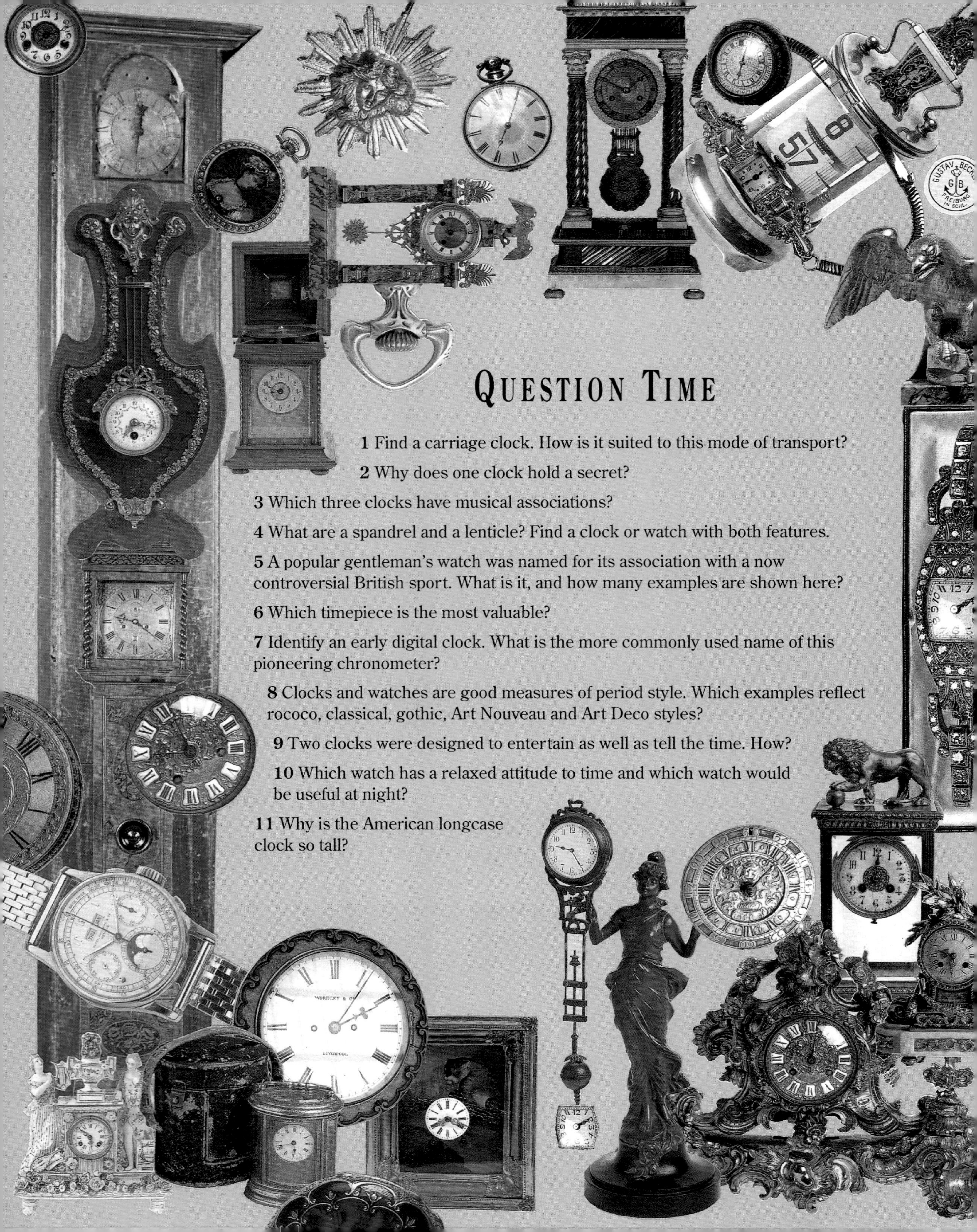

QUESTION TIME

1 Find a carriage clock. How is it suited to this mode of transport?

2 Why does one clock hold a secret?

3 Which three clocks have musical associations?

4 What are a spandrel and a lenticle? Find a clock or watch with both features.

5 A popular gentleman's watch was named for its association with a now controversial British sport. What is it, and how many examples are shown here?

6 Which timepiece is the most valuable?

7 Identify an early digital clock. What is the more commonly used name of this pioneering chronometer?

8 Clocks and watches are good measures of period style. Which examples reflect rococo, classical, gothic, Art Nouveau and Art Deco styles?

9 Two clocks were designed to entertain as well as tell the time. How?

10 Which watch has a relaxed attitude to time and which watch would be useful at night?

11 Why is the American longcase clock so tall?

W.H. YOUNG
BOSTON
NEW HAVEN CLOCK CO.
NEW HAVEN, CONN. U.S.A.
Thomas
Lincoln
PENNEY
Cambridge
GLOUCESTER

Question Time

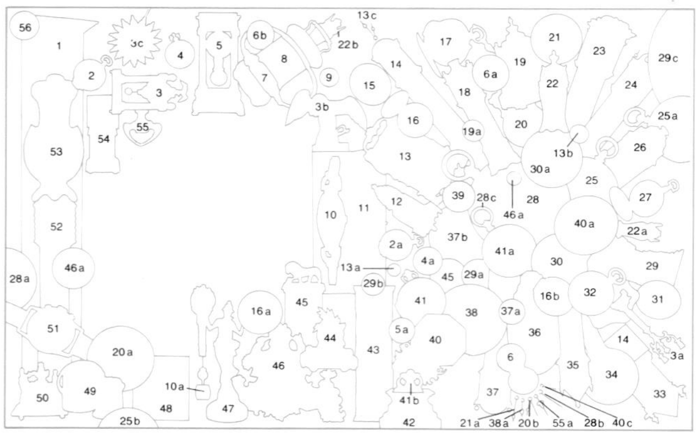

1 American longcase clock mounted in a simple painted pine case. The movement and face are English. 1730s. 5ft 8in. ***(G)***
2 Enamelled gold pocket watch set with split pearls and two minute rose diamonds. Made in Switzerland, probably for the Chinese market. Obverse side **(2a)**. 1890. 1¼in. ***(D)***
3 English mantel set consisting of a clock and two candelabras **(3a)** devised to complement Victorian mantelpieces. Fashioned from veined marble with gilt brass figures of Egyptian maidens, eagles **(3b)** and a spagnolette or 'sunburst' pendulum bob **(3c)**. 1880. Clock 21in. ***(E/F)***
4 Silver pair-cased, or farmer's, verge watch. Made in England, this design **(4a)** was introduced in 1800 and remained popular for the next 60 years. Pair-cased refers to the outer case which gives extra protection. 1825. 2¼in. ***(B)***
5 Rare French portico clock (four columns supporting a platform or entablature) made of ribbed blue glass with ormolu mounts. Engraved face **(5a)**. 1840. 2ft. ***(G)***
6 Early English watch, with verge escapement, signed by the watchmaker Richard Riccard. The silver dial **(6a)** is engraved with stylized tulips, which also appear as pinwork decoration on the leather case **(6b)**. 1660. 3in. ***(G)***
7 Fashionable cocktail watch with diamonds mounted in platinum and a 9ct white gold bracelet. 1935. ¾in face. ***(C)***
8 Flick clock made by the German company Junghans. It is visually a forerunner of digital clocks developed later in the century. Tiny pointers hold back the time cards. 1905. 5in. ***(C)***
9 Trademark of Gustav Becker from Freiburg, Germany, and found on the movement of the firm's Black Forest mantel clocks.

55b

10 Diamond and platinum bracelet watch with lozenge-shaped dial **(10a)** and stirrup shoulders typical of its period. The maker is unidentified. 1920s. 3in long. ***(E/F)***
11 White gold wristwatch made by Audemars Piguet for the Swiss watchmakers Gubelin of Lucerne, with a minute repeating movement unusual in a watch this size. 1930s. 1in. ***(G)***
12 English novelty clock carved from wood to appear medieval with gilt face and supports. 1860s. 9in high. ***(C)***
13 Full-calendar clock made by the English watchmaker Dent. The cast case, with masks, fruit and scroll work, is very ornate for the mid-19th century. Two of its three subsidiary dials are shown **(13a,b)**. Hands **(13c)**. 1860. 6in. ***(E)***
14 Swedish painted longcase clock with mouldings picked out in gold leaf. The square dial **(14a)** with arched top is a feature widely found in continental Europe. 1750s. 8ft. ***(F)***
15 Gilt face from English bracket clock. Late 19th C. 4in.
16 Early verge watch by the English maker Peter Garon, with engraved dial in chased silver and gilt **(16a)**. An outer case with glass lid keeps out dust **(16b)**. 1690. 2½in. ***(E)***
17 American hunter-cased gold watch with a chain and fob made for sale in the English market. 1890. 2¼in. ***(D)***
18 Miniature longcase clock made in France. Polished mahogany case with an arched brass dial, inscribed *Tempus fugit* ('Time flies'). 1885. 2ft 2in. ***(B/C)***
19 French mantel clock produced for export to Britain. What appears to be marble is in fact steel with gilt decoration. The movement is signed 'Marti à Paris', but the dial **(19a)** is by British clockmaker John Bennett. 1880. 17in. ***(C)***
20 Striking wall clock from northern England finished in walnut veneer and carved **(20a)**. Hands **(20b)**. 1850. 15in. ***(D)***
21 Dial and minute hand **(21a)** from an American eight-day mantel clock by Boston maker W. H. Young. 1850. 19in. ***(D)***
22 Elaborate pierced metal mantel clock set. The bombé (bulging) style of the clock case is repeated in the two accompanying vases **(22a,b)**. 1890. 15in. ***(C)***
23 Walnut longcase clock with panelled marquetry by

PRICE GUIDE: ***A*** less than £100 ($150) ***B*** £100–250 ($150–400) ***C*** £250–500 ($400–800) ***D*** £500–1000 ($800–1600) ***E*** £1000–2000 ($1600–3200) ***F*** £2000–3000 ($3200–4800) ***G*** over £3000 ($4800)

Robert Dingley of London; the original green staining on the marquetry leaves can still be seen. 1690. 6ft 6in. ***(G)***
24 Scottish longcase clock by Alexander Nicol of Arbroath. The painted arch shows a battle scene and on the spandrels are representations of the seasons **(24a)**. 1800. 6ft 8in. ***(E)***
25 Engraved gold dial from a Swiss pocket watch by 'Le Comte' of Geneva with typical Swiss engraving and translucent blue enamelled case **(25a)**. The spiral pattern **(25b)** is created on a special lathe. 1875. 1½in. ***(C)***
26 Ebony and metal mounted mantel clock by Thwaite and Reid of London, with chiming movement. 1860s. 3ft. ***(G)***
27 Single-cased verge watch with a small, or half-hunter, window exposing the inner chapter ring when the lid is closed. Made in England. 1820. 2in. ***(B)***
28 London-made gentleman's lever watch in 18ct gold, with a gold balance wheel inside. It has a scrolled double 'frame' or cartouche in the centre **(28a)**, attractive hallmarked winder **(28c)** and hands **(28b)**. 1877. 1¼in. ***(C)***
29 American shelf clock by the New Haven Clock Co. **(29c)** with pressed wood (gingerbread) surround, metal inlaid enamel dial **(29a,b)** and eight-day movement. 1900. 22in. ***(B)***
30 Lacquered English wall clock with 'drop dial' face **(30a)** and mother-of-pearl inlay. 1860. 2ft. ***(C/D)***
31 Dial from a German architectural style mantel clock made by the Hamburg American Clock Co. 1900. 20in. ***(A)***
32 Swiss-made enamelled gold watch. When the winder is pressed the repeating mechanism restrikes the preceding hour; rare in a watch of this size. 1890. 1½in. ***(F/G)***
33 American architectural shelf clock in ebonized and gilded pine with pointed finials on the hood. 1885. 19in. ***(A)***
34 English mahogany teardrop shaped wall clock signed by the maker Jno (John) Nevil of Norwich. 1790. 4ft 2in. ***(G)***
35 Victorian longcase clock in a light oak case signed Gaze Ebrors, London. An allegorical Father Time is depicted on the partly gold ground. 19th C. 8ft 2in. ***(E/F)***
36 Long pendulum wall clock by the London clockmaker Richard Hindmore, decorated with chinoiserie on the case. 1725. 5ft 9in ***(G)***
37 George III mahogany longcase clock by Conyers Dunlop of London. The top dial can be set to strike or silent **(37a)**. Detail of main dial **(37b)**. 1770. 7ft. ***(F/G)***
38 Elegant wall clock with mahogany frame and heart-shaped hour hand **(38a)**; made in England and signed Penney of Cambridge. 1875. 15in. ***(C)***
39 Dial with roman numerals from a classic American shelf clock. 1895. 6in.
40 Hexagonal wall clock which strikes the hours on a bell. Signed on face **(40a)** by Thomas of Lincoln. 1870. 16in. ***(E)***

41 English silver pair-cased pocket watch. The dial **(41a)** is decorated with a frigate and, instead of numbers, bears the owner's name: Thomas Baldwin. Details of winder **(41b)**, hands **(41c)**. 1793. 2¼in. ***(E)***
42 Steel mantel clock, transfer-printed to resemble slate or marble. Mass-produced in America for export overseas. 1879. 18in. ***(A)***
43 Watchstand made by American whalers from bone and marine ivory, known as scrimshaw, and enclosed in a wooden frame. 1833. 2ft. ***(E)***

30

44 Louis XVI-style striking mantel clock in marble and ormolu. 19th century revival items closely resembled their 18th century originals. 1850s. 12in. ***(D/E)***
45 'Four glass' clock – all four sides are glass – made in Germany's Black Forest. The lion and base are not brass, but spelter, an alloy of zinc. 1895. 16in. ***(A/B)***
46 French gilt-brass mantel clock in a blend of earlier Louis XV and XVI styles forming a hybrid shape that never existed in the 18th century. Dial **(46a)**. 1875. 15in. ***(D)***
47 Bronzed soft metal clock made in France; the clock **(47a)** and pendulum are held aloft by a figurine. 1900–10. 12in. ***(B)***
48 German picture clock with an eight-day movement by the well-known clockmaker Sattele Eisenbach. The face is protected by a glass mounted frame. 1860. 12in. ***(E/F)***
49 Miniature oval carriage clock with fitted case made in France by A. Dumas. 1870. 4in. ***(C)***
50 Ceramic mantel clock handmade in Dresden with two Grecian figures representing the arts. Late 19th C. 15in. ***(E)***
51 Gold chronograph made by Patek Philippe & Co., with stopwatch, perpetual calendar and day, month and phases of the moon. 1945. Dial 1¼in. ***(G)***
52 Longcase clock signed by the English clockmaker Daniel Smith. The case is walnut inlaid with floral marquetry; a glass lenticle exposes the pendulum. 1720. 8ft 2in. ***(F/G)***
53 Lyre-shaped clock from France with red marble and ormolu case, backed by a velour mount. 1900. 16in. ***(C)***
54 Novelty mantel clock in oak, with a musical movement made by the British company Symphonion. 1900. 10in. ***(C)***
55 Winder and hands **(55a)** in Art Nouveau style from a silver-plated motoring watch **(55b)**. 1910. ***(C/D)***
56 Face from a German 'faux marbre' (fake marble) wooden mantel clock. 1890. 5in.

24a

PRICE GUIDE: ***A*** less than £100 ($150) ***B*** £100–250 ($150–400) ***C*** £250–500 ($400–800) ***D*** £500–1000 ($800–1600) ***E*** £1000–2000 ($1600–3200) ***F*** £2000–3000 ($3200–4800) ***G*** over £3000 ($4800)

G-ADHL
PORT OF POOLE
EMPIRE AIRWAYS
1940
Chamberlains
Worcester
ROYAL WORCESTER
MADE IN ENGLAND
PATENT IRONSTONE
CHINA

CHINA STALL

1 Find four teapots disguised as a building, metal, flora and fauna and wickerwork.

2 China decoration takes many forms. Find something painted, printed, plated and pierced.

3 Find pieces associated with seafood, lighting, drinking coffee and drugs.

4 Find pieces purporting to be ancient Egyptian, classical, Renaissance and rococo.

5 Which pieces have theatrical, literary and film associations?

6 Which pieces depict travel by land, sea and air?

7 Find examples of saltglaze, parian and slipware.

China Stall

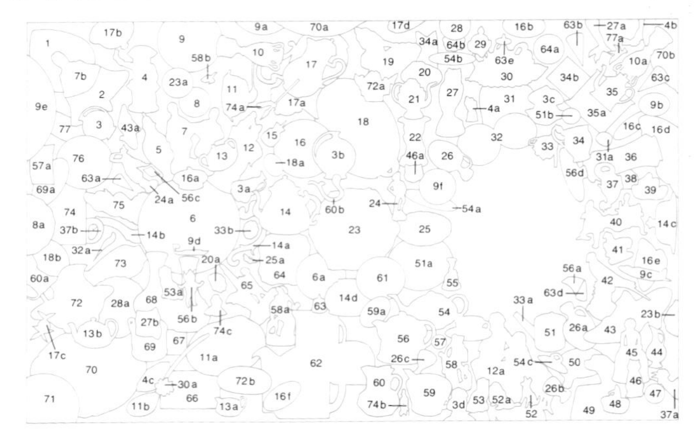

1 Wemyssware dressing-table tray. 1905. 11in. ***(C/D)***
2 Wemyssware egg basket. 1910. 8in. ***(C/D)***
3 One of two Doulton jugs advertising Dewar's whisky **(3b)**. Other jug **(3a)**. Called 'Rembrandtware' after the portraits **(3c,d)** which mimic the artist's style. 1910–20. 7in. Each ***(B)***
4 German Toby jug of a town crier **(4a,b)** ringing his bell and wearing the traditional tricorne hat **(4c)**. 1890. 8in. ***(A)***
5 Unusual Mason's Ironstone vases gilded and painted in the Japanese Imari style. 1830s. 2ft 4in high. Pair ***(E)***
6 Worcester plate with family crest **(6a)**. 1813. 9¼in. ***(E)***
7 Worcester sweetmeat figures. 1865. 8in high. ***(D)***
8 Meissen gloss-gilded plate. The intricate pattern **(8a)** was painted on in liquid gold. 1840s. 11in. ***(B)***
9 Poole pottery plate commemorating the landing in Poole Harbour of the Empire Airways flying boat. The designer's and painter's names appear on the back **(9f)**. Details **(9a–e)**. 1940. 15in. ***(E)***
10 Pair of neo-classical Dresden vases based on an 1815 design. Late 19th C. 16in. ***(E/F)***
11 Painted and gilded Worcester sauce tureen with lid **(11a)** and ladle **(11b)**. 1775. 7in. ***(E)***
12 Art Nouveau piece from Royal Dux, Bohemia. The moulding of the nymphs' faces **(12a)** is of high quality. *c.*1900. 16in. ***(C)***
13 Wedgwood silver-plated earthenware sugar bowl, milk jug **(13a)** and teapot **(13b)**. 1900. Teapot 4in. Set ***(B)***
14 Early Meissen teapot, with scrolled handle **(14a)** and curved gilded spout **(14b)**. The pot's enamelled lid is also gilded **(14c,d)**. 1723. 5in. ***(G)***
15 Pre-Columbian whistling pot from Peru. *c.*1300. 9in. ***(A)***
16 Minton soup plate, covered dish **(16a)**, dinner plates **(16b,c)**, fruit bowl **(16d,e)** and large dish **(16f)** in an oriental pattern. 1805. Dinner plate 10in. Each ***(A)***
17 Meissen chocolate pot and cover in the Japanese Arita style **(17c)**. The lid **(17a,b)** has a hole through which to stir the chocolate and a gold rim **(17d)**. 1740s. 8in. ***(E)***
18 Worcester taper or candlestick painted in a Japanese 'finger and thumb' pattern **(18a)** with the Chamberlains mark **(18b)**. 1800–1805. 4in wide. ***(B)***
19 English earthenware crowned lion on base, probably painted by child workers. *c.*1780. 4½in. ***(D)***
20 Lid for a Belleek basket; unusual delicately coloured flowers **(20a)** add to the value. 1880. 10in. Basket ***(F)***
21 Cabbage teapot with a snake forming handle and spout; revival of French 17th-century style. Late 19th C. 7in. ***(A/B)***
22 Majolica conservatory seat modelled as a winged harpy with lion's legs. *c.*1875. 17in. ***(E)***
23 Minton's majolica dish, meant for oysters as the fish design **(23b)** shows. Sauce dish **(23a)**. 1889. 11in. ***(B)***
24 Meissen statuettes of *Commedia dell'Arte* figures by craftsman Peter Reinicke. Figure **(24a)**. 1743. 7in. ***(E)***
25 Chelsea porcelain plate, painted with vegetables, insects and a butterfly typical of the makers **(25a)**. *c.*1755. 9in. ***(D)***
26 English pink and yellow vase in antique Greek style. Details of top **(26b,c)**. Other vase **(26a)**. 1860. 6in. Pair ***(B)***
27 Martinware stoneware bird, with outsize clawed feet **(27a)** and detachable head **(27b)**. London. 1898. 11in. ***(G)***
28 Meissen plate with gloss-gilding **(28a)**. 1840s. 11in. ***(B)***

57b

59b

PRICE GUIDE: ***A*** less than £100 ($150) ***B*** £100–250 ($150–400) ***C*** £250–500 ($400–800) ***D*** £500–1000 ($800–1600) ***E*** £1000–2000 ($1600–3200) ***F*** £2000–3000 ($3200–4800) ***G*** over £3000 ($4800)

71

29 Monkey's head cover for a Minton majolica teapot **(29a)**. 1890. 5in. ***(C)***
30 Belleek basket with perfectly formed flowers **(30a)** and handles and feet imitating coral. 1904. 11in. ***(D)***
31 Detachable beaker, made to resemble an owl's head, from a Staffordshire slipware jug. Detail of the eye **(31a)**. 17th C. 3in high. Jug ***(G)***
32 Two of six pearlware plates made in Yorkshire and decorated with painted birds **(32a)**. *c.*1820. 8in. Set ***(E)***
33 Miniature creamware teapot, part of a child's tea set. Details show the spout **(33a)** and the painted flowers **(33b)**. *c.*1810. 4in high. ***(B/C)***
34 Napoleon-style cup based on a Sèvres original. Detail of the foot **(34a)**. Painted mark **(34b)**. 1900. 3½in high. ***(B)***
35 Saltglaze teapot by John and Thomas Wedgwood in the shape of the Big House at Burslem **(35a)**. 1750. 5in high. ***(E)***
36 *Maiolica* jar from Palermo, Sicily. The picture of St. Lucy carrying eyes on a plate indicates the jar was meant for eye ointment **(36a)**. *c.*1580. 12in. ***(F/G)***
37 Minton's majolica novelty teapot; the hen's head **(37a)** forms the spout, and its tail **(37b)** the handle. 1872. 8in. ***(C/D)***
38 Meissen mark used during the 1840s.
39 Belleek mark for the period 1891–1926.
40 Rare Coalport copy of a domestic scene taken from the German makers Meissen. *c.*1840. 10in. ***(E)***
41 One of a pair of Staffordshire painted pottery zebras. 1850. 8½in high. Pair ***(C)***
42 Canary from Bow, London. 1760. 3in. Pair ***(E)***
43 Realistic china court shoe by Royal Worcester with gilt 'seeding' **(43a)**. 1919. 7¾in long. ***(G)***

36a

44 Royal Crown Derby jug. 1900. 10in high. ***(B)***
45 Very rare naive Staffordshire saltglazed stoneware figure of a bell lady. 1740. 4in high. ***(G)***
46 The Cheshire cat, from a rare series of Royal Worcester *Alice in Wonderland* figures. Detail **(46a)**. 1950s. 3in. ***(D)***
47 Date mark from French makers Sèvres for the year 1880.
48 French faience figure of a girl with baskets, probably used for holding salt at table. 1790. 8in. ***(E)***
49 Very rare Rockingham dog. 1830. 4in long. ***(D)***
50 Belleek earthenware bedpan. 1870–80. 10in. ***(A)***
51 Derby yellow-ground 'cabinet' cup and saucer **(51a)** decorated with painted scenes **(51b)**. *c.*1790. 3in. ***(C)***
52 Walt Disney pottery characters **(52a)** from *The Lady and the Tramp*. 1950s. 5–6in. Each ***(A/B)***
53 One of a pair of Staffordshire spaniels modelled on more expensive porcelain. Other spaniel **(53a)**. 1850. 11in. ***(B/C)***
54 Irish Belleek teapot, cup and saucer and cake plate **(54a)** in the Shamrock pattern; detail of the inside of the cup **(54b)** and the teapot lid **(54c)**. 1895. Plate 6½in. Set ***(D/E)***
55 Stoneware Tinworth mouse menu-holder. *c.*1885. 4in. ***(D)***
56 Mabel Lucie Attwell teapot with transfer-printed outline and hand colouring **(56c)**. The orange spout **(56a)**, hand and knop **(56d)**, and kewpie figure **(56b)** are typical of the period. 1925. 5in. ***(A)***
57 Decorative detail and band **(57a)** from an unusual earthenware ewer made by Bishop and Stonier in England. Complete ewer **(57b)**. 1875. 13½in high. ***(C)***
58 Front and back view **(58a)** of a painted Staffordshire figure of a huntsman. Detail **(58b)**. *c.*1850. 12in. ***(B)***
59 Art Deco teapot and sugar bowl from a breakfast set **(59b)**. Detail of geometric design **(59a)**. 1930. Teapot 4in. Set ***(B)***
60 One of two Mason's Ironstone octagonal jugs. Other jug **(60a)**. Green dragon handle **(60b)**. *c.*1840. 10in. ***(A)***
61 Vienna-style cabinet plate with portrait. 1890. 9in. ***(C)***
62 Clarice Cliff Art Deco tea service in 'Bizarre' design. 1930s. Teapot 5in high. Set for six ***(D/E)***
63 Clarice Cliff mustard pot and lid **(63e)**, pepper **(63a,b)** and salt shakers **(63c,d)**. 1930s. 3½in high. ***(B)***
64 Imari-type pattern Worcester dessert plate with 'gothic' oak leaves **(64a)**. Detail of centre **(64b)**. 1808. 8in. ***(B)***
65 Mantelpiece ornament by German makers Sitzendorf, probably used for holding spills. 1890. 10in high. ***(A)***
66 Original maker's mark for Mason's Ironstone.
67 Maker's mark for Royal Worcester. *c.*1910.
68 Pair of Dutch porcelain vases from the Oude Loosdrecht factory following a popular Meissen style. 1770s. 7in. ***(E)***
69 Rockingham porcelain mug, with typical rococo-style gilded decoration **(69a)**. *c.*1835. 4in. ***(D)***
70 Nymphenburg plate painted with flowers and insects **(70a,b)** by Josef Zachenberger. *c.*1760. 9in. ***(G)***
71 Armorial-style dish made in China. 1730. 9in. ***(D)***
72 Typical Sunderland ewer and basin printed with verses **(72a)** and local views **(72b)**. *c.*1840. Bowl 12in; jug 9in. ***(C)***
73 Rare 19th-century white Sèvres vase with Art Nouveau style decoration in enamels and gilding. 1881. 5¼in. ***(C/D)***
74 Stacey Marks Minton tile panel with falconry scene in Art Nouveau style. Details **(74a–c)**. 1871. 12in. ***(C)***
75 Irish Belleek parian crouching Venus. Late 19th C. 17in. ***(G)***
76 Copy of a 16th-century Italian *maiolica* charger from the Della Robbia factory at Birkenhead. 1894. 12in. ***(E)***
77 Wedgwood majolica bowl with silver-plated mount in the popular fan pattern with birds **(77a)**. 1879. 10in. ***(C)***

29a

PRICE GUIDE: ***A*** less than £100 ($150) ***B*** £100–250 ($150–400) ***C*** £250–500 ($400–800) ***D*** £500–1000 ($800–1600) ***E*** £1000–2000 ($1600–3200) ***F*** £2000–3000 ($3200–4800) ***G*** over £3000 ($4800)

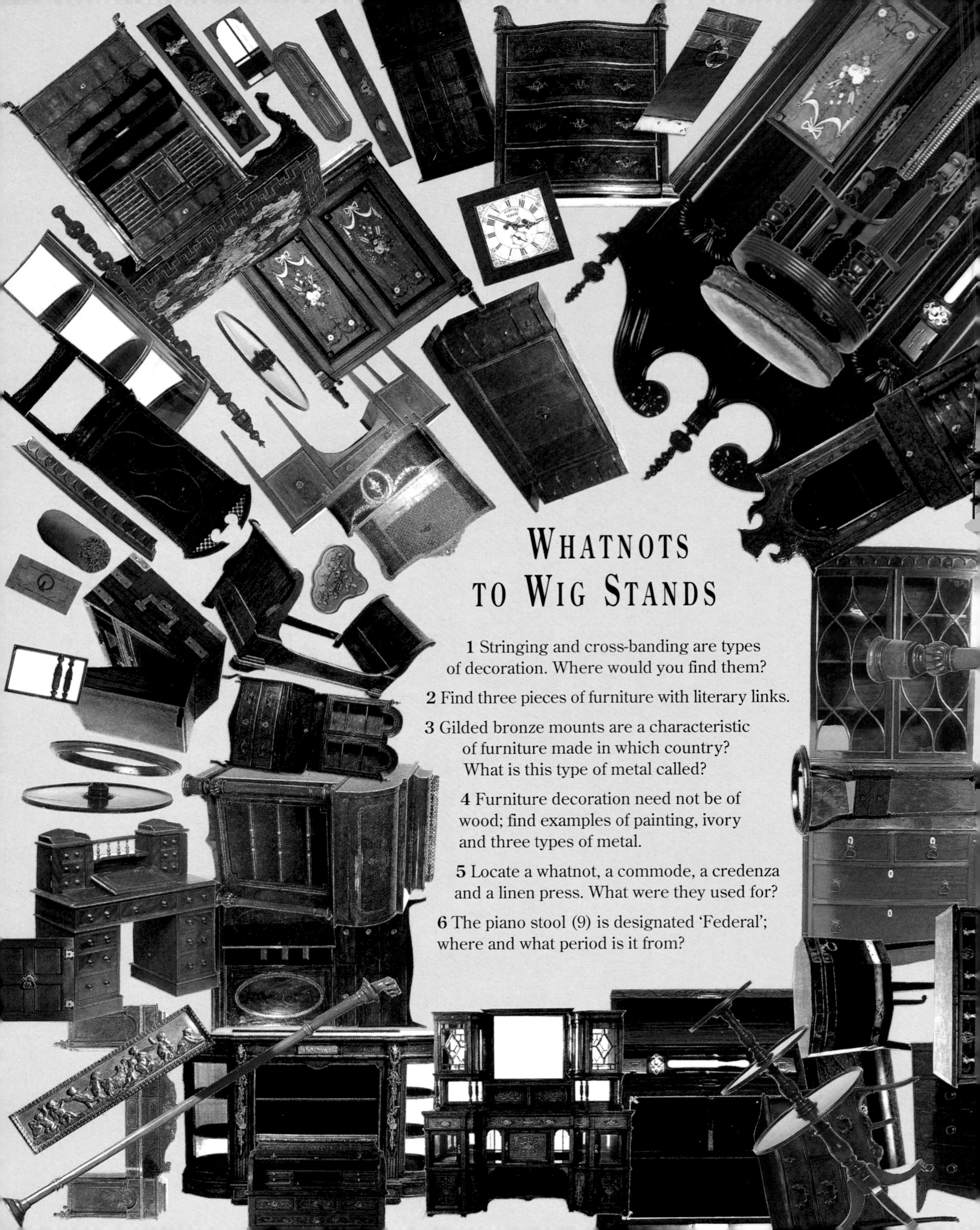

Whatnots to Wig Stands

1 Stringing and cross-banding are types of decoration. Where would you find them?

2 Find three pieces of furniture with literary links.

3 Gilded bronze mounts are a characteristic of furniture made in which country? What is this type of metal called?

4 Furniture decoration need not be of wood; find examples of painting, ivory and three types of metal.

5 Locate a whatnot, a commode, a credenza and a linen press. What were they used for?

6 The piano stool (9) is designated 'Federal'; where and what period is it from?

Whatnots to Wig Stands

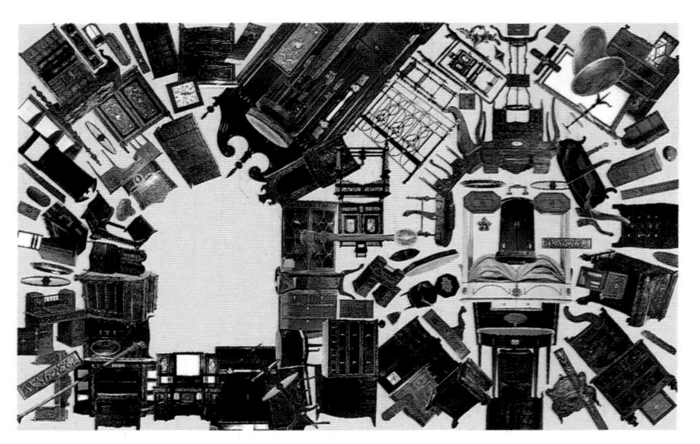

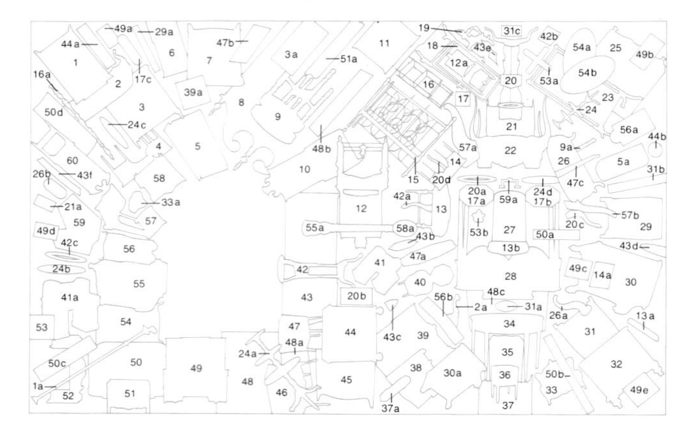

19a

1 *Secrétaire à abattant* with figured mahogany grain, made in Altona, Denmark. Turned column and carved foot **(1a)**. 1840. 4ft 10in. ***(E)***
2 Victorian stool with scrolled rosewood legs **(2a)**. *c.*1850. 2ft 6in x 4ft. ***(F)***
3 English satinwood cabinet with hand-painted panel surrounded by ebony border **(3a)**. 19th C. 4ft. ***(G)***
4 Sheraton revival sideboard. Early 20th C. 4ft 6in long. ***(D)***
5 Art Deco sycamore sideboard by French designer Jacques Adnet. It is banded in stainless steel with glass panels covering the top **(5a)**. 1925–30. 7ft long. ***(G)***
6 Early Victorian glazed-door cabinet in mahogany with cupboards and a drawer. 1845. 8ft. ***(F)***
7 Danish walnut veneered commode, or chest of drawers, with gilt detailing and rococo-style handles. The wooden top is painted to resemble marble. 1775–1800. 2ft 9in. ***(G)***
8 Mahogany six-shell desk and bookcase made by American cabinet maker John Goddard. 1760–70. 10ft 10in. ***(G)***
9 Federal mahogany piano stool with reeded legs **(9a)** and base. Made in New York. *c.*1800–10. 2ft 6in. ***(F/G)***
10 Maltese bureau bookcase with olivewood and walnut veneering and scrolling cornice. 1780. 6ft. ***(G)***
11 Secret compartment from a bureau bookcase. A catch within the small cupboard releases the hollow right-hand pillar. Bureau bookcase **(11a)**. 1730s. 6ft 5in. ***(G)***
12 Italian cabinet veneered in ebony with ivory marquetry. The central panels are engraved with classical scenes in Renaissance style **(12a)**. 19th C. 5ft 6in high. ***(F)***
13 English walnut writing table with built-in writing box **(13a)**. The simple table top **(13b)** and ornately carved legs reflect the eclectic style of the Victorians. 1840s. 3ft 6in. ***(F)***
14 George III mahogany sideboard from England with bowed top and tulipwood cross-banding on the drawer and doors **(14a)**. 1790. 4ft 2in long. ***(G)***
15 Cast iron and brass bedstead with looped design. 1870. 4ft 6in wide. ***(D)***
16 Four-tier whatnot with spiral turned columns **(16a)**. 1870. 6ft high. ***(D)***
17 'Perspective' panel in handcut veneers from a 17th-century oak chest **(17d)**. Drawer fronts **(17a–c)**. 1660. 3ft high. ***(G)***

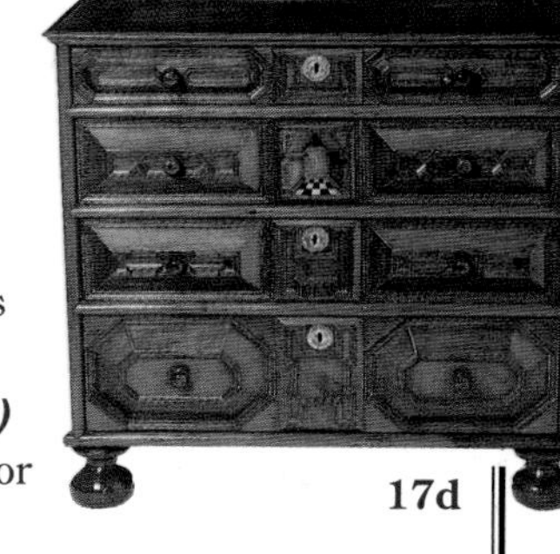

17d

18 Full-sized cheval, or four-legged, mirror in mahogany with original brass candle holders. 1820–30. 6ft 6in. ***(D/E)***
19 Asymmetrical rococo drawer handle in gilt from a Swedish commode **(19a)**. 1775–1800. 2ft 8in high. ***(G)***
20 Mahogany wig stand. A circular frame supports a bowl for powdering wigs **(20a)** and drawers beneath **(20b)** hold the necessary materials. Detail of foot **(20c)** and carved vertical support **(20d)**. 1755–60. 2ft 7in high. ***(F)***
21 Dutch walnut *bureau à cylindre*, with diamond parquetry on the roll top and cross-banding around the drawers **(21a)** and top. 1780s. 3ft 7in high. ***(F/G)***
22 Lady's writing desk, or *bonheur du jour*, in the mixture of French styles known as *tous les Louis*. Made from burr walnut, with kingwood cross-banding. 1860. 3ft 7in wide. ***(F)***
23 Chippendale-style cheval mirror. 1900. 6ft high. ***(E)***
24 Mahogany three-tiered dumbwaiter, one of a pair **(24a)**. Food was left on the trays so that guests could help themselves. *c.*1775–85. 4ft. Pair ***(G)***
25 Miniature mahogany chest with stud feet and elegant shaped apron beneath bottom drawer. 18th C. 12in high. ***(B)***
26 Doll's house sofa upholstered in olive silk **(26b)** on a stained wooden frame **(26a)**. 1890. 9in long. ***(A)***
27 Georgian mahogany corner cupboard with bow front and brass fittings. Made in England. 1780s. 4ft high. ***(D/E)***
28 Painted dressing table with gilt mounts and fabric apron. Made in America. Late 18th C. 3ft. ***(G)***
29 English George II bureau with highly figured walnut

PRICE GUIDE: ***A*** less than £100 ($150) ***B*** £100–250 ($150–400) ***C*** £250–500 ($400–800) ***D*** £500–1000 ($800–1600) ***E*** £1000–2000 ($1600–3200) ***F*** £2000–3000 ($3200–4800) ***G*** over £3000 ($4800)

11a

veneer exterior showing off the grain, and oak drawer linings. Front of drawer with fittings **(29a)**. 1735. 3ft high. ***(G)***
30 Burr walnut davenport. Side drawers provide space for personal possessions and documents **(30a)**. 1870. 2ft wide. ***(G)***
31 Mahogany bureau with sloping fall front decorated with inlaid marquetry panel **(31a)** and boxwood lines on drawer fronts **(31b)**. Interior door panel **(31c)**. 1780. 3ft 6in. ***(D)***
32 Miniature English chest of drawers in oyster veneer with marquetry inlay and button handles. 1790s. 14in high. ***(C)***
33 French Louis XV-style bedstead in walnut with beading and carved footboard **(33a)**. 1895. 4ft 6in wide. ***(E)***
34 American Hepplewhite-style card table made from mahogany with green baise surface. *c.*1790–1810. 3ft high. ***(G)***
35 Bedside commode with false drawer fronts concealing a chamber pot compartment. The term 'commode' can also refer to a chest of drawers. 1778. 2ft 8in high. ***(D)***
36 Washstand, or dressing chest, in Hepplewhite style with fold-over top which opens out to provide tray spaces, a mirror and useful compartments. 1800. 2ft 10in. ***(E)***
37 Serpentine-shaped commode or chest of drawers from Malta decorated all over with fine marquetry inlays and applied veneer parquetry **(37a)**. 1775–1800. 5ft. ***(G)***
38 English Edwardian oak bedstead with typically elegant and restrained carving. 1910. 4ft 7in wide. ***(C)***
39 Housekeeper's cupboard in oak with cross-banding on the drawers and fitted clock **(39a)**. 1820. 6ft 6in. ***(C)***
40 George III mahogany wine cooler with a lead-lined interior for holding ice. 1770. 2ft 2in high. ***(G)***
41 Child's kneehole writing desk with leather writing slope and desktop furniture **(41a)**. Mid-19th C. 23in x 22in. ***(G)***
42 Triangular mahogany washstand or wig stand designed to fit into a corner. It has three scrolling legs **(42a)**, drawers **(42b)** and a bowl holder **(42c)**. 1765. 2ft 7in. ***(E)***
43 Bureau bookcase made from mahogany in 18th-century revival style with authentic period detailing **(43a,d,f)** and outstanding glass front **(43b,c,e)**. 1920. 6ft 10in high. ***(F)***
44 William and Mary laburnum chest of drawers. The 'oyster' veneer is cut across the grain to resemble an oyster shell, hence its name **(44a)**. Turned ball foot **(44b)**. 17th C. 3ft 4in. ***(G)***
45 Bow-fronted mahogany chest of drawers with splay feet. 1800–10. 3ft 3in high. ***(D)***
46 Free-standing French-style commode with gilded mounts. 19th C. 3ft high. ***(G)***
47 Large Hepplewhite period wine cooler with brass bands and handles **(47b)**. The four tapering square legs have castors **(47c)**. Lid **(47a)**. 1770. 2ft 4in. ***(G)***
48 Inked-in burr walnut writing slope with original inkwell, leather-covered tinder boxes with gilt-metal lids (used to light candles for melting sealing wax), agate quill holder and gilt-metal paperknife **(48b)**. Closed box with cylindrical lid **(48a)** and open leather writing surface **(48c)**. 1850s. 18in. ***(D)***
49 18th-century or classical revival cabinet in rosewood decorated with marquetry panels **(49e)**. The edges of the mirrors and cabinet doors have bevelled or sloping glass **(49a–d)**. Late 19th C. 6ft 2in high. ***(D)***
50 Fine walnut credenza with high-quality figured veneers and a gilded plaque **(50a,c)** and mounts **(50b)**. It has quarter-circle ends **(50d)** and a single door. 1860. 3ft 7in. ***(G)***
51 French revival *bureau à cylindre* based on a 1760s design, with marquetry and gilded mounts **(51a)**. It takes its name from the slatted pull-down cover. 1900–20. 3ft 7in. ***(E)***
52 Scottish mahogany pedestal sideboard. The table frieze is banded with brass and fitted with three drawers, flanked by a pair of pedestals on turned feet. 1825. 8ft 4in long. ***(G)***
53 Cupboard door from an Arts and Crafts style dresser **(53c)**. This movement promoted handcrafted rather than machine made furniture; shown in the heavy panelling **(53a)** and large metal mounts **(53b)**. 1910–20. 5ft 6in high. ***(F)***
54 Linen press in veneered mahogany with flame mahogany oval panels bordered with satinwood cross-banding and ebonized border **(54a,b)**. 1800–10. 10ft. ***(F)***
55 Cylinder fall davenport in burr walnut. On top is a lockable stationery box and below, framed by turned columns **(55a)**, are shelves to hold music. 1865. 3ft. ***(F)***
56 Double-domed bureau bookcase from Malta. The bookshelves are glass-fronted **(56a)** and the bureau drawers attractively veneered and inlaid **(56b)**. 1790. 6ft 3in. ***(G)***
57 French *lit en bateau*, boat-shaped day bed, made of mahogany in the Empire style. The plain side was pushed against the wall. Splayed leg **(57a,b)**. 1850. 3ft wide. ***(D/E)***
58 Louis XV-style bedstead from France with canework panels. A rococo-style garland motif decorates the footboard **(58a)**. 1895. 4ft 6in wide. ***(F)***
59 Military-style writing slope in polished mahogany with flush-fitting handles **(59a)**. 1850s. 21in wide. ***(D)***
60 Revival glass display case with Chinese Chippendale-style fretting on the cornice and a Sheraton-inspired cabinet and legs. 1900. 6ft 2in. ***(D)***

53c

PRICE GUIDE: ***A*** less than £100 ($150) ***B*** £100–250 ($150–400) ***C*** £250–500 ($400–800) ***D*** £500–1000 ($800–1600) ***E*** £1000–2000 ($1600–3200) ***F*** £2000–3000 ($3200–4800) ***G*** over £3000 ($4800)

1 Find an early example of the weapon still used by British policemen.

2 Which two swords might have crossed at the grim end of a legendary rebellion?

3 Locate something no well-groomed escapee would dare leave behind.

4 Not all the weapons shown here were designed to harm: find one with a medical purpose.

5 Spot two works of art created in off-duty moments.

6 What was the gambler's best friend?

7 Which conflict brought together a cap, a flag, a pack of playing cards and a hand gun?

Call to Arms

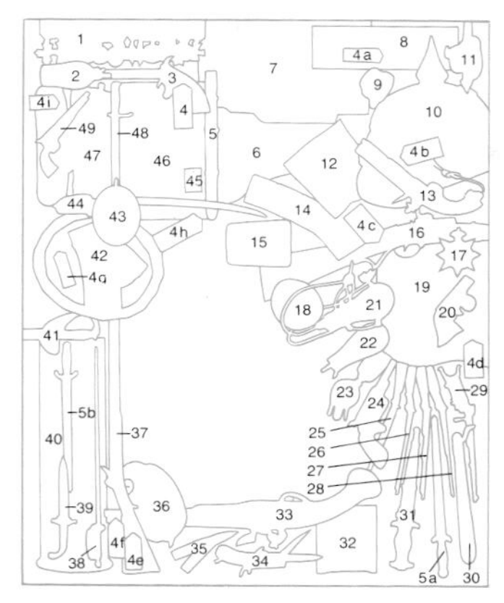

1 Medals awarded to British officer Lt. Col. E. C. Maxwell, dating from the Boer War to WWII. 1904–45. ***(B)***
2 English gun flask containing powder, bullets and percussion caps. 1840. 5in. ***(A)***
3 Wheelan's patent rimfire pistol with rotating double barrel. Made in the USA and used as a concealed weapon. 1867. 5in. ***(B)***
4 Shoulder flashes **(4a–i)** from the Imperial German Army and Navy. 1870–1919. ***(A)***
5 Scabbard of dyed and polished sharkskin (shagreen) accommodating a pair of Chinese shortswords **(5a,b)**. 1850. 23in. ***(A)***
6 Leather holster for a German Mauser pistol. 1914. 7in. ***(A)***
7 Contemporary scale-model of the French three-decker warship *Le Lion,* sporting 100 guns. 1792–1815. 3ft 4in. ***(D)***
8 Rare German Stoermer-Herzberg percussion gun, with interchangeable shotgun and rifle barrels. 1830. 3ft 9in. ***(F)***
9 Standard-issue Confederate cap or 'kepi'. 1861–65. ***(C)***
10 Spiked helmet or 'Pickelhaube' with cockade worn by German soldiers until the end of WWI. 1900. 9in. ***(C)***
11 Basket-hilt of a Scottish backsword, probably made for a Highland Militia Regiment. 1740. 3ft 9in. ***(C)***
12 Confederate battle flag used in the American Civil War; replaced the earlier 'Stars and Bars' of the South. 1865. ***(D)***
13 Holster pistol issued to troops serving the East India Co., a British, Far East-based trading concern. 1840. 15in. ***(C)***
14 Playing cards from the American Civil War. 1864. ***(B)***
15 Christmas gift, containing tobacco, sent to WWI British servicemen by Princess Mary. 1914. 6in long. ***(A)***
16 Hall's Patent Rifle, made in the USA. Breechblock and lock can be removed for use as a pistol. 1831. 3ft 11in. ***(D)***
17 British officer's gilt helmet plate from the 11th (North Devon) Regiment. 1878. 2in. ***(B)***
18 'Gun money' coin minted by the former British monarch James II (1633–1701), who was forced to melt down his cannon to pay his Irish troops. 1689. 1½in. ***(A)***
19 Silver lace 'wing' epaulettes worn by a British officer of the 5th Royal Lancashire Militia. 1840s. 7in. ***(B)***
20 Remington Derringer pistol with a ring-grip trigger and four barrels; made in America. 1866. 4in. ***(B)***
21 Gun-metal powder flask with brass fittings made by Flask Co. of Meriden, Conn., USA. 1850. 7in. ***(A)***
22 Lacquered brass powder flask embossed with the American eagle. 1860s. 4in. ***(B)***
23 Rare German Telegraphist's belt buckle from WWI with a drum attachment. 1915. ***(A)***
24 Slocum's 320 rimfire patent revolver with sliding tubes and chambers; made in America. 1863. 5in. ***(C)***
25 English shotgun made by Moore & Woodward. 1840. 3ft 6in. ***(D)***
26 Double-barrelled shotgun made by the English firm Blanch. 1840. 3ft 10in. ***(E)***
27 Shotgun manufactured by the English gunmakers Rigby. 1840. 3ft 10in. ***(E)***
28 Belgian shotgun by makers Lassence-Rong. 1840. 3ft 10in. ***(D)***
29 Target-shooting gun by Swiss gunsmith Paul. 1840. 3ft 11in. ***(D)***
30 Decorated boxwood truncheon bearing the British Crown's insignia. 1815. 12in. ***(A)***
31 German presentation dagger issued to officers of the elite SS (*Schutzstaffel*). 1939–45. 14in. ***(D)***
32 Military portrait of Lt. Col. Sir Robert Harvey painted by Thomas Heaphy (1775–1835). 1815. 23 x 26in. ***(E)***
33 Dragoon holster pistol made in England with brass buttcap or 'skull crusher' for bludgeoning. 1741. 12in. ***(E)***
34 Unwin & Rogers rimfire knife pistol. 1870. 7in folded. ***(C)***
35 Pocket fleam with tortoiseshell handles. 1850s. 5in. ***(A)***
36 Hairbrush from WWII, with concealed map compass and hacksaw blade. 1940. 4in. ***(B)***
37 English Flintlock sporting gun made by William Ryan & Son in Birmingham. 1825. 4ft 2in. ***(E)***
38 Scottish small sword with silver hilt inscribed: 'Carried for his Prince by Patrick Fea of Airie 1746' **(38a)**. 3ft. ***(E)***
39 Doubly lethal knife-pistol made in France; the gun barrel is concealed by a stiletto blade. 1860. 8in. ***(B)***
40 Shell case with intricate decoration. 1914–18. 11in. ***(B)***
41 Spanish sword with 'bilboe' hilt, named after the city of Bilbao where the design originated. 1770. 3ft 4in. ***(B)***
42 Regalia of a Knight Grand Cross of the British Order of St. Michael and St. George. 19th C. ***(F/G)***
43 Miniature portrait of an officer painted on ivory as a keepsake. 1820. 3in. ***(C)***
44 Hilt of an Indian Army sabre, probably issued to a detachment of Mountain Artillery. 1915. 3ft. ***(B)***
45 WWI Turkish soldier's belt buckle. 1915. 3in across. ***(A)***
46 Ackermann print of Scots Fusilier Guards officer from 'Costumes of the British Army'. 1820. 10in. ***(A)***
47 German cartridge pouch made for Mauser rifle cartridges. 1888. 8in. ***(A)***
48 WWI German bayonet, with serrated back. 1912. 14½in long. ***(A)***
49 Colt New Army pistol from the American Civil War. 1864. 9in. ***(E)***

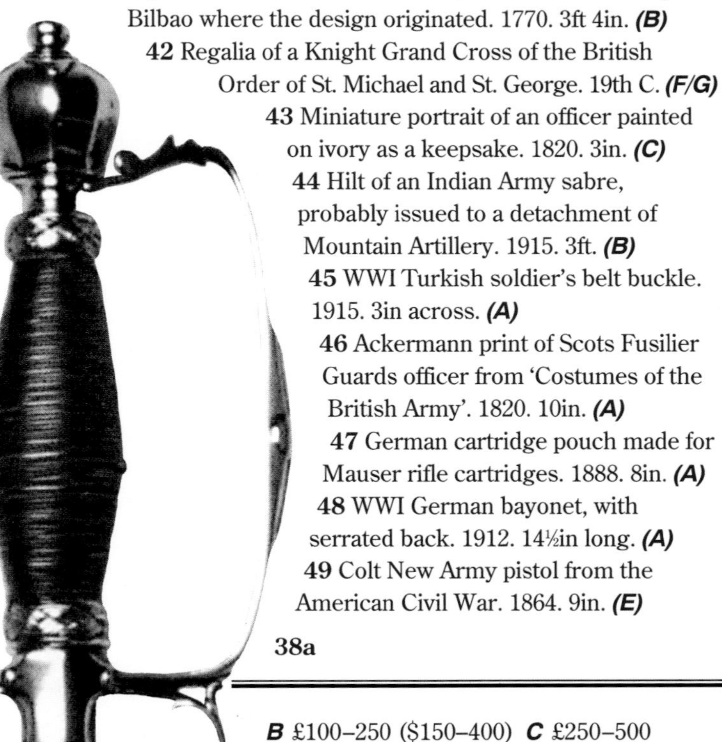

38a

PRICE GUIDE: ***A*** less than £100 ($150) ***B*** £100–250 ($150–400) ***C*** £250–500 ($400–800) ***D*** £500–1000 ($800–1600) ***E*** £1000–2000 ($1600–3200) ***F*** £2000–3000 ($3200–4800) ***G*** over £3000 ($4800)

METAL MISCELLANY

1 Metalwork is decorated using a variety of techniques. Find a single item with examples of chasing, casting, repousée and engraving.

2 How would you use a quaich, a vinaigrette and an epergne?

3 Find objects useful for the nursery, the smoker and for the bedroom.

4 Name the style period of the following articles: candlestick (36), jug (47) and tea set (71).

5 One piece shown is especially valuable; which is it?

6 Which item is permanently out of doors?

7 How many different metals are represented here?

Metal Miscellany

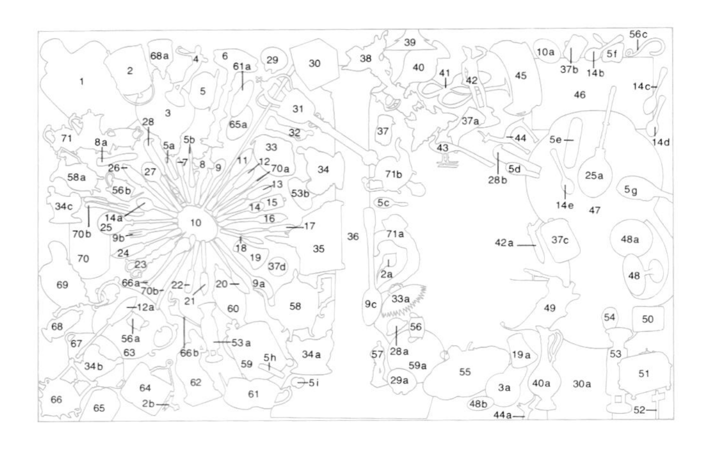

1 Silver hip flask, made in Sheffield. 1929. 6in. ***(A)***
2 Copper and brass portable heater, with floral relief pattern **(2a)**; perhaps Middle Eastern. 19th C. 18in high. ***(B/C)***
3 Scottish silver quaich commemorating a marriage, and the bride's posy ring **(3b)**. 1654. Quaich 7in. Set ***(E)***
4 English bronze of David about to slay Goliath, showing the influence of Rodin. 1895. 11in. ***(F/G)***
5 Silver dressing-table set with tray and buttonhook; clothes brushes **(5a,e,h)**; cuticle shaper **(5b)**; hairbrushes **(5c,d,g)**; hand mirror **(5f)**; and cosmetic jars **(5i)**, decorated in romantic fashion. 1900. Mirror 12in long. ***(D)***
6 One of a pair of cast silver candlesticks in typical mid-18th-century design. Late 19th C. 10in. Pair ***(F)***
7 Bone-handled butter knife, Birmingham. 1834. 6in. ***(A)***
8 Baby's gold rattle with bells, a whistle and a coral teether **(8a)**. Made in London. 1860. 7in long. ***(G)***
9 French silver dessert spoon with patterned back **(9a)**, fork **(9b)** and serving spoon **(9c)** from set of 12. 1724. 8in. Set ***(G)***
10 George III silver punch ladle with a beaded edge to the bowl **(10a)** and twisted whalebone handle. 1780. 14in. ***(B)***
11 Silver fiddle-pattern butter knife with milkmaid engraving. Hyam Hyams, London. 1869. 8in. ***(A)***
12 Butter knife with silver blade and stained ivory handle by John Daly of Dublin. Detail **(12a)**. 1795. 8½in. ***(A)***
13 Broad-bladed butter knife with ivory handle. Made in France. 1820. 7½in. ***(A)***
14 Silver egg spoon with gilded bowl and Lewis Carroll-type figure on the handles. One of a set of six **(14a–e)**. 1890. 4½in. One spoon ***(C)***
15 Silver match case with a striker on the base. Late 19th C. 1½in. ***(A)***
16 Silver butter knife in palm pattern by George Adams, London. 1878. 8in. ***(A)***
17 Butter knife with silver-gilt blade and polished horn handle. 1809. 9in. ***(A)***
18 Bone-handled butter knife. 1813. 5in. ***(A)***
19 Swedish silver beaker with stylized flower work and plain silver beaker **(19a)**. 1726 and 1735. Both 3½in. Each ***(C)***
20 Butter knife with silver blade and stained ivory handle by Peter and Anne Bateman, London. 1796. 8in. ***(A)***
21 Butter knife with engraved silver blade and rectangular agate handle. George Unite, Birmingham. 1836. 8½in. ***(A)***
22 Butter knife with silver scoop blade and bone handle by Joseph Willmore, Birmingham. 1810. 7½in. ***(A)***
23 Sheffield plate snuffer scissors. 1835. 7in. ***(A)***
24 Silver fiddle-pattern butter knife with cow engraving by Charles Boyton, London. 1871. 8in. ***(A)***
25 Silver-gilt spoons made in Cologne; the smaller **(25a)** bears the mark of Peter Kaff. 1650–70. 7 and 7½in. Each ***(D)***
26 Butter knife with stained ivory handle. 1800. 9in. ***(A)***
27 Rare Scottish 'Puritan' spoon with plain, plank-shaped stem. Only four such are known. 17th C. 5in. ***(E/F)***.
28 Silver butter knife with curved blade **(28a)** and a gemstone inset at the end of the handle **(28b)**. 1900. 6in. ***(C)***
29 Brass ashtrays inset with the faces of Oliver Cromwell and King Charles I **(29a)**. 19th C. 3in wide. Each ***(A)***
30 Rare chest-shaped silver caddy with lock and key, by Robert Makepeace and Richard Carter of London, and Chinese scenes on the sides **(30a)**. 1778. 3½in. ***(G)***
31 Enniskillen (N. Ireland) town mace, bearing the town arms, the Irish harp, the rose of England and the arms of Queen Anne. 1706. 3ft 2in. ***(G)***
32 French bronze Venus, a popular subject for Victorian statuary. 1890. 12in. ***(D)***
33 One of a pair of silver vegetable dishes and covers with acanthus leaf decoration **(33a)**. Made by Paul Storr of London. 1794. 7in high. ***(G)***
34 Silver-gilt salt by Paul Storr from a set of four **(34a–c)**. 1811–13. 5in. ***(G)***
35 Silver 'mosque' inkstand by Elkington & Co., a presentation piece. 1898. 12in. ***(G)***

39a

PRICE GUIDE: ***A*** less than £100 ($150) ***B*** £100–250 ($150–400) ***C*** £250–500 ($400–800) ***D*** £500–1000 ($800–1600) ***E*** £1000–2000 ($1600–3200) ***F*** £2000–3000 ($3200–4800) ***G*** over £3000 ($4800)

36a

36 Silver candlestick, one of a set of two pairs. One pair **(36a)** made 1781, the other in 1787. 11in high. Set ***(G)***
37 Silver match cases. Further examples **(37a–d)**. 1860–1910. 1–1½in. Each ***(A)***
38 Victorian centrepiece for fruit with a cut and frosted glass dish on a silver stem of fruiting vines. 1869. 19in. ***(E/F)***
39 Glass dish from a silver epergne **(39a)**; the glass dishes are interchangeable with candle sconces. 1835. 18in. ***(G)***
40 Large Sheffield-made silver claret jug; one of a pair **(40a)**. When the handle is gripped, the lid opens automatically. 1898. 16in. Pair ***(G)***
41 Child's spoon and pusher with distinctive handles. Made in Birmingham. 1914. 4in and 5in long. ***(A)***
42 Gladiator, with sword held aloft **(42a)**, one of a pair made in Germany of spelter, a low-grade zinc alloy which can look like bronze but is not so heavy. 1910. 20in. ***(B/C)***
43 Copper weathervane in the shape of a peacock. Made in America. *c.*1870–1910. 16in high. ***(A)***
44 Inscribed brass figure of a deer, probably Middle Eastern. Detail of head **(44a)**. 19th C. 6in long. ***(A)***
45 Boat-shaped silver fruit basket with fly-punching, a mechanical piercing technique ideal for mass production. 1890–1910. 12in long. ***(D)***
46 Italian plaque in chased gold relief, mounted on lapis with cornelians at the corners. Made for the Borghese family by Gugliemo della Porta as part of a cabinet. 16th C. 10in. ***(G)***
47 American Rookwood earthenware jug with electroplated pattern of flowers and foliage in silver. 1890. 6in. ***(D)***
48 Machine-made silver bonbon dish with an enamel centre in a medieval style **(48b)**. The hammer marks on the base **(48a)** were added later. 1908. 4in diameter. ***(C)***
49 Electroplated silver gondola rosebowl with original glass liner and grill. Made in Germany. 1900. 16in. ***(G)***
50 Ornate silver match case with ridged striker on the bottom. Late 19th C. 1½in. ***(A)***
51 Dutch marriage casket in silver, engraved with scenes of courting couples. In very fine condition. 1630. 3in long. ***(G)***
52 Detail from a bronze group 'Monkey Steeplechase' **(52a)** by Paul-Joseph Gayrard, Paris. 1850. 10in long. ***(E)***
53 Front and rear view **(53a)** of a silver figure of a chauffeur. The base **(53b)** bears a Chester hallmark, but it was most probably made in Birmingham. 1906. 4in. ***(D/E)***
54 Novelty brass match case modelled on the popular prime minister William Gladstone. Late 19th C. 2½in. ***(A)***
55 Child's miniature silver tea and coffee service. 1905. Tray 6in. ***(C)***
56 Sugar bowl from silver tea set in a Japanese style, reflected in the exotic shape. Teapot **(56b)**. Milk jug **(56a)**. Detail of handle **(56c)**. 1879. Teapot 5in high. ***(E)***
57 French or Florentine classical-style bronze after a marble original of Belvedere Antinous; paired with a Medici Venus. Late 17th C. 20in high. ***(G)***
58 Electroplated teapot and milk jug **(58a)**, part of a French service by Frenais. 1880. Teapot 9½in. Pair ***(B)***
59 Silver tankard with pomegranate feet and thumbpiece. The inscription on the base **(59a)** records its presentation in 1662 to British envoy Sir Philip Meadows. 16in high. ***(G)***
60 Scandinavian silver spice container. 19th C. 3in. ***(A)***
61 Rare pair of silver teapots, made by Robert Garrard in late 18th-century style. The lids are engraved 'green' **(61a)** and 'bohea' for green and black tea. 1822. 5in. Pair ***(F)***
62 'Man against Nature', French bronze statue on a marble base of a man wrestling a lioness. 1880. 2ft. ***(E/F)***
63 Silver caudle cup made by Robert Sanderson in Boston, America, possibly for a wedding. A caudle cup was used for making hot gruel. Mid-17th C. 5in high. ***(G)***
64 Rare silver-gilt vinaigrette made after the Battle of Trafalgar. A bust of Nelson is engraved on the front and the cast and pierced grille shows the *Victory*. 1805. 1½in. ***(G)***
65 Electroplated tea caddy with a beautifully engraved lid **(65a)** and neo-classical swags. 1880. 5in high. ***(A)***
66 George IV bronze and copper urn. The legs **(66a)** have animal feet and mask faces at the top, the handles **(66b)** are in the form of a dragon's head. 1830. 15in high. ***(B)***
67 Oval silver tray with 'rayed' effect; the reeded edge encloses a decorated border. 1870–80. 23½in. ***(F)***
68 Silver sugar caster made in London. The style, but not the decoration **(68a)**, mimics 1740s style. 1898. 7in. ***(B/C)***
69 Silver copy of a mid-18th-century three-legged sauce boat with engraved monogram. 1888. 5½in. ***(C)***
70 Complete Sheffield-made box of cutlery with silver handles. The knives **(70a)** have steel blades and the forks **(70b)** two steel prongs. 1770–80. Knife 9½in. Set ***(F)***
71 Irish silver copy of a mid-19th-century rococo revival tea set with typically ornate decoration, particularly the scroll work and the female figure on the teapot **(71b)**. Detail of handle **(71a)**. 1915. Teapot 6in high. Set ***(G)***

52a

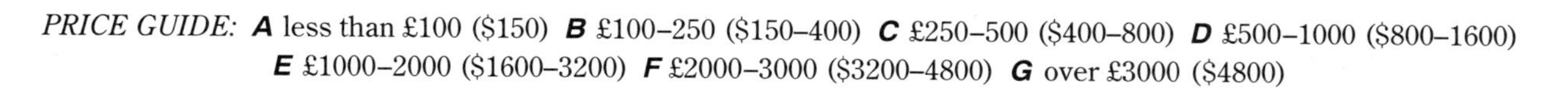

PRICE GUIDE: ***A*** less than £100 ($150) ***B*** £100–250 ($150–400) ***C*** £250–500 ($400–800) ***D*** £500–1000 ($800–1600) ***E*** £1000–2000 ($1600–3200) ***F*** £2000–3000 ($3200–4800) ***G*** over £3000 ($4800)

THE END OF THE HUNT

RHAPSODY IN BLUE

1 The Ming pen tray (39) would grace any desk. The ewer and basin (64) was a bathroom feature before running hot water. The quintal vase (58), invented in Holland, brought bulbs into the home. The salt (30) takes its name from the condiment it holds.
2 The daikon, or white radish, appears in the Hirado pottery (4).
3 The willow pattern, a standard design emulating Chinese style, was actually invented in Britain in the late 18th century. Examples can be seen on plates (3, 17, 59) and the spirit decanters (42). The pattern on plate 17c has been reversed.
4 The ordinary looking tea bowl (11) made in the 15th century was sold for £363,000.
5 Both have decorative uses. A garniture (49) is used to embellish or 'garnish' a mantelpiece. The lambrequins, a scalloped decoration, are used to decorate the edges of cups (26) and plates.
6 The Florian vases (24) were inspired by jugs found at the Roman town of Pompeii. Porcelain makers Sitzendorf have attempted to pass themselves off as their rival Meissen by using a similar mark (72).
7 Spirit decanters, labelled 'W' for whisky (42a) and 'B' for brandy (42b), capture the spirit of Scotland and fire of France.
8 Plate 32 has a portrait of the British prime minister William Gladstone, who gave his name to the Gladstone bag.
9 The Spode plate (65) depicts oxen and a camel in an exotic landscape, a scene not normally associated with blue and white.
10 A sedate tea drinker can be seen on a teapot (55); the golfer teeing off (48d) is on a plate (48).

MYSTERIES OF THE EAST

1 The moonflask (18) was made in England by Minton. The elegant jardinière (14), by Christofle, is French and the Japanese-style tea set (15) was made in America by Gorham.
2 The embroidered panel (20) was made in Turkey, then considered part of the orient. The bridge cloth (8) is Indian and the wall hanging (12) Japanese.
3 Cloisonné (14, 17, 26) inlays coloured enamels into wires soldered on to a metal vessel. Parquetry (22) creates a pattern by inlaying different types of wood into a wooden background. Shibayama (21) inlays precious metals and other materials into a base metal such as iron or bronze.
4 Traditional Japanese clothing lacks the pockets found in western dress and an inro (19) is used for small personal possessions. It comprises a series of compartments secured by a cord and a decorative toggle known as a netsuke (6, 31). The okimono (11, 37) is a carved figure, used for household decoration.
5 Until the end of the 18th century it was cheaper for westerners to order dinner services with personalised designs (3, 5) from China. The work table (25) was made especially for western markets, as there were no such items in the East. The Swiss-made watch (24) was lacquered in Japan and returned to Europe for sale.
6 The fisherman (33) was carved from an ivory walrus tusk. The kingfishers (29) are made from elephant ivory and stand on a stag antler leaf. The box (23) is decorated with cinnabar lacquer, which is made from crushed beetle wings.
7 Magnificent cranes appear on pieces 14 and 19; geese appear on pieces 34 and 19. The elephant's ball (39) is topped by an eagle.
8 The ebony elephant (39) with inlaid shibayama ball is the most valuable, at £10,000–£15,000.
9 The god Hotei plays Go with a young boy inside a tiny wood carving (32).

WONDERS OF SCIENCE

1 The pantograph (14) was used to copy maps. By adjusting the hinges the image could be either enlarged or reduced at will.
2 At sea, the sextant (12) or octant (23), used with a chronometer (30), determines latitude and longitude. The orrery (2) could provide space travellers with a guide to our solar system. The surveyor's or miner's dial (20) indicates direction without points of visual reference.
3 The block instrument (1) used telegraphic messages to determine whether a railway line was clear. The nautical telescope (6), with inset flag guide, was essential for reading signals at sea.
4 The collection of weather guides (5) was used by the British polar explorer Robert Falcon Scott (1868–1912) on his fatal expedition to the Antarctic in 1910. The worn ebony and brass octant (23) assisted in the search for Sir John Franklin, the explorer who was lost while trying to find the North-West passsage.
5 A compass (4a, 5b) is essential for finding direction. The ivory draughtsman's rule (24) is an elegant measure of distance. Two sets of balance beam scales (10, 18) provide accurate weight readings. Thermometers (4b, 5) measure temperature.
6 The Edison phonograph (15) brought music into the home and gave pleasure to thousands. The best views at the opera could be enhanced through a pair of opera glasses (11, 21). Restful birdsong would have come from the singing birds in the gilded cage (3).
7 They are all kinds of barometer using different methods to measure air pressure and so predict the weather. The stick barometer (7, 17, 22) uses a column of mercury to register pressure change. The aneroid barometer (4c, 5d) has a partial vacuum chamber to detect changes in pressure and was developed for use at sea. The wheel barometer (8) also uses a mercury tube, but achieves a more accurate result by activating a pointer. These were also known as banjo barometers because of their shape.
8 The military surgeon's kit (19) brought help to those injured in the trenches of WWI.

COUNTRY STYLE

1 The panelled oak chest (49) was made as a blanket box. The two commodes (14, 63) conceal chamber pots beneath lift-up seats. The raised chest (36) kept baker's dough in good condition.
2 Country furniture used readily available woods. Pine can be seen in dressers (19, 21), chests (22, 61) and tables (67); oak in benches (29), boxes (37, 49, 50), dressers (38, 62), bedsteads (43) and tables (45); and beech in chairs (16, 32).
3 The canterbury (40) was used in the 18th century as a plate-holder. In the 19th century it stored sheet music.
4 Although samplers fulfil a decorative function (35, 64), they were originally created as a catalogue of stitches (39).
5 The table (10) is considered to be one of the finest examples of the work of the Shaker religious community, renowned for its craftsmanship. The other two are a set of drawers (52) and a rocking chair (15).
6 The Orkney chair (27) was made from driftwood as there are no trees on the island. The small drawer was used for tobacco and whisky.
7 The Windsor chair with desk extension (28) was made in America.

JEWELLERY BOX

1 The dragonfly is on a diamond and peridot brooch (65), the 'fairy' is 10. The lion is on a mother-of-pearl cameo (112) and the dove (87a) is a detail of the Pliny's Doves brooch (87).
2 The gemstone associated with seas and oceans is the aquamarine. It is found in the diamond pendant (100), the diamond brooch (98) and earring (95a).
3 The torpedo cufflinks (15, 15a) are by Peter Carl Fabergé (1846–1920).
4 Both the 19th-century plaque (28), made from shell cameo, and the 19th-century bangle (27) in gold and mosaic depict this scene from classical mythology.
5 The gold turtle brooch (86) carries a pearl on his back and the oval locket (11) is made from a hawk's bill turtle shell.
6 The good luck wishbone brooch (37) could have been plucked from a chicken.

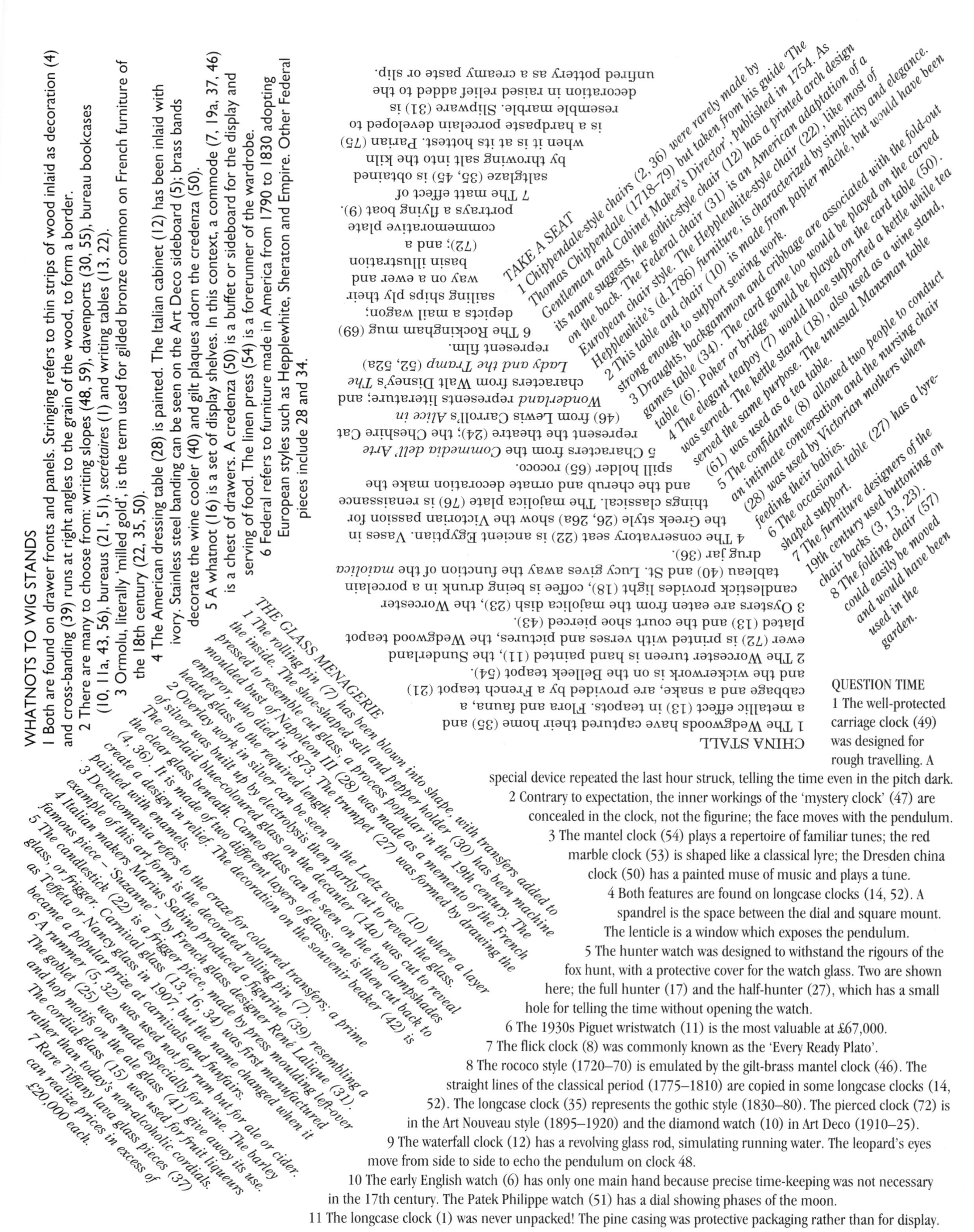

WHATNOTS TO WIG STANDS

1 Both are found on drawer fronts and panels. Stringing refers to thin strips of wood inlaid as decoration (4) and cross-banding (39) runs at right angles to the grain of the wood, to form a border.

2 There are many to choose from: writing slopes (48, 59), davenports (30, 55), bureau bookcases (10, 11a, 43, 56), bureaus (21, 51), *secrétaires* (1) and writing tables (13, 22).

3 Ormolu, literally 'milled gold', is the term used for gilded bronze common on French furniture of the 18th century (22, 35, 50).

4 The American dressing table (28) is painted. The Italian cabinet (12) has been inlaid with ivory. Stainless steel banding can be seen on the Art Deco sideboard (5); brass bands decorate the wine cooler (40) and gilt plaques adorn the credenza (50).

5 A whatnot (16) is a set of display shelves. In this context, a commode (7, 19a, 37, 46) is a chest of drawers. A credenza (50) is a buffet or sideboard for the display and serving of food. The linen press (54) is a forerunner of the wardrobe.

6 Federal refers to furniture made in America from 1790 to 1830 adopting European styles such as Hepplewhite, Sheraton and Empire. Other Federal pieces include 28 and 34.

CHINA STALL

1 The Wedgwoods have captured their home (35) and a metallic effect (13) in teapots. Flora and fauna, a cabbage and a snake, are provided by a French teapot (21) and the wickerwork is on the Belleek teapot (54).

2 The Worcester tureen is hand painted (11), the Sunderland ewer (72) is printed with verses and pictures, the Wedgwood teapot plated (13) and the court shoe pierced (43).

3 Oysters are eaten from the majolica dish (23), the Worcester candlestick provides light (18), coffee is being drunk in a porcelain tableau (40) and St. Lucy gives away the function of the *maiolica* drug jar (36).

4 The conservatory seat (22) is ancient Egyptian. Vases in the Greek style (26, 26a) show the Victorian passion for things classical. The majolica plate (76) is renaissance and the cherub and ornate decoration make the spill holder (65) rococo.

5 Characters from the *Commedia dell' Arte* represent the theatre (24); the Cheshire Cat (46) from Lewis Carroll's *Alice in Wonderland* represents literature; and characters from Walt Disney's *The Lady and the Tramp* (52, 52a) represent film.

6 The Rockingham mug (69) depicts a mail wagon; sailing ships ply their way on a ewer and basin illustration (72); and a commemorative plate portrays a flying boat (9).

7 The matt effect of saltglaze (35, 45) is obtained by throwing salt into the kiln when it is at its hottest. Parian (75) is a hardpaste porcelain developed to resemble marble. Slipware (31) is decoration in raised relief added to the unfired pottery as a creamy paste or slip.

TAKE A SEAT

1 Chippendale-style chairs (2, 36) were rarely made by Thomas Chippendale (1718–79) but taken from his guide The Gentleman and Cabinet Maker's Director, published in 1754. As its name suggests, the gothic-style chair (12) has a printed arch design on the back. The Federal chair (31) is an American adaptation of a European chair style. The Hepplewhite-style chair (22), like most of Hepplewhite's (d.1786) furniture, is characterized by simplicity and elegance.

2 This table and chair (10) is made from papier mâché, but would have been strong enough to support sewing work.

3 Draughts, backgammon and cribbage are associated with the fold-out games table (34). The card game loo would be played on the carved table (6). Poker or bridge would be played on the card table (50).

4 The elegant teapoy (7) would have supported a kettle while tea was served. The kettle stand (18), also used as a wine stand, served the same purpose. The unusual Manxman table (61) was used as a tea table.

5 The confidante (8) allowed two people to conduct an intimate conversation and the nursing chair (28) was used by Victorian mothers when feeding their babies.

6 The occasional table (27) has a lyre-shaped support.

7 The furniture designers of the 19th century used buttoning on chair backs (3, 13, 23).

8 The folding chair (57) could easily be moved and would have been used in the garden.

THE GLASS MENAGERIE

1 The rolling pin (7) has been blown into shape, with transfers added to the inside. The shoe-shaped salt and pepper holder (30) has been machine pressed to resemble cut glass, a process popular in the 19th century. The moulded bust of Napoleon III (28) was made as a memento of the French emperor, who died in 1873. The trumpet (27) was formed by drawing the heated glass to the required length.

2 Overlay work in silver can be seen on the Loetz vase (10) where a layer of silver was built up by electrolysis then partly cut to reveal the glass. The overlaid blue-coloured glass on the decanter (14a) was cut to reveal the clear glass beneath. Cameo glass can be seen on the two lampshades (4, 36). It is made of two different layers of glass; one is then cut back to create a design in relief. The decoration on the souvenir beaker (42) is painted with enamels.

3 Decalcomania refers to the craze for coloured transfers; a prime example of this art form is the decorated rolling pin (7).

4 Italian makers Marius Sabino produced a figurine (39) resembling a famous piece – 'Suzanne' – by French glass designer René Lalique (31).

5 The candlestick (22) is a frigger piece, made by press moulding left-over glass, or frigger. Carnival glass (13, 16, 34) was first manufactured as Teffeta or Nancy glass in 1907, but the name changed when it became a popular prize at carnivals and funfairs.

6 A rummer (5, 32) was used not for rum but for ale or cider. The goblet (25) was made especially for wine. The barley and hop motifs on the ale glass (41) give away its use. The cordial glass (15) was used for fruit liqueurs rather than today's non-alcoholic cordials.

7 Rare Tiffany lava glass pieces (37) can realize prices in excess of £20,000 each.

QUESTION TIME

1 The well-protected carriage clock (49) was designed for rough travelling. A special device repeated the last hour struck, telling the time even in the pitch dark.

2 Contrary to expectation, the inner workings of the 'mystery clock' (47) are concealed in the clock, not the figurine; the face moves with the pendulum.

3 The mantel clock (54) plays a repertoire of familiar tunes; the red marble clock (53) is shaped like a classical lyre; the Dresden china clock (50) has a painted muse of music and plays a tune.

4 Both features are found on longcase clocks (14, 52). A spandrel is the space between the dial and square mount. The lenticle is a window which exposes the pendulum.

5 The hunter watch was designed to withstand the rigours of the fox hunt, with a protective cover for the watch glass. Two are shown here; the full hunter (17) and the half-hunter (27), which has a small hole for telling the time without opening the watch.

6 The 1930s Piguet wristwatch (11) is the most valuable at £67,000.

7 The flick clock (8) was commonly known as the 'Every Ready Plato'.

8 The rococo style (1720–70) is emulated by the gilt-brass mantel clock (46). The straight lines of the classical period (1775–1810) are copied in some longcase clocks (14, 52). The longcase clock (35) represents the gothic style (1830–80). The pierced clock (72) is in the Art Nouveau style (1895–1920) and the diamond watch (10) in Art Deco (1910–25).

9 The waterfall clock (12) has a revolving glass rod, simulating running water. The leopard's eyes move from side to side to echo the pendulum on clock 48.

10 The early English watch (6) has only one main hand because precise time-keeping was not necessary in the 17th century. The Patek Philippe watch (51) has a dial showing phases of the moon.

11 The longcase clock (1) was never unpacked! The pine casing was protective packaging rather than for display.

CALL TO ARMS
1 This sturdy truncheon (30) would have been used by a hired watchman to quell village lawlessness in the days before the British police force was formed in 1829.
2 The elegant small sword (38) might well have locked blades with the basket-hilted backsword (11) in April 1746 at the infamous Battle of Culloden in Scotland, which destroyed the forces of Bonnie Prince Charlie and ended the Jacobite rebellion seeking to restore him to the English throne.
3 This hairbrush (36) from WWII provided the Allied prisoner-of-war with the resources to dash for freedom. Although many were made, few have survived.
4 The pocket fleam (35) was used by a military surgeon for blood-letting, to remove supposed impurities from the patient's blood.
5 The first example, a crafted brass shell case (40), is a fine piece of 'Trench Art' from WWI. Such works were a popular pursuit among soldiers, who fashioned vases, ashtrays and walking-stick stands from spent artillery ammunition. The second example is a model battleship (7) made from carved bone and dating from the Napoleonic Wars.
6 The Remington Derringer pistol (20) was uniquely tailored to a gambler's needs. As well as being compact and easy to conceal, its four barrels allowed the user to keep firing without reloading.
7 All these objects (9, 12, 13, 49) were brought together during the fighting and lulls of the American Civil War (1861–65).

METAL MISCELLANY
1 The caudle cup (63) made by American silversmith Robert Sanderson in the 17th century has cast caryatid handles and a now slightly faded chased (using a hammer to depress a design), repousée (small hammer blows that raise the design) and engraved design consisting of a turkey centred between flowers.
2 A quaich (3) is a shallow two-handled drinking cup used on special occasions such as a betrothal. First used in the 17th century, a vinaigrette (64) is a small decorative box containing a tiny sponge soaked in spiced vinegar. It was used to ward off evil smells or as 'smelling salts'. An epergne (39) is a dining table centrepiece with trays for sweetmeats.
3 The baby's rattle with coral teether (8) would live in the nursery. For the smoker there are brass ashtrays (29) and match cases (37, 54). Any dressing table would welcome the handsome dressing-table set (5).
4 The candlestick is classical, taking its shape and design from a Roman column. The jug has the naturalistic flourishes of turn-of-the-century Art Nouveau. The ornate tea set has the exuberance of the rococo (18th century).
5 The timeless lure of gold is proved by this 16th-century plaque (46) worth £30,000–£50,000.
6 The painted weathervane (43) is exposed to all weathers.
7 There are nine metals in total: gold, silver, bronze, steel, iron, brass, copper, spelter (zinc based) and electroplate (silver on nickel).

ACKNOWLEDGEMENTS

Picture credits
American Museum at Bath: p10 *10, 15*; p11 *28*
David Battie: p6 *66*; p7 *7, 15, 21, 23, 25, 27, 30, 31, 45, 66*; p14 *23*; p32 *6, 73*; p33 *20, 43, 45*
Bonhams: p26 *17*
Bridgeman Art Library: p6 *65*; p7 *18, 43, 44*; p20 *5, 7/8, 12*; p26 *1*; p29 *23*; p42 *30*
Christies Colour Library: p11 *46*; p22 *56, 58*; p28 *5*; p36 *5, 8, 52*; p37 *8, 14*; p42 *9*
Crane Gallery/Museum of English Naive Art, London: p10/11 *2, 8*
Esto, New York: p10 *52*; p11 *33*; p23 *15*; p36 *9*; p37 *28, 34*; p43 *43* (Richard Kendzierski/James C. Frasca Collection); p40 *14*
Chris Linton: p40 *9*
Sotheby's, London: p6 *2, 11*; p6/7 *8, 10*; p7 *26, 34, 48, 54*; p26 *15, 42*; p33 *27, 37*
Marshall Editions Developments (© DACS): p26 *31*
Museum of American Folk Art, New York/Esto, New York: p10 *7*
Eileen Tweedy/by courtesy of the Board of Trustees of the Royal Armouries: p40 *49*
Victoria & Albert Museum: p37 *41*
Virginia Historical Society: p40 *12*
Wallis and Wallis, Lewes: p40 *8, 17, 19*
Winterthur Museum, Winterthur, Delaware: p42 *63*
Jerry Young: p10 *54*; p23 *13, 26, 28, 34*; p26 *13*; p33 *21*; p42 *29*; p43 *44*

Whilst every effort has been taken to contact the source and owner of each piece featured, the publishers apologise for any omissions.

Thanks to
John Bly Antiques, Tring, Hertfordshire; Bruford and Heming, London; Brympton d'Evercy, Yeovil, Somerset; Cheshire Military Museum; City Clocks, London; Roger Dew; Fairfax House (York Civic Trust), York; Paul Farrelly, Tring, Hertfordshire; Hanbury Hall, Worcestershire; Haworth Art Gallery (Hyndburn Borough Council), Lancashire; Japanese Gallery, London; Coral Mula; The Parker Gallery, London; Seventh Heaven (Antique Bedstead Centre), Clwyd; George Somlo Antiques, London; Sotheby's, London; Up Country, Tunbridge Wells, Kent; Welholme Galleries, South Humberside.

Special thanks to Phillips auctioneers for allowing us to use a selection of pieces in Jewellery Box on pages 16–19.

Editor	Tim Probart
Design and collages	Roger Kohn
Illustrator	János Márffy
Picture researcher	Elizabeth Loving
DTP editor	Mary Pickles
Editorial assistant	Simon Beecroft
American consultant	Susan Ward
Editorial Director	Ruth Binney
Production	Barry Baker, Janice Storr

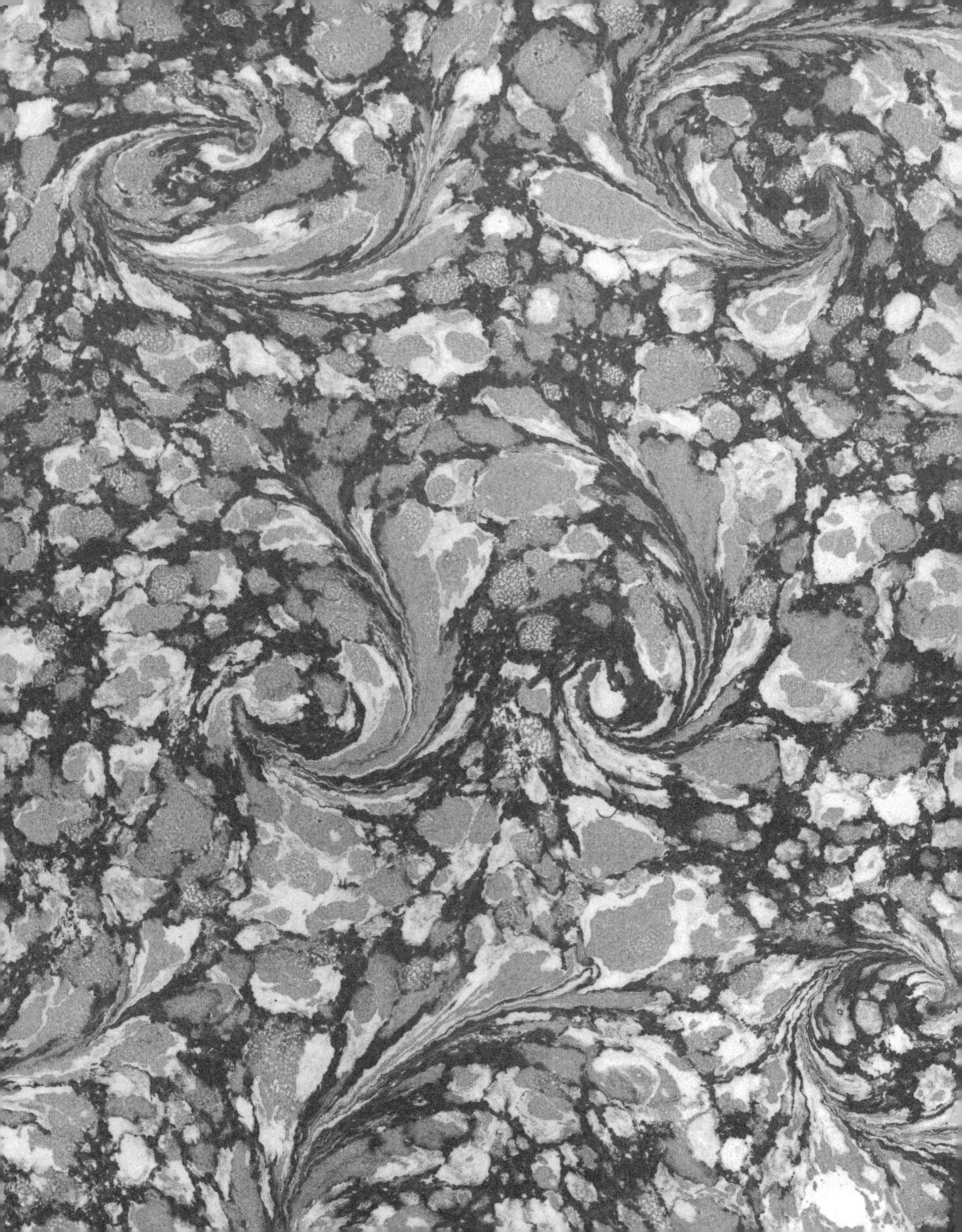